Warriors'
Words

**Recent Titles in the
Praeger Series in Political Communication**
Robert E. Denton, Jr., General Editor

The Modern Presidency and Crisis Rhetoric
Edited by Amos Kiewe

Governmental Commission Communication
Edited by Christine M. Miller and Bruce C. McKinney

The Presidential Campaign Film: A Critical History
Joanne Morreale

High-Tech Campaigns: Computer Technology in Political Communication
Gary W. Selnow

Rhetorical Studies of National Political Debates: 1960–1992
Edited by Robert V. Friedenberg

Campaigns and Conscience: The Ethics of Political Journalism
Philip Seib

The White House Speaks: Presidential Leadership as Persuasion
Craig Allen Smith and Kathy B. Smith

Public Diplomacy and International Politics: The Symbolic Constructs of Summits and
International Radio News
Robert S. Fortner

The 1992 Presidential Campaign: A Communication Perspective
Edited by Robert E. Denton, Jr.

The 1992 Presidential Debates in Focus
Edited by Diana B. Carlin and Mitchell S. McKinney

Public Relations Inquiry as Rhetorical Criticism: Case Studies of Corporate Discourse
and Social Influence
Edited by William N. Elwood

Bits, Bytes, and Big Brother: Federal Information Control in the Technological Age
Shannon E. Martin

Warriors' Words

A Consideration of Language and Leadership

Keith Spencer Felton

Praeger Series in Political Communication

PRAEGER

Westport, Connecticut
London

Library of Congress Cataloging-in-Publication Data

Felton, Keith Spencer.
    Warriors' words : a consideration of language and leadership /
Keith Spencer Felton.
        p.   cm.—(Praeger series in political communication, ISSN
1062-5623)
    Includes bibliographical references and index.
    ISBN 0-275-94992-3 (alk. paper)
    1. Political oratory—History—20th century.   2. Rhetoric—
Political aspects—History—20th century.   3. Communication in
politics—History—20th century.   4. World politics—20th century.
I. Title.   II. Series.
PN4193.P6F45   1995
808.5'9358'0904—dc20   94-37392

British Library Cataloguing in Publication Data is available.

Library of Congress Catalog Card Number: 94-37392
ISBN: 0-275-94992-3
ISSN: 1062-5623

First published in 1995

Praeger Publishers, 88 Post Road West, Westport, CT 06881
An imprint of Greenwood Publishing Group, Inc.

Printed in the United States of America

The paper used in this book complies with the
Permanent Paper Standard issued by the National
Information Standards Organization (Z39.48-1984).

10 9 8 7 6 5 4 3 2 1

Copyright Acknowledgments

The author and publisher gratefully acknowledge permission to quote from the following sources:

Barbara Sicherman, *Alice Hamilton: A Life in Letters* (Cambridge, Mass.: Harvard University Press, 1984). Reprinted by permission of the publishers. Copyright © 1984 by the President and Fellows of Harvard College, Editorial © 1984 by W. Rush, G. Hamilton, Letters.

Frederick G. Fisher, "Where the Tall Grass Grows." Unpublished memoir. Reprinted by permission of Frederick G. Fisher.

For Jean Spencer Felton,
doctor of medicine,
lover of words,
teacher, father

There are those to whom fact is not fact unless it has been transmuted by lyricism.

—Kay Boyle,
from the prologue to
"The Spirit's High Mountain"

Contents

Series Foreword

Those of us from the discipline of communication studies have long believed that communication is prior to all other fields of inquiry. In several other forums I have argued that the essence of politics is "talk" or human interaction.[1] Such interaction may be formal or informal, verbal or nonverbal, public or private but it is always persuasive, forcing us consciously or subconsciously to interpret, to evaluate, and to act. Communication is the vehicle for human action.

From this perspective, it is not surprising that Aristotle recognized the natural kinship of politics and communication in his writings *Politics* and *Rhetoric*. In the former, he establishes that humans are "political beings [who] alone of the animals [are] furnished with the faculty of language."[2] And in the latter, he begins his systematic analysis of discourse by proclaiming that "rhetorical study, in its strict sense, is concerned with the modes of persuasion."[3] Thus, it was recognized over 2,300 years ago that politics and communication go hand in hand because they are essential parts of human nature.

Back in 1981, Dan Nimmo and Keith Sanders proclaimed that political communication was an emerging field.[4] Although its origin, as noted, dates back centuries, a "self-consciously cross-disciplinary" focus began in the late 1950s. Thousands of books and articles later, colleges and universities offer a variety of graduate and undergraduate coursework in the area in such diverse departments as communication, mass communication, journalism, political science, and sociology.[5] In Nimmo and Sanders' early assessment, the "key areas of inquiry" included rhetorical analysis, propaganda analysis, attitude change studies, voting studies, government and the news media, functional and systems analyses, technological changes, media technologies, campaign techniques, and research techniques.[6] In a survey of the state of the field in 1983, the same authors and Lynda Kaid found additional, more specific areas of concerns such as the presidency, political polls, public opinion, debates, and advertising to name a few.[7] Since the first study, they also noted a shift away from the rather strict behavioral approach.

A decade later, Dan Nimmo and David Swanson argued that "political communication has developed some identity as a more or less distinct domain of scholarly work."[8] The scope and concerns of the area have further expanded to include critical theories and cultural studies. While there is no precise definition, method, or disciplinary home of the area of inquiry, its primary domain is the role, processes, and effects of communication within the context of politics broadly defined.

In 1985, the editors of *Political Communication Yearbook: 1984* noted that "more things are happening in the study, teaching, and practice of political communication than can be captured within the space limitations of the relatively few publications available."[9] In addition, they argued that the backgrounds of "those involved in the field [are] so varied and pluralist in outlook and approach. . . . it [is] a mistake to adhere slavishly to any set format in shaping the content."[10] And more recently, Nimmo and Swanson called for "ways of overcoming the unhappy consequences of fragmentation within a framework that respects, encourages, and benefits from diverse scholarly commitments, agendas, and approaches."[11]

In agreement with these assessments of the area and with gentle encouragement, Praeger established the Praeger Series in Political Communication. The series is open to all qualitative and quantitative methodologies as well as contemporary and historical studies. The key to characterizing the studies in the series is the focus on communication variables or activities within a political context or dimension. As of this writing, nearly forty volumes have been published and there are numerous impressive works forthcoming. Scholars from the disciplines of communication, history, journalism, political science, and sociology have participated in the series.

I am, without shame or modesty, a fan of the series. The joy of serving as its editor is in participating in the dialogue of the field of political communication and in reading the contributors' works. I invite you to join me.

Robert E. Denton, Jr.

NOTES

1. See Robert E. Denton, Jr., *The Symbolic Dimensions of the American Presidency* (Prospect Heights, Ill.: Waveland Press, 1982); Robert E. Denton, Jr., and Gary Woodward, *Political Communication in America* (New York: Praeger, 1985; 2nd ed., 1990); Robert E. Denton, Jr., and Dan Hahn, *Presidential Communication* (New York: Praeger, 1986); and Robert E. Denton, Jr., *The Primetime Presidency of Ronald Reagan* (New York: Praeger, 1988).

2. Aristotle, *The Politics of Aristotle,* trans. Ernest Barker (New York: Oxford University Press, 1970), p. 5.

3. Aristotle, *Rhetoric,* trans. Rhys Roberts (New York: The Modern Library, 1954), p. 22.

4. Dan Nimmo and Keith Sanders, "Introduction: The Emergence of Political Communication as a Field," in *Handbook of Political Communication,* ed. Dan Nimmo and Keith Sanders (Beverly Hills, Calif.: Sage, 1981), pp. 11–36.

5. Ibid., p. 15.

6. Ibid., pp. 17–27.

7. Keith Sanders, Lynda Kaid, and Dan Nimmo, eds., *Political Communication Yearbook: 1984* (Carbondale: Southern Illinois University, 1985), pp. 283–308.

8. Dan Nimmo and David Swanson. "The Field of Political Communication: Beyond the Voter Persuasion Paradigm," in *New Directions in Political Communication,* ed. David Swanson and Dan Nimmo (Beverly Hills, Calif.: Sage, 1990), p. 8.

9. Sanders, Kaid, and Nimmo, *Political Communication Yearbook: 1984,* p. xiv.

10. Ibid.

11. Nimmo and Swanson, "The Field of Political Communication," p. 11.

Acknowledgments

Books about words are rife with minutiae, and it requires great generosity to lend their authors a hand. Special thanks, therefore, go to Professor Lawrence R. Jannuzzi for his reading of the manuscript; to Kathleen Pabst and the staff of the Mechanics' Institute Library in San Francisco for undaunted helpfulness in using their fine and historic research facility; to Steve and Kathy Fedor for their computer advice; to Brian Strahl for his superior sleuthing; to the management of Tobin & Tobin for sanctioning a book-finishing furlough; to Dr. Keith Miller for his counsel on the realities of foundation life; and, most of all, to Digby Diehl for three decades of encouragement.

Introduction

In a 1988 radio interview,[1] Israel's former foreign minister Abba Eban, commenting on promising peace negotiations between his country and Egypt, referred to the talks as having a "salutary reckoning."

He might instead have predicted for them a "good result," or even an "auspicious conclusion." After all, his native language is Hebrew, and English is his only by studied acquisition. Rather, he chose a phrase which, while ringing of commerce with diplomatic circles, was one he offered conversationally, without pretense.

In this one interviewing response, a diplomat has demonstrated the importance of elevating the level of language. "A good end" would have handled the first dimension of Eban's response to the question; "a salutary reckoning" probes deeper, gives off resonances, harmonics of meaning which vibrate long after the speaker has moved on to other phrases, other contexts.

Contained in this situation is much of what drives the present book. It is a book about how an elevated use of language can magnify meaning, and motivate beyond the facile measure. It is about the persuasive import of oratory, and is an attempt, through selection and responsive commentary, to see a coherent pattern of language in the great swath of events in modern Western experience.

There is power in purposive oratory. When poetic in its reach, when deservedly acclaimed, oratory outlives the moment of utterance, and enters a universal lexicon of expression to become a permanently recorded part of the march of ideas. The influence of language upon history is ineluctable; mindful of this power, the present text celebrates the lift of language, and observes with respect how exemplary oratory buoys civilization over its perennial perils.

Winston Leonard Spencer Churchill, Britain's most formidable, and most rhetorical, prime minister, perhaps best exemplified this buoying effect. To history

he is legendary and exalted; yet, to his student, he is compellingly, even touch-
ingly human. Exaltation of spirit, and humanness of aspect, will be found essential components in men of oratorical genius. Churchill had both qualities in
abundant measure; and surely, were the figures discussed here in competition
with each other, there would be no doubt as to the "winner."

But the concept of competition would demean this book's intentions; all the
statements surveyed are on equal footing, for all fit the book's premise: They
represent words uttered in public (or written for public appreciation) which made
a difference to both their contemporary audience and posterity's reviewing public. Seen collectively, they become in a certain measure a valuable historical-
psychological silhouette which delineates the Western profile in moments of
crisis.

Not all types of oratory strive for ennoblement. Among the exalted of spirit
cited here can be found exponents of the oratory of tyranny. The exceptional
dissemination of nefarious ideas, however heinous, is nonetheless oratory; and
in the cases cited here, tyrannical oratory met the qualifications of (1) motivating
people, and (2) changing the course of ideas. In turn, of course, positive oratory
can be provoked by the actions (and concomitant oratory) of an unchecked
tyrant. As demagoguery sank to uncharted depths, so the oratory of salvation
rose to new heights to meet the challenge.

As this preface attempts to impart, this text leans toward the general questions
which rhetoricians' active listeners and readers—their *receivers*—tend to ask.
The questions are in fact basic to probing the meanings of these exchanges:
What is the purpose of oratory? Is it to inform? And if it is to inform, what are
the best means of doing so? If it is in the form of a speech, why is delivery so
important?

What is it about an effective speech which invades our feelings, and changes
our attitudes? Why do our emotions become sensitized? What is it that touches
us? What is the difference between a speaker's style and his substance? When
is style substance, and substance style? Why are both often effective in exciting
responses in us? And, finally, how can common words move us to unusual
conclusions? These questions and considerations, embracing both spoken and
written rhetoric, will be posited about each rhetorician we encounter ahead.

This book attempts to elucidate rhetoric from two perspectives:

First, the text takes the view that certain historical figures have helped insti-
gate significant social change through the instrument of oratorical address. By
speaking at key times, eloquently and from the heart, and zeroing in on critical
problems, these leaders brought themselves into intimate touch with people. We
will look at some of these figures, examine their notable words, and consider
them personally, within the context of the events which gave rise to their rhetoric.

The second part of this book's thesis is that just as spoken language has
influenced history, so did the written record of this language influence the *study*
of that history. This phenomenon is, in essence, an historical echo: The words

which gave rise to the deeds (and hence, as Professor Jamieson puts it in *Eloquence in an Electronic Age,* were words which *became* deeds) also became the words which gave rise to the *understanding* of the original deeds, in retrospect. Put in different terms, the history of the Blitz, or Dunkirk, or the Battle of Britain, or Midway, or Normandy well could be told in lists of ordnance and catalogued troop movements; but these events are far better understood when remembered in the context of a pronouncement such as "We shall fight them on the beaches. . . ." The effect of historical events upon modern readers (or hearers) invariably distills down to the "hook" of history. That "hook" is often the memorable phrase. Like a small artifact which survives time, such a phrase can become a talisman for the appreciating scholar of a succeeding age.

Part of rhetoric's history was fundamentally altered by the advent of broadcast media. These means of mass communications have been used for over sixty years to bring leaders' actual voices to their citizenry. In that time, the oratorical skills of the world's leaders have made the difference in the outcome of wars, political elections, and social movements. And the skill of the rhetorician, both in developing his ideas and in projecting them, was as important in 1988 (a U.S. presidential election year, and the concluding year for oratory under discussion) as it was in 1928, when Marconi's wireless device was first exploited politically by public broadcast of the Democratic convention bombast. We shall note and feel the most impact of the media upon ideologically trembling mid-1950s America.

In times before the advent of electronic media, delivery of a speech of historical moment had little or no immediate effect, and required publication and the passage of time for its meaning to be appreciated. (Lincoln's words at Gettysburg, delivered to a word-weary and inattentive crowd, required years of repetitive printing before "Fourscore and seven years ago" and "of the people, by the people, for the people" became bulwark Americanisms.)

A more modern and equally hope-filled message had a disastrously negative effect. England's Neville Chamberlain sacrificed himself and his government with the four words "Peace in our time!" and administered his own coup de grace with three more words: "Peace with honor!" These phrases evoked swift, summary, and retributive citizen action. On the floor of the House of Commons in 1940, the words of Cromwell to the Long Parliament were exhumed by Member of Parliament Leo Amery and thrown in Chamberlain's face: " 'Depart, I say, and let us have done with you. In the name of God, go!' " The rhetoric of one age can be invoked to decry the errors of another.

Electronic media represent a revolution in changing communications equaled only by the dawn of printing; before that time (excepting the limited scope of the labors of scribes), cultural wisdom achieved passage only by word of mouth. Yet this oral-and-aural choice has to do with more than technical invention. Even now, well into the visions of fiber optics, much of what we remember as being momentous comes in the form of *expressions*—public utterances—by our leaders. These exemplars use language to set the standards for our conduct, to enunciate the laws by which we live, and to define the scale of values against which we measure the progress of our lives.

As a sign of this phenomenon, in the age of print our vehicles of expression turned from utterance to impress, and yet the new conveyances retained a vocal nomenclature: Newspapers were named "The World *Herald,*" "The San Francisco *Call,*" "The Village *Voice.*"

The import of vocalization—directness of being spoken to—has meanings deeply rooted in psychobiology and in mysticism. Even in the secular epoch, the preacher's sermon is an in*voca*tion, and is personally felt by listeners; the same idea on paper is a treatise, and tends to stand apart from, and not dependent upon, a receiver. The treatise's lack of communication by vibrating currents of air alters, and in some ways absolves us of, our responsiveness, our responsibility.

An article in a journal or a speech equally can develop an idea; but passion in a speaker's rendering also provides an immediacy unavailable from the muteness of the page. When wax, and then wire, and then iron oxide, and then optical sound tracks made vocal reproduction possible, history gained an exquisite gift: *presence.* What color does to the psyche through the retina and the optic nerve, sound accomplishes with comparable vividness and psychological effect by the alchemy of vibrant air, and the dance of tympanum and stapes. There are things we need, as citizens, which only the spoken word can provide. This book will bring some of these words to bear, and by their placement in the canon of meaningful utterances, appreciate again their fortuitous provision.

Each chapter of *Warriors' Words* intends to suggest a path for inquiry into that chapter's subject or subjects. Such a path bears the periodic guideposts of the subject's verbal relationships and interplay with its times.[2] An epoch of history is an immensity, a tangle of meanings. My approach to each vignette is to reach inside it, and free from its whale-mass the ambergris of its essence. I want, with this book, to open up history, to make a moment's essence available.

In its organization, the text of this book draws oratorical highlights from four epochs of our country's history. These include voices of social conscience from turn-of-the-century adolescent America,[3] and the words of leaders from the periods before, during, and after the Second World War. Finally, postwar oratorical legacies to modern American experience are cited, with examples from presidents and other figures. Most notable in this section are the words of a citizenry in the grip of the crises which collectively have become known as McCarthyism.

Each section begins with a prefatory "assay." In the metallurgical sense, an assay is an analytical means of determining the amount of a particular metal in an ore or alloy. By this quantitative process, the amount of gold or silver in coin bullion was determined. In the most facile metaphorical borrowing, the historian can attempt to obtain a qualitative measure of which elements of his subject's efforts are precious, and which are base. Each section of *Warriors' Words* will begin with an assay as a trial at obtaining perspective and, hence, historical objectivity.

Included throughout are contributions from figures who were not of a formal leadership stature, but whose utterances, either formal or informal, had the qualities of being pivotal to public thought, or exemplary of critical times. Among this group of comments or statements is a seminal argument of the early-twentieth-century legal figure Clarence Darrow; the courageous congressional-hearing words of the Boston lawyer Joseph N. Welch; and, from the modern era, the verbal insurgency of Reverend Jesse Jackson.[4]

Some notes of explanation: Dr. Martin Luther King, Jr., perhaps the most persuasive orator since Churchill, appears here absent familiar phrases. The civil rights movement, for which his voice was clarion, has been the victim of years of neglect; at present his words, already deservingly well disseminated, are going through the crucible of canonization. For this book's purposes, we will examine portions of one of his lesser-known addresses, his Nobel Prize acceptance speech. And President Kennedy's inaugural words to the young, which are also honored with overexposure, here are skirted for similar reasons. The balanced cadences of exortation give way (for our purposes) to words of debate which won for him his presidency in the first televised encounter between political opponents. Indeed, Mr. Churchill's innumerable watchwords give way here to his skills at eulogy; perhaps his most important words (other than those which fortified besieged British spirits) were those which gave public approbation to separating out a patrician's (Chamberlain's) bad judgment from his essential worth. The positive uplift of such approbation suggests the supportive value of rhetoric as well.

It should be noted that the figures discussed here reflect the author's oratorical cultural bias. I am a native English speaker; my ear, my hand, my emotions all resonate to the English tongue.[5] Therefore, the profundity of expression of the world's leaders has reached me in this language, which (saving an oddly grouped Gandhi and Hitler) is native to all of them as well. And it was true of Gandhi, as with most prominent Indians of the colonial and postcolonial epochs, that English, though not native, was certainly his operative tongue—his *lingua franca.*

A multifaceted view of history is a happy by-product of research into rhetoric. If this view of events and their words contributes to fuller understanding of the meanings underlying human currents, then the collective oratory represented and discussed here will have achieved yet another level of fulfillment.

In one way or another, the speakers whose words appear here are persons of conviction and commitment. These strong personal currents seek outlet. Sometimes, as in the case of the Axis dictator, these currents contain pathology. And sometimes, as it is for a Churchill, living a life of deep feelings can generate expressions which convey all the colors of poetry.

An orator's first task is to convey the colors of his own feelings to others, using the most moving verbal means available to him. His other task, in so doing, is to arrive at such a poetic plane that his words convey the colors of the feelings of us all.

Experiencing rhetoric is a direct way of appreciating it. *Examining* rhetoric, however, suggests a possible need for explication skills in many fields of study, including literary, scientific, political, sociological, and even philosophical explorations. The academician's tools, on the other hand, are not always readily available, or necessarily always desirable. This introduction will assay some of an earnest, but lay, receiver's possible keys for converting rhetorical personalities and verbal productivity into advances in understanding the subject matter (or the individuals) under discussion.

It is easy to see, from the text's grouping of rhetoricians, that we are talking about the movers and shakers, the exceptional people; and, to be sure, we expect from such people no dissimulation, no disingenuousness, no cant or *sub-rosa* intent of injury. We stand, on our side, as naive, novitiate, and hence open and vulnerable. We want, by such posture, to indicate our trust. How, then, do we explain the rhetorician who appears sincere, but seems (as some see them) guilty of being misguided, or unintentionally deceptive (a Nixon, a MacArthur, or on the other pole, a Kennedy, a Roosevelt)?

A fruitful way to regard rhetoric, from the standpoint of "getting something out of it" about the rhetorician as well as his subject, is to ask two questions:

1. What do these words tell me about the *exterior* person?—about his beliefs, the workings of his intellect, the way his mind has ordered his universe?
2. What do these words tell me about the *interior* person?—about his emotions, his fears, his instincts, his prejudices; in short, about his responses over the long haul to the ways in which the universe has impinged upon him?

These questions might be extrapolated further:

1. What does this rhetoric tell me about that which the rhetorician *knows* (the world he sees, the hypotheses he posits, queries he dares to make and scrutiny he is willing to undertake)?
2. What does this rhetoric tell me about that which the rhetorician does *not know* (his own psychological underpinnings and fallabilities, the "Garry Wills" treatment of Nixon[6])?

A third question emerges: What do we expect from all these words? That is, where should rhetoric *lead* us? What should rhetoric *leave* with us?

Any powerful rhetoric should accomplish two functions for the receiver:

1. It should invite him to challenge his belief systems, with the active intentions of change/alteration or affirmation; and
2. It should enable him to adapt the elements of the "new thinking" to his own identity, tools, and workable point of departure.

Finally, the most heralded element of rhetoric is also its most memorable: its eloquence. When Churchill meets with Roosevelt for the first time, and is heartened by the solemn camaraderie of the hymns sung by servicemen of the English-speaking world, and reveals his thought that this bond is "the only hope, to combat merciless degradation," we realize that such a rhetorician is capable of moving us with his words, because *he* is moved, deeply moved, inside his own spirited being.

Rhetoric—an elevation, an elongation—an exaltation of language, is a civilizing force. It should affect us, in some ways, like music, and even in some ways, like language's sublime extension: poetry. It should *affect* us, because (to force the tautology) it should reach our *affective* side. As speech in man is a refinement of his animalism, so is refinement of speech a way of protecting civilization from its animalism. And what, on this ship's deck, suggests this surety for Churchill? It is the undergirding by a certain brotherhood; a communication. Language—as Winston Churchill demonstrated—can save us.

One of oratory's liabilities is that an oration invariably suffers when abridged, or, worse, is extruded in abstracted form through other media. For example, the high, strident, carefully built rhythms in the speech-making style of Jesse Jackson do not work when excerpted for news broadcast in segments. And, when his sermon-like orations are transcribed, they require the reader's imagination if the Black leader's vocally insistent sentiments are to receive full appreciation. (His words are abridged here for an unfortunate but necessary textual economy.)

Similarly, the effect of a written polemic is different from that of its spoken cousin. For all his spoken effectiveness, Hitler's *Mein Kampf* was clearly a written exercise, the teeth-grinding ruminations of an incarcerated madman whose larval ideologies took on weight in a prison cocoon. This written record of the fledgling *Fuehrer's* harsh, gestational psychopathology does not have the shrieking tones of his later public address, the attack of which even the virulence of his thinking cannot fully convey.

An aspect of rhetoric common to the most famous and infamous of the rhetoricians represented here is the *persuasive* intentions of their speeches. Rhetoric is defined as "the art of speaking or writing *effectively*. . . . skill in the *effective* use of language [emphasis added]. . . ."[7] It is also "the art or science of using words effectively in speaking or writing, so as to influence or persuade. . . ."[8] Skillful speaking which achieves a desired effect, a moving to action of one's listeners, the creation of a change in apperception, or the winning to one's side of those holding opposite views are some of the responses which rhetoric of quality can induce. All else is not rhetoric but grandiloquence, pretty but hollow vocal entertainments.[9]

The principal figures cited in this volume attest to the power of directed speech, the importance which ideas, conviction, delivery, *and the readiness of an audience and its openness to change* can have in completing the cycle of action which is rhetoric.

A comparatively recent use of the word *rhetoric* suggests a pejorative meaning: The notion of a "rhetorical question" persists in parlance, implying that such a question was a lame tautology, begging itself or, worse, an attempt at obfuscation. When such expression is attributed to a politician, the receivers of the message more firmly imprint the link of "rhetorical" with subterfuge. This may be so; however, the fate of language is movement and change; and sometimes, the change is from positive to negative.[10]

The logical, if bowdlerized, outcome of such current pejorative thinking about rhetoric is manifest in the smile of humorous tolerance given, always askance, to the soapbox at "speakers' corners" where every crackpot can "orate" his grievances to the derisive wanderers-by. He—the last "rhetorician"—is a creature of abuse and scorn, laughable to a community too long removed from the elegance and persuasive import of the serious speaker with a communicative mission.

Mention is made of these baser rhetorical connotations because so much of this text deals with words, or their speakers, who inherited an elevated plane of parlance. Lincoln's simplicity of language is ineffable. The driving force of Churchill's phrases, conveyed with his singular guttural lisp, helped preserve a nation and a concept of civilization that were ten centuries old. That some practitioners—historical as well as contemporary—make leaden notions seem aerial with the momentary propulsive puffery of flowery sounds does not diminish the strength in words—well-chosen and well-placed words—which make us wonder, words which make us feel a coldness in the lungs, an emotional rush in the throat, an at-homeness with values that in our quotidian, shortsighted lives we forget are there. These values *are* there, within us; they are our ballast, and steadying as it is, that ballast is driven forward by the gyroscopic force of words.

Finally, there is value to be reaped from rhetoric which is not practicable, not applicative as is mathematics, or useful as is plumbing. This value resides in the sublime results of the pursuit of others' organized words; and much of it begins its suffusing process in our formative years.

Often I have wondered why schoolchildren are expected to memorize passages of famous speeches, or significant writings from the ages. Surely it is more than the desire to foster acquaintance with legendary word passages which prompts teachers to assign the Hamlet soliloquy, a verse of Burns, Lincoln's battlefield-canonizing cadences, a roseate sonnet, or even (in the all-wise college years) the concluding, affirming climax of Joyce's Dublin epic.[11] These assigned commitments to memory must, in fact, be more than any rote learning: They must represent the desire to encourage the habit of acquiring not small passages of words, but small disciplines. By such habits are magnified our experience and our wealth; as with any washing in sacred water, one is cleaned, and one is also cleansed.

To harmonize one's time with revered and repeated wordage is a way of instilling rhythms in the soul, as harmonizing with one's mother's heartbeat by physical proximity is the infant's bulwark against the unexpressed fears of being *ex utero*.

Extrapolating from this notion to rhetoric as value, a well-hewn piece of persuasive exposition can be felt as an incantation, and its speaker or author a kind of surrogate priest. One looks up to clergy, for comfort if not for answers; and by this unspoken liturgical kinship the rhetorician claims our respect—at least at the outset, as we await his words. In Mark Antony's terms, we lend our ears; but if the music is right, we give our hearts.

NOTES

1. Broadcast on the program "Weekend Edition," National Public Radio, February 20, 1988.

2. Part I's chapter on Alice Hamilton and Jane Addams depicts two subjects of equal significance. These two pioneers of America's social history worked much in common cause.

3. Among these American voices an Asian speaks: the philosopher and religious leader Mohandas K. Gandhi, a Hindu from the Indian subcontinent. Not only is Gandhi universally appealing, but his influence has been of fundamental value to such U.S. luminaries as Martin Luther King, Jr.—and thus has helped to foster America's history as well as that of the country he helped liberate.

4. The fact that Jackson's 1988 presidential candidacy was thwarted is irrelevant; what is important is that he is the first seriously regarded Black contender for the presidency, and part of the reason why he became a compelling figure had to do with his arresting and unique use of language. These facts, together with his background as a preacher, make noteworthy the quality of his utterances.

5. A recent and noteworthy study indicates that infant native-language discernment and cognitive separation from foreign sounds has been found throughout a range of cultures in babies as young as six months. (National Public Radio: "Weekend Edition," February 15, 1992.)

6. See Part IV's discussion of John F. Kennedy.

7. *Webster's Ninth New Collegiate Dictionary.* Merriam-Webster, Springfield, Mass., 1987.

8. *Webster's New Universal Unabridged Dictionary,* Second Edition, Simon and Schuster, New York, 1983.

9. Music has its equivalent requirements: A score of notes offering a theme and refrain for the purpose of selling soap or automobiles or blue jeans can swell a room with the sounds of strings and brass; such sounds, however, *cannot* be considered music.

10. Garry Wills, in his formidable 1970 book *Nixon Agonistes,* dissects Richard Nixon's use of language to reveal its patent cunning; condescension when embodied in language makes the distasteful tort of patronage into the reprehensible crime of misjudgment. For a politician, such a mistake can be fatal.

11. One modern dancer was proud of her high-school-era memorization and performance of the Prologue to the *Canterbury Tales;* her gruel-mouthed utterances from an earlier incarnation of English were as slothful as her Terpsichore was lithe. And a writer of thirty years named the only piece he had committed to his memory while young: a statement of Santayana's on the meaning of death, a piece the writer remembered and recited at his mother's funeral.

Part One

Prophets of the New Century

Assay: The Autumnal God—The Moral Crisis of Coming to Terms with a Postwar World, 1918–1938

When a country experiences a moral crisis, of the magnitude which America felt following the Civil War, and again following the First World War, it undergoes to some extent a natural resurgence of interest in the fundamental religious values which characterized the country during its "upbringing." Facing the moral vacuum following the 1914–1918 debacle—a calamity made more disappointing because it followed so quickly upon the heels of the twentieth century's touted glories to come—America proved itself no different from any other nation.

For a time, in this period of American history, the influence of religion and religionists soared to a white heat. From this intensity, and because of several converging historical circumstances, as the decades passed religion's heat fell to a tepidity and ultimately it settled into an uneasy quietude, where it sits today.

Religion reached its greatest intensity in America with a movement which flourished in the first quarter of the twentieth century. To speak of this development as a movement is inaccurate; this moral-seeking energy was much more amorphous than the word *movement* suggests. However, it is a discernible phenomenon. Leaders in this movement were born around the time of the Civil War, and died between the two world wars of the present century. Conflicts between nations or other sharply defined factionalisms were beginning to be recognized as a lamentable but permanent feature of human activity. Indeed, much of the narrative color and pattern in biblical lore comes from the clashes of nations, states, cults—philosophies. It is not inconsequential that religious leaders, in an effort to forestall the demise of their influence in the United States, redoubled their efforts to create out of a battle-fatigued nation a parish of converts.

In a sense, religionists borrowed the remaining energy from the dissipating nationalistic fervor, and harnessed it to what was undeniably a less harmful set of what they deemed defensible concepts; and so they built churches and developed battle strategies.

Moral rectitude has always figured highly in the public discourse of religious persons; and this human eccentricity is also, of course, a key element of public proclamation in military crises.[1] It makes an odd realization that the first dealing in military surplus items may have been with a stock of attitudes, and not footlockers or wool shirts. Invocation to one's God, with the intention of seeking blessing for the violent manifestation of one's territoriality, has colored the rhetoric of political leaders throughout history.

Into this philosophical vacuum, in post-Wilson America, hurried an eager group. Like the sharply divided classes already extant in America, they tended to separate along lines of what was then called "breeding." From the lower classes (and if not *from* them, certainly appealing *to* them) came a cast of characters right out of the "carny" circuit; and the public clamored for such personae upon whom to shower their interest. They covered the gamut of Police-Gazette personalities: There was the Religio-Political Legend (in the rotund form of William Jennings Bryan); there was the Carotid-Throbbing Evangelist (William S. "Billy" Sunday, who also was precursor to the Astringent Sanctimonious Ideologue of the next decade, one Father Charles Coughlin, an opportunist whose turned-around collar hid a larynx full of screams for totalitarian values); and there was the Glamorous Fraud (Sister Aimee Semple MacPherson). I doubt the most morbid biogeneticist could conceive of a more interesting faculty for the schooling of religious principle than this group, which held the shaky, shell-shocked hand of America as it moved into the century of apocalypse.

Perhaps at last, after revolution, continent conquering, civil war, industrial burgeoning, and world war, this was now the time when America was ready to go through its rite of passage. War, as President Kennedy would comment a generation later about another world conflict, could temper a nation; and now this war, this First World War at the end of the teens, would pry the lid of insulation open on the inwardly directed self-satisfaction of the United States. But along with these upturns of enlightened behavior came the multiple ills of much negativity and parochialism: The cumulative effect of immigration, rapid population growth, and the beginning efforts at sorting out questions of civilized behavior made America vulnerable to provocation and a pushover for zealots giving encouragement to the violence-prone, the young, and the ignorant. No "foreign," "Commie," "leftist radical" diatribe ever did the violence to the lip-served American canon of shibboleths than the narrow and hateful parochial Klansmen and the other secret societies of religio-commercio-politico fraternities ilk.

And yet, for so long at the center of the ring of fire, leading the faculty of the rabble-rousing collegium, were the likes of these two "ministers of the faith" whose presence guaranteed America the certainty of moral backsliding.

Father Coughlin, this proto-Nazi with a clerical tunic, added his virulence to the cauldron of difficulties of the 1930s. He was in fact a vituperative charlatan, a man whose "rhetoric" accomplished nothing in our catalogue of rhetoric's requirements; rather, his words carried hatred, deception, a noise of baiting and constructive lying which established a specimen of virulence whose impact would be felt throughout the turbulent times ahead in the country—most notably in the fetid political atmosphere of the 1950s.

The earlier preacher, Billy Sunday, was a less lethal variety of zealot. He developed a feverish following not because of any oratorical (let alone liturgical) talent, but because of sheer energy. When preaching, he was able to whip things up into such a frenzy that, like a singer who has no real voice but who has lots of "personality," he was able to "put his song over" with a vividness that passed for magnetism.

These men had no credentials for claiming eminence; but in that critical growth period between McKinley's assassination and the Scopes trial of 1925, the country's character was being laid down layer by layer, and in the eyes of many, libertinism was becoming overt, and religion, serious religion with invested principles, was becoming—worse than covert—covered over for good.

America, expanded by 1912 to the full ranges of the continent, still felt itself young, malleable, driven. The lawless streak which characterized the romantic Old West, with its boomer-sooner kind of "first one there grabs what he can" ethos, struggled nonetheless with the Calvinist and other fundamental religious fibers deeply embedded in its muscle. A few splenetic hatemongers in pulpits, or, their obverse, the comically neurasthenic Protestant-preacher-characters of Everytown, did not and could not bring to America a divinity of consequence, a godhead of reckoning, a deity concept with sufficient depth and breadth to help it through this painful insurgence of geographical and cultural expansion.

Was this the best a great nation could produce in the way of philosophical leadership? What had gone wrong? And how had it gone wrong so quickly? It seemed only yesterday that there was such robustness and acclaim for the new times, times of great national encouragement. The century itself had turned—a feat about which people took great pride, despite their having done nothing to bring it about—and provided the opportunity for endless metaphors of renewal. The Isthmus of Panama was breached (1914) by the ingenuity of de Lesseps and Goethals, which act carried the enthusiasm of century surviving into the higher gear of continent splitting and ocean binding. The Great War in Europe, which Hynes[2] and others have poignantly shown took a fundamental toll on the confidence of a generation of women and men of England, Germany, and France, meted out extinction to a not insignificant number of American boys, but left the taste of adventure in the mouths of many, a taste which whetted appetites for later escapades. World fairs, like San Francisco's 1915 Pan Pacific Exposition and the earlier (1904) exhibition in St. Louis, gave official sanction to the notion that America was becoming something, becoming "somebody." If you were an American, it was hard not to feel good about it! So, the atmosphere was charged, people were growing in sophistication, the intellectual climate was expectant; there was opportunity in the air, and the "air" itself, an atmosphere for entertaining ideas, was ready for something to happen. One of the things which happened was that the arguments over fundamentalist beliefs were due for an elevation in the level of religious inquiry.

One of the most revered of the era's voices of God was a tired, flabby, bald old man who had made a name for himself in a way, in politics, and was going into senescence wearing the glorious robes of the believer. William Jennings Bryan had been a member of the House of Representatives; he had run in 1908 for president against William Howard Taft; he served as Woodrow Wilson's secretary of state (his one high-level office); he had made a speech at the 1896 Democratic convention about the gold standard which electrified his audience, and those beyond, for decades; and when he had a mere handful of days left to live, he offered up his sanctimony and his piety and his well-earned burden of representation of the believers of the world upon the sacrificial altar of a case at bar. He knew his Bible; he could quote from any verse of Scripture. He knew the ways of his audience and the people of the times, and he knew that he could sway them, for he had eloquence on his side. He knew he was on friendly ground when he went from his home in Nebraska to the little Tennessee town of Dayton, where a shy, slender schoolteacher a half century his junior had brought out (for all his pupils to see) the wretched notion that man, made in God's image, actually somehow had leapt out of the womb of apes! He knew that he had a chance now, despite his respectable adversary, a clever old lawyer from Chicago, to put the finishing touches on a career which espoused traditional values, by making the hallowed contribution to humanity, before his death, of restoring faith to the people.

This was a noble wish. This desire was worthy of the respect of the people, and earned the solicitude of all the folks in the town of Dayton, Tennessee, and it earned the respect of the man with the hair in his eyes and the flaccid galluses who looked about as much like a fancy lawyer as a monkey looked like a man! And the lawyer *did* respect the famous proselytizer, and respected him for his beliefs; for it was that kind of respect which had made the lawyer remain positive about people, positive about human nature itself.

In a career which would include pleading for the lives of murderers and crafting arguments to persuade damaged and grieving souls to forgo retribution, Clarence Darrow had formed bedrock respect for human beings, for the ordinary, common man, and for the somewhat inflated but still common man like William Jennings Bryan.

So, here were two men of astonishing repute, amazing skill and electric personalities, pitted against each other. If the winner was modernity and enlightenment, the loser was not a discredited old preacher. There wasn't a cell of meanness or cynicism in Clarence Seward Darrow; he put Bryan on the stand as an adversarial witness and he destroyed the old believer's argument, with its naive insistence upon theistic catchwords; but he never intended to destroy Bryan himself. The famous photograph of the two of them during the Scopes trial says more than all the words written about them: It says things, in fact, quite biblical. It says things which in all probability would have occurred to Darrow, as he gazed upon the eminence who had been his witness: Love thy neighbor, love thine enemy. The Kingdom of Heaven is within. Charity begins at home, and the home, always, is the heart. Ravage an argument, pulverize an outmoded idea; love a man.

There in Dayton, two men sat sweating in the heat and emotion of a cymbal-clash of ideas. One was offering testimony for eons of blind history. One was counsel for daring ideas that were central to a whole new age, a whole new century. (They looked like a couple of old cornball pensioners, swatting flies to keep awake in the heat.)

In fact, the dialogue they had enough courage to engage in gives more credit to the mind of man than almost anything that yet had transpired in the new century. America was slowly being released from the bonds of traditionalist thinking. Bryan, meaning well, lent his name to the defense of parochialism, and he should receive great respect for this willingness. Darrow, knowing better, practiced his profession in service of ideas; and he earned more than respect for this act. He earned a foothold, in the early morning of the American day, for the kind of maturity of thought required of a nation which, in a score of years, would have to reckon with another disastrous war of global scope, and with the warping, cureless agony of nuclear fission's force.

Into the spring of the new century came the enthusiasts of traditional religion; the only problem was that the God they searched for, and preached about, and held up for the masses to contemplate, was a late God, an autumnal God, who in fact already had arrived: He was a God *passé;* and with the departure of Bryan, this God's leaves of learning turned orange and fell onto the ground.

A new and different God was needed. And if America would admit it, it was a secular God it needed, or rather a God-force in man which would face squarely the ills of the new century's society, and attempt to reconcile the need of the Word of God with the other needs of the human race.

That "God," that spirit of revitalization and reform, came in part in the fashion of three Americans and a man from the Asian subcontinent of India, all four of whom symbolized the appeal to a higher ethical standard. These persons—true reformers in that they did not see themselves in that role but only as persons of deep conviction acting upon their beliefs—gave their energies toward the betterment of those around them. In so doing, the three Americans changed the face of a nation's concept of social responsibility; and the Indian showed an astonished world that the best weapons for fighting wars of conviction were courtesy, abstinence, self-denial, a posture of noncombativeness, and the absolute necessity of preserving one's enemy's dignity.

NOTES

1. "A date which will live in infamy.... Always will we remember the character of the onslaught.... the American people in their righteous might will gain the inevitable

triumph, so help us God'': These were Franklin Delano Roosevelt's first words of public notice to Japanese belligerents following the attack on Pearl Harbor.

2. Writer Samuel Hynes bears a surname similar to that of the great photographic portraitist, historian, and chronicler Lewis Hine. Hine's astonishing pictorial record of the early twentieth century included coverage of the same war-torn and displaced Europeans for whom Alice Hamilton implored Congress to send humanitarian aid.

Chapter One

Let There Be Light:
The Genesis of a Social Conscience in the New Century (Jane Addams and Alice Hamilton, M.D.)

What doth the Lord require of thee, but to do justly, and to love mercy, and to walk humbly with thy God?

—Micah

"First, let's eat; *then* we'll talk about art!"
—A 1960s artist-turned-Reagan-era-entrepreneur

In the Chicago telephone directory of 1991, under the heading "Social" in its "Yellow Pages," there are a dozen distinct categories of agencies of public service. Their individual areas of focus include ethnicity, religion, sexual orientation, problems of the aged, problems of youth, problems of sensory deprivation. There are, additionally, nine pages of entries for agencies listed in other, related categories of social service—some clinical, some charitable, some educational, some rehabilitative. In all, no fewer than 1,352 agencies are listed for social services.[1]

Equally remarkable about these statistics is what they suggest about a tenet of the American Constitution: the separation of church and state. It is true that the missions long had been undertaking social betterment in the form of their "good works"; but this was essentially insular and centripetal, as seems even today to be characteristic, for example, of Catholic charities. The majority in Hull House's project and its 1,300 Chicago legatees alone came from the *secular* world; yet from that secular world came, nonetheless, exalted and splendid achievement. What the Lord did require, according to Micah, could be true also of the elevated inner standard of the figure, cast in the Jane Addams mould, who would become the social worker.

As we have seen, at the beginning of the century such humanitarian focus would have been impossible. But because of the driving force and conviction of a virtual handful of persons, a new concept of social responsibility and conscience had a chance to germinate, take hold, and develop. Much of this humanitarian concern stemmed from two sources: the unstinting and long-unappreciated work of Jane Addams, at her settlement house in Chicago called Hull House; and the contributions of Alice Hamilton, M.D., based on her training in the eastern United States in medicine and social service.

Hamilton, a young woman from a prestigious Fort Wayne, Indiana, family,[2] was one of the early female recipients of an M.D. degree from an American university (Wayne State University), and the very first woman M.D. on the faculty of Harvard University Medical School (where she served with great distinction from 1919 until 1934). In about 1910, she began developing an interest in the safety conditions for workers in industry, out of which the great fields of industrial medicine, occupational health, and industrial hygiene were derived. Earlier, in 1897, Dr. Hamilton had gone to Chicago, where she joined forces with Jane Addams. Forty-six years later, in 1943, Dr. Hamilton's seminal book, *Exploring the Dangerous Trades,* appeared; a work of great sensitivity, it not only established Dr. Hamilton's pioneer credentials, but it fostered standards in the workplace for anyone engaged in physical effort or under any kind of physical stress. And, because of her related social work, the book's contributions to industrial mental health ushered in the physician's need to be concerned with all the parts of the employee-patient.

Unlike other subjects of the present book, neither Dr. Hamilton nor Addams said or wrote any single statement whose pith succinctly catalogues its author's contributions to human welfare. However, the career efforts of each of them, at work in an area which was nonexistent before their participation and which became a staple of modern social concern after their departure, serve well as sources of their wisdom and achievements.

Dr. Alice Hamilton would survive Jane Addams by thirty-five years; and considering the generation this period represented (from 1935 to 1970), this physician should be included among the more farsighted scientists of our time. As with so many physicians who abandon or eschew private practice, Alice Hamilton turned to an academic career, and it too felt the impress of her qualities. Joining Harvard Medical School's new industrial hygiene program in 1919 enabled her to add that distinction of being the institution's first female professor. What is true of so much pioneering work obtained with Dr. Hamilton's investigations; for it is only within the century's latter decades that the full meaning of Alice Hamilton's achievements and insights has become evident to industry. Indeed, governmental regulatory bodies are only now putting into effect the consequences, in the form of strictures, of work done by the Harvard professor before the beginning of the Depression.

As her impact has been felt by modernity, this point in the narrative about Dr. Hamilton is propitious, perhaps, for a personal anecdote of more recent vintage. In 1916, Alice Hamilton and her sisters moved to a house in Hadlyme,

Connecticut. That early-nineteenth-century home, as Professor Barbara Sicherman describes it, "sat fairly high on the east bank of the Connecticut River, next to the ferry landing."[3] Hoosier by upbringing, after 1916 Alice was by temperament and residence a New Englander. Anyone looking at that lively face, with the intelligent eyes and the thin but expressive mouth, would assume, moreover, that this was a deeply thoughtful New Englander.

At least, that was one writer's judgment. By good chance and a young man's brash thoughtlessness, I made an autumn trip to Connecticut in 1962, and called, unannounced, at the house in Hadlyme. An attendant greeted me, accepted my introduction at face value, and then called in Margaret Hamilton. Learning the nature of my visit (my father, an industrial physician and professor of preventive medicine and public health, for years had spoken of Dr. Hamilton in reverential terms), Alice's younger sister informed her famous sibling that a colleague's son had come to call.

We waited for Alice to collect herself from an afternoon nap. ("She'll just take a moment," her sister defended her. "She's doing fine, for ninety-three," the attendant whispered.)

I spent a memorable and in some ways embarrassing visit with Alice. She queried me sharply about "that fellow, Nixon!" who was at the time attempting to unseat Pat Brown as California's governor. Cloistered at school in Grinnell, Iowa, I was not current on California politics; but this Easterner, born four years after Lincoln's murder, revealed her clear and pointed opinions on the latest West Coast news. Her views on the former vice president were consistent with the values of the impatient and forward-thinking physician who had accompanied Jane Addams to Germany after the First World War, in an effort to pressure the Allies to release stockaded food supplies for Europe's starving children.

When our visit concluded, following a session of mutual fussing-over between the older Alice and the younger Margaret, I realized as I walked away from this Hadlyme idyll that I had been in the presence of someone who was not just famous or worldly, but whose depth and strength were on a level of profundity: These qualities had, after all, enabled this quiet, elderly lady to be an innovator of immense accomplishment and prestige. She had been a person of depth and strong will in her twenties, when medicine, and the decision to take on the toxicological concerns of industry, were new to her; she had been so in early middle age, at Hull House and in pursuit of women's emancipation; she certainly was so at ninety-three, when I visited. She would be even more so, by dint of a survival capacity which stemmed at least in part from her attitudes toward good health and her genial wisdom, when, outliving Margaret, she died a few years later, at the age of 101.

The darkness of the nineteenth century's industrial medical backwardness which the young Alice Hamilton encountered had been allowed to persist for a considerable period of time. It was true that the growth of the country and the betterment of people's ways of living were intricately and directly linked with the rise of successful practical applications of this and the previous century's scientific creativity. And yet, in the pathetic way characteristic of our system of enterprise—of allowing society only gradually to elevate its level of sophistication in some areas while according a few persons quick and galactic wealth—that same system was making monsters and morons out of young boys as they pushed coal cars along rails in the mines literally by the force of their brows; and girls in spinning mills along the rivers of the eastern industrial cities inhaled enough flax dust to make the coverlets they would need later in the hospital when resultant diseases claimed their health and their lives. Commerce, and sometimes the greed behind it, is a metastatic process; it can, and in nineteenth-century America did, consume public morals at the same time that it gave terminal illnesses (such as the varieties of the one called, in fact, "consumption") to the wretched children, illiterates, immigrants, and others in society who had to take what they could get. Some suffered collapsed lungs, or bashed brains, or exhaustion from sixteen-hour days of toil; others would be destroyed by excessive and substandard alcohol, or desiccated by malnutrition, or crazed by the consequences of ignorance and sexual disease. It was not a pretty picture.

And then, in the 1880s, on tour in Europe with a friend, Jane Addams discovered the London settlement house called Toynbee Hall. Returning to the United States, they secured the vacant and unkempt Charles Hull mansion in a run-down Chicago ward, where their own settlement experience would begin. In time, this effort was able to thrust the "bootstrap" settlement concepts onto the national scene. Addams' timing was close enough; while hers was a nation not overly hospitable to social enlightenment, at least somehow, by some miracle, it did allow it to take root.

It was an inevitability, the connecting of these two lifelong spinsters with the visionary sensibilities. They were a good match for each other, as social worker and physician. Their stories interweave in interesting ways. And as their efforts coincided, gradually, the social climate about them became, little by little, more accommodating to their impress.

Consider a few of the social achievements in the years between the turn of the century (1900) and the entry of the United States into the Second World War (1941):

1903 Emmeline Pankhurst founded the National Women's Social and Political Union.

1904 France established a ten-hour limit on the work day.

1906 Upton Sinclair's novel *The Jungle* incited interest in Chicago stockyard procedures leading to establishment of the U.S. Pure Food and Drug Act.

1910 Florence Nightingale died; a long life (she was born in 1820) enabled her caregiving to influence those of like mind in the new century.

1913 Mrs. Pankhurst brought violent impatience to her suffragette cause, and went to jail; Albert Schweitzer opened his Lambaréné hospital.

1916 Margaret Sanger took part in opening the first birth control clinic in Brooklyn, New York.

1917 Suffragism crossed the Atlantic—women were arrested for demonstrating outside the White House.

1919 The death penalty was abolished in Austria; a law restricting the use of child labor was passed in the United States.

1920 Great Britain and Austria created unemployment insurance.

1922 Dr. Marie Stopes held birth control meetings in London.

1926 Turkey undertook reforms in regard to women.

1927 The Industrial Health and Safety Center opened in London (and none too soon—that same year, aerial crop dusting with insecticide began).

1928 Mrs. Pankhurst died in London.

1932 Trade union membership in Great Britain hit 4.4 million.

1935 The Committee for Industrial Organization (reorganized in 1938 as the Congress of Industrial Organizations) was formed by John L. Lewis; Alcoholics Anonymous was conceived in New York City.

1938 The United States established the forty-hour work week.

1942 Oxfam was founded (by Gilbert Murray).

The emphatic changes in life which these developments suggest made deep dibble-punches into the loam of American (and British) societal concerns. Once seeded, social reform developed in its manifest aspects—health, family planning, medicine, labor law, women's rights, and, perhaps most dramatic of all, the movement of charitable activity. This new "cause"—moving away from the fashionable guilt-salving "Ladies' Aid" kind of frippery and toward the dedication of professionals to long-term betterment projects—brought advances of health care to indigents, identified pockets of disease, and dealt with what would now be called "Third World" dilemmas of famine and family size. All these issues are natural extensions of the activities of Jane Addams and Alice Hamilton.

A telling key to Jane Addams' vivacity and presence in her chosen theater of operations can be found by reading only a portion of the subject index which follows Allen F. Davis' biography *American Heroine: The Life and Legend of Jane Addams* (New York: Oxford University Press, 1973). Here (with ellipses replacing page numbers) is a verbatim listing under the subheading "Addams, Jane: *reputation and image*":

adoration . . . as community symbol . . . contrast between legend and reality . . . as most dangerous woman in America . . . declining reputation . . . as heroine and feminine conscience of nation . . . as mother figure . . . as priestess and sage . . . as "symbol of purity" . . . as "representative American" . . . restoration of reputation . . . as role-model . . . treated as saint . . . as villain and fool. . . .

Clearly, Addams was kept in a constant posture of public tension regarding the many agenda items she laid out for local, state, and national governments to reckon with, and to reconcile.

I expressed that I felt Ms. Addams and Hamilton to have been a "good match" for each other. From my readings, I have concluded this was not because they were complementary opposites in character, but because each had a certain tenor of energy—warm/emotional/human, or distant/objective/analytical—at different times and on different issues. For example, some visitors to Hull House described Addams as seeming "aloof"; and throughout the works of Davis, Wise, and Addams herself, everywhere nouns of high emotionality and praise are mated with adjectives which modify with grounded qualities. Hence, Davis gives us a chapter entitled "Practical Saint"; and the Nobel committee chose Addams in 1931 because she was one "of the finest representatives of American *practical idealism* [emphasis mine]."[4] Indeed, the exalted, "laying on of hands" sort of character might make for some lachrymose appreciation, but a true *reformer* is a work-oriented person. Practical experience is inextricably linked with effort; effort is a serious business. High moral purpose is fine, even noble; but the motivator with goals to meet and attitudes to alter is a sleeve roller. The true scenes of Jane Addams are not bedside melodramas, or tender little hands locked in her strong, bountiful ones; they are of fiercely determined Jane extorting $10,000 out of Henry Ford, of all people—for a women's peace march!

The two main foci of Addams' life—women's rights, and peace—came together in her Women's International League for Peace and Freedom. Hard fighter though she was, she fought on terms she defined, and she defined them in ways which stressed their feminine aspect. She saw peace not as "the absence of war but the unfolding of world-wide processes making for the nurture of human life." One of her most poignant arguments was in referring to the "peculiar revulsion" mothers feel when their sons go off to die.[5]

This mixture of the earthbound realist with an eye on higher human attainments was a part of her thinking from earliest adulthood. "The opening of the ages has long been waiting for this type of womanhood," she said in her valedictory address to her college class. "Now is the time for a faint realization of this type, with her faculties clear and acute, from the study of science, and with her hand upon the magnetic chain of humanity." Jane Addams, I venture, "studied science" in the sense that men "studied war"; that is, she was studious about the imposition of logical thinking upon her plans. Predetermined results, from deductive appraisal, were useful. Jane Addams sought *useful* things.

How, then, was Jane Addams at other times on other planes, planes of emotionality and intuition—those "feminine" characteristics? Like all deep thinkers, and like all assiduous workers (especially those who sustain significant ideals over many years), Jane Addams probably never felt that she would fail; because to conceive of her ideals—a peaceful world, a world of gender equality—I wager it was necessary for her to formulate, and then accept, the notion that *these goals were noble, but not outside the grasp of humankind.* She could stand in awe of the kind of perfection of which humanity is capable, however infinitesimal the pragmatic evidence for it. To be certain about one's ideals in this way is necessary to begin the kind of work this woman did; to continue to work, year after year, decade after decade, does not come from one's genius side, but from some kind of inner determinism, of which one is probably unaware.

This is the character of the woman who created Hull House, and with it, largely, the field of social work. This is also a woman who, among others, developed the concept of the League of Nations. This is also the woman who was a founder of the American Civil Liberties Union.

Such a person necessarily becomes politically involved. This Jane Addams did, in her support for Theodore Roosevelt in the 1912 election. At the Progressive Party convention, she presented herself before the crowd, and endorsed the candidate:

> I rise to second the nomination stirred by the splendid platform adopted by this convention. Measures of industrial amelioration, demands for social justice, long discussed by small groups in charity conferences and economic associations, have here been considered in a great national convention and are at last thrust into the stern arena of political action.
>
> A great party has pledged itself to the protection of children, to the care of the aged, to the relief of overworked girls, to the safe guarding of burdened men. Committed to these human undertakings, it is inevitable that such a party should appeal to women, should seek to draw upon the great reservoir of their moral energy so long undesired and unutilized in practical politics. . . .
>
> I second the nomination of Theodore Roosevelt because he is one of the few men in our public life who has been responsive to the social appeal and who has caught the significance of the modern movement. Because of that, because the programme will require a leader of invincible courage, of open mind, of democratic sympathies, one endowed with power to interpret the common man and to identify himself with the common lot, I heartily second the nomination.[6]

Though she intended no shrewdness in this act, it nonetheless added to her canonization as the saint of social justice. The vicissitudes of war, five years later, which earned her an equal dose of scorn and vilification, did not deter Addams from her goals, any more than had praise. For her stance against war, and for other reasons, the candidate considered most likely to receive a Nobel Peace Prize was nominated and passed over several times, starting in 1916, before it was awarded to her in 1931, four years before the end, and at a time when she was least capable of harnessing attention to her causes.

Alice Hamilton continued her contact with Addams. As illustrious as her friend was, the industrial physician's achievements on her own are among the most astonishing for any person, at any time. For a woman to have accomplished them, and in the years she accomplished them, is almost unbelievable.

Imagine a slight, unprepossessing woman coming into the office of your plant. From her looks, she might be the receptionist's mother, bringing a forgotten sack lunch; but the fantasy would be quickly dispelled when the lady turns out to be an expert on the toxicology of lead, and when she demands to see every tool, die, and open-hearth blast furnace within the bowels of your noxious, body-crippling manufactory.

Here was a woman whose correspondents included Walter Lippmann and Felix Frankfurter. Here is also a woman, writing her cousin Jessie from shipboard in 1925, watching the ship's band's "second violinist, a slim, fair boy with the most sensitive hands. I don't know why he is so different from an American boy but I cannot imagine our ever producing anything like him. He is at once pathetic and impudent, babyish and old, appealing and cold. I should feel quite helpless with him."

And two months later, the same individual, with the same sensibilities and heart waiting to be touched, moved herself and her cause along by the power of her intellect in a communication (written on Harvard University School of Public Health letterhead) to Professor Robert Morss Lovett of the University of Chicago.[7] Here was her "outline of the plan for expenditure of funds in the interest of workers' health," which was embodied in a scheme to attack the substance benzene, which she was one of the first to discover had lethal properties:

> There are two needs at present in American industry which are not being fully met. The first is scientific research in the field of the newer industrial poisons. No organization has undertaken this, although from time to time various centers of scientific research, such as Harvard, Yale, Syracuse University, and Columbia, have carried on studies of this kind, but the field is not by any means covered. One poisonous substance which came into prominence during the war and whose use has increased rapidly ever since is coal-tar benzol. An association of employers, the National Safety Council, has undertaken an inquiry into the actual conditions under which benzol is used in industry, but certain features of benzol poisoning which can only be determined by animal experimentation [this is 1925, remember!] are still unsolved and it will be impossible to fully control benzol poisoning in industry until these dark spots have been cleared up. I should therefore suggest as one line of work the provision of $25,000 for three years to be devoted to the thorough study of benzol and I would suggest that Harvard Medical School is best equipped to carry this out.
>
> The second need is to secure expert information concerning the dangerous dusts and vapors encountered in industry. In such industrial countries as England and Germany for instance, the central factory inspection department is responsible for this field. If any accident arises from a new

compound used in a trade, the experts from this department visit the plant, examine the workmen, and if necessary assign to the pharmacological department of some university the experimental work necessary to determine the nature of the poison. If it is a question of a well-known substance which is causing unusual trouble, the experts decide what means for protection are necessary to prevent such trouble.

In the United States we have no such experts. The Federal Public Health Service has no authority to make investigation unless invited to do so by the employers. They have not even a body of experts who can pass on a theoretical question. No state department of labor or department of health is equipped to deal with such problems. They cannot even undertake to analyze a mixture used in industry in order to determine its nature. It is therefore highly important that some consultative body with access to appropriate laboratory facilities be constituted in this country. It should have its seat in New York City and it should be widely advertised throughout the country, not only to trade unionists but also to employers of labor, for it is of the utmost importance that this body of experts be known as absolutely impartial, capable of dealing with these questions in the spirit of pure scientific inquiry. . . .

The Workers' Health Bureau of New York City to which the American fund has already contributed has already established far-reaching relations with organized labor. I have followed its work from the beginning and can assure you that it has a record of achievement which is very admirable. Their technique is as follows: They approach a trade union and establish relations with it, then they select an individual in a given plant, instruct him in the sanitary standards which apply to his industry and give him a questionnaire which he is to fill out concerning conditions in his plant. This is then checked up by one of the two directors of the Workers' Health Bureau; they then compare it with the sanitary code covering the locality and if there are violations report them to the proper authority. If, however, the sanitary code, as is often true, is inadequate for the protection of the workers, they work out in consultation with employers and employed a new detailed sanitary code and endeavor to have it accepted as a working agreement. They have succeeded in introducing a large number of these, especially in connection with the painters' trade.

They also undertake to study the health hazards of an industry; for instance, they have begun work with the stone cutters. We know already the injurious character of different kinds of natural stone so that in connection with granite, marble, sandstone and limestone cutters no examination of the stone is needed. For artificial stone cutters it is necessary to have analyses made of the stone dust. This the Workers' Health Bureau is doing. After this they must select typical groups of cutters numbering at least one hundred, and have thorough physical examination made including an X-ray of the chest and an expert interpretation of the X-ray. This is the only way to determine the actual injury done by dust.

The unions affiliated with the Workers' Health Bureau pay for its services but it is impossible to ask them to pay for this kind of research. An examination such as the above costs between $5 and $10 apiece and the stone cutters could not possibly pay for it. A similar piece of work ought to be done for the garage workers who are exposed to poisonous exhaust gases, but these men earn from $28 to $35 a week and they could not pay for such a study.

The Workers' Health Bureau needs a clinician on full time, an extension of its laboratory facilities, and a fund to pay for X-rays. Perhaps $15,000 a year would cover what it needs to extend the work as it should be extended, for it has already gone far out into the field and is capable of much further development.

A very close relation should be established between the Workers' Health Bureau and the consulting committee of experts, but the details of this will have to be worked out very carefully.

This is the pioneer at work, the medical equivalent of Jane Addams' first-ever social worker. Hamilton's letter is astonishing for her recognition of the issues, the clarity with which she saw their import, and the thought contained in her plan of attack. This is 1925: There is no National Institute of Health; there is no Occupational Safety and Health Administration; there is no Federal Drug Administration; there are no routine procedures to induce wealthy pharmaceutical houses to deliver fabulous research grants; there are no parameters for laboratory investigation. Medicine, in Alice Hamilton's learning days, was a lot like the Wright brothers' bicycle shop: What came out of it could fly through the air in ways da Vinci did not dream; but it was still a bicycle shop, with its processes more the heat and hammer of a smithy than the hum of programmed assembly in the industrial America which loomed on the horizon.

As it was with Pasteur, with Semmelweis,[8] with Banting,[9] and with Freud, so was it with Hamilton: Genius is inextricably linked to originality; advancement is ineluctably tied to hard work. The oldest alchemy in the world—the fervor of a curious mind, a positive spirit, and an indignant consciousness—merged into one, in the form and soul of a wisp of a woman with a penetrating gaze. The substances she called into question, the procedures she recommended, are in every preventive medicine text today. Occupational safety and health, despite their current hapless position as the rope in the tug-of-war between liberal and conservative governments, will remain urgent matters whose insistence for due regard will not go away. Alice Hamilton is the reason why.

The romantic side lived on in this woman, to be sure. This was not romantic in the domestic sense (for neither Hamilton nor Addams ever married; and only Addams seems to have had an attachment which might have developed into marriage). One of the hundreds of people who wrote to Jane Addams for help, or simply to unburden, was a woman who identified herself as a prostitute. Davis tells the story of Alice Hamilton's deciding to respond to this letter, in Addams' momentary absence from Hull House. Alice took up a correspondence with the woman, expecting a "thrilling glimpse into a terrible, unknown world filled with helpless victims of man's lust." Apparently, the woman would write her letters early in the morning before her clients arrived, and she gave the impression of herself as "a captive bird beating herself against the bars." At length, Dr. Hamilton decided to visit the woman, after first advising a local charity to notify the police if she failed to return by the end of the afternoon. "I found a home luxurious but vulgarly ugly," Hamilton later wrote, "and a woman of mature years, handsome, dignified, entirely mistress of herself. The pitiful little bird in the cage was a ludicrous picture."[10] The experience apparently gave the physician to conclude that women so engaged were actually more culpable than their clients, because of their mercenary attachment to the experience. It is one of few instances where parochialism got the better of this wise individual.

The Hamilton family of luminaries and Jane Addams (alone from her clan in the limelight) all survived into old age. By 1931, Jane Addams was able to see forty-odd agencies in Chicago, each fundamentally indebted to her. Alice Hamilton, who celebrated more than a century of birthdays, was, like her Chicago friend of earlier days, known throughout the world. She had come into medical science at a time when bright young men were learning new things in established fields. When she left life, she had long ago been the bright young woman, who taught new things in an unfathomed field. Love of learning and long life had been great gifts, totally deserved.

By the time America had stopped resisting, and then embraced, and finally incorporated the philosophy and accomplishments of Addams and Hamilton, it was pointed at last in a more progressive social direction. With child labor laws, and preventive controls on industry, some semblance of enlightenment worthy of a new century had become evident. With its social turmoil somewhat soothed, America was at last off on a good footing now—just in time to look up into the cyclone of a depression, and another world war.

But there was the rest of the world, far away from the shores of America, which, with the Old World's handicaps, had not fared so well nor rebounded so quickly from the problems following the Armistice. In fact, at this very point which finds an America blowing hot and cold with adolescent anxiety, and a world in a roiling swirl of actions which led inevitably to global war, another deep-thinking and deeply committed reformer was caught up in the maelstrom of bringing *his* culture into the twentieth century. Thus comes the one subject of this book whose roots are not Western.

How might Americans, or anyone else for that matter, lift their sights from the unremarkable likes of their neighborhood preacher, with his acceptably intoned litanies and his brow lined from inner suffering, to discover a figure—indeed, one of the first international figures of the twentieth century—whose distilled beliefs and simple statements revealed the rarity a person could possess, and the intricacy of which a human being could be capable? How might one apprehend a figure absorbed in bringing the perfection of God to the wretched lives of his human family?

A figure of this stature, in the form of a living man, would not have been possible in the America of Father Coughlin, or the Austria of Martin Buber, or even the Tibet of the Dalai Lama. The majestic continents which included these countries had to defer to another land, an impoverished and desiccated subcontinent, in order to locate one of this mystical greatness. A goodness so great, in a man, that it could permeate mankind, not just in his lifetime but for generations, had come on only one part of the earth's surface: It had come on the subcontinent of India, in an individual, in a man; and it had come in our lifetime.

NOTES

1. Sixty years ago, when Hull House had attained the age of four decades, Robert Morss Lovett, writing for *The New Republic,* indicated there were at least forty such early agencies listed. This, before FDR. (In fact, the future chief executive only recently had become disabled himself; with abundant funds and astonishing motivation, he was able to do the work on himself which Addams was required to do for so many others.)

2. Among family members were her sister Edith Hamilton, the great classicist; a sister Ruth, who was an accomplished artist; a brother, Arthur, an educator; and another sister, Margaret Hamilton, who dedicated her career to library science.

3. Sicherman, Barbara. *Alice Hamilton: A Life in Letters.* A Commonwealth Fund Book. Harvard University Press, Cambridge and London, 1984.

4. This term has evolved into many variants from others' descriptions of Gandhi.

5. Wise, Winifred E. *Jane Addams of Hull House.* Harcourt, Brace and Company, New York, 1935.

6. Davis, Allen F. *American Heroine: The Life and Legend of Jane Addams.* Oxford University Press, New York, 1973, p. 189.

7. Lovett is the same man who wrote *The New Republic*'s article on Jane Addams; he was a personal friend of both Addams and Hamilton.

8. This Hungarian physician discovered and attacked the problems of sepsis in the late 1800s.

9. In 1921, the Canadian Sir Frederick G. Banting and his assistant Charles Best devised the process whereby insulin could be isolated from the pancreas.

10. Sicherman, *Alice Hamilton,* pp. 291–294.

Chapter Two

Mohandas Karamchand Gandhi: Goat's Curds and Flax, and the Wisdom of the Ages

Mohandas Karamchand Gandhi started his professional life with all the canny tools of a flashy little man: a lawyer's glib tongue, cravatted Western garb beneath the coffee-bean face, the usual knowledge of torts and misprisions which was ready to be dispensed at fees appropriate to the power of a bailout man. He ended life clothed in dhoti simplicity, sustained by goat's curds, self-abnegation, and a projected serenity which grew like a lily from his belief in man.

The attraction to the simple ways came later; after jail and beatings, astonishment at the treatment of some human beings carved and nudged at him until, a man of the people, he emerged a prophet. For that flowering belief evinced a strength of commitment to transcendence which is greatness, and which is the kind of spirituality and polity from which others' greatness can come. Gandhi, the celibate prophet, sowed the seeds of *ahimsa*—noninjury to animal life, or nonviolence—that carried down through the travails of the twentieth century with enough momentum to motivate another subject of this book to incorporate Gandhian principles in the racial struggles of modern Alabama.

Between his May 1893 South African train trip from Durban to Pretoria, during which the newly enfranchised lawyer with the brown skin was forced out of his first-class seat, and the gathering for morning prayers on January 30, 1948, when an amateur radical named Godse fired revolver bullets point-blank into his chest, Mohandas Karamchand Gandhi, the little Hindu from Porbandar, whittled away at his earthly possessions, his mental concerns, and his words, until there came from him an expressiveness as sublime as the truth force, *satyagraha,* and as immediate as the beat of a heart. For these reasons, Gandhi must be viewed, and studied, as a foremost "orator": preaching compassion, depth of commitment, and a religiosity of respect for mankind which flows over, and obliterates, the narrow coordinates of sect.

The subcontinent of India seems long to have held the fascination of many in the West. The bright exoticism of almost every facet of life for Hindu, Brahmin, and Sikh appears as rare and special colors to those from England and America. The unbelievable blanket formed by the masses lay across the land, a blanket of so many, many people! The sights and sounds, the free interplay of large beasts of burden right in the centers of commerce; the rich curries, the costumes, the prayers, the beggars who live in the streets, the masses being purified by a Ganges flowing with the whole exudate of a society—how the English ever let themselves get close enough to this land to stamp it into serfdom is mysterious in itself. The English reserve has not opened up many Britons to the charms of the peoples of India. Even as exceptional a figure as Churchill held Gandhi, the foremost Indian of all, in striking disdain. And though Lord Irwin (''Halifax'' in the later era of the war) played the diffident aristocrat when he and Sir Winston engaged in their quiet duel with King George VI for appointment as prime minister, as one of the last viceroys preceding independence he had no difficulty executing Indians for what the English representative saw as capital crimes. To Churchill, Gandhi's intervention on behalf of three condemned men revolted him as a ''nauseating and humiliating spectacle of this onetime Inner Temple lawyer, now a seditious fakir, striding half naked up the steps of the Viceroy's palace, there to negotiate and parley on equal terms with the representative of the King-Emperor.''[1]

And yet, Americans have felt a compelling pull toward the Mahatma. This has been especially true of journalists; two renowned writers of the prewar and wartime eras, Vincent Sheehan and William Shirer, have written books of their experiences with Gandhi. Also, photographer Margaret Bourke-White created some of her best-known images from the slender little body in the dhoti.

Why had this simplicity-seeking, self-castigating man had this effect? These Americans, particularly, were seasoned journalists, not teenagers prey to an inebriating fancy. Their story in 1931—the initial rationale for contact—was understandable: The picture of an Indian of the Indian National Congress standing up against the British government and having so many successful encounters could not be turned down. And Gandhi's ploys, his appeal to the opposite (a basic Christian turnaround, such as ''Love thy neighbor'') in the forms of *ahimsa,* his fasting so that a country might live, his absolute candor on any subject, including his endless struggles with *brahmacharya* (sexual abstinence), his astonishing ability to discern just the right response to the latest British oppression, could only whet the fascination of a professional newspaperman.

So it was with Vincent Sheehan, an American journalist who found in Gandhi a force of sufficient magnitude to change his life. Sheehan ended up in a novitiate's posture, sitting with Gandhi (or taking walks, as was Gandhi's custom), so as to absorb something of this unique individual's irreplaceable wisdom. Much of his writing on the Indian leader (in his book *Lead, Kindly Light*) characterizes the diminutive Gandhi as being in absolute control, and the extremely tall Halifax as oafish, stumbling over the courtesies each of this odd duo gave in respect to the other, as they danced the courtly dance on whose movements the lives of millions depended. While Shirer remained merely an admirer of Gandhi, Sheehan moved swiftly into the role of a philosophical disciple, a role which brought him several lengthy interchanges with Gandhi within the few days preceding his murder. He was on the garden grounds of Birla House in New Delhi, having sought the Master out because of a premonition of his death, when he heard the shots which Nathuram Godse pumped into the greatest Indian in a subcontinent of countless Indians.

The writings of Gandhi which the Mahatma seemed to feel most deeply are those which, in a literary sense, serve as his hand laid upon the anguished breast of an angry people. These are the words of a counsel of peace, the plea of a prophet for unceasing effort to be devoted by man to the conquering of his instincts of hatred, as Gandhi struggled with what he considered his own base instincts.

Here is his "doctrine of the sword" (dating from 1920):

I do believe that when there is only a choice between cowardice and violence, I would advise violence. I would rather have India resort to arms in order to defend her honor than that she should in a cowardly manner become or remain a helpless victim to her own dishonor. But I believe that non-violence is infinitely superior to violence, forgiveness is more manly than punishment.

Forgiveness adorns a soldier. But abstinence is forgiveness only when there is power to punish; it is meaningless only when there is no power to punish; it is meaningless when it pretends to proceed from a helpless creature. A mouse hardly forgives a cat when it allows itself to be torn apart by her. . . . But I do not believe India to be helpless, I do not believe myself to be a helpless creature. . . .

Let me not be misunderstood. Strength does not come from physical capacity. It comes from an indomitable will. . . .

I am not a visionary. I claim to be a practical idealist. The religion of non-violence is not meant merely for the rishis and saints. It is meant for the common people as well. Non-violence is the law of our species as violence is the law of the brute. The spirit lies dormant in the brute, and he knows no law but that of physical might. The dignity of man requires obedience to a higher law—to the strength of the spirit.

I have therefore ventured to place before India the ancient law of self-sacrifice. For satyagraha and its offshoots, non-cooperation and civil resistance, are nothing but new names for the law of suffering. The rishis who discovered the law of non-violence in the midst of violence were greater geniuses than Newton. They were themselves greater warriors than Wellington. Having themselves known the use of arms, they realized their uselessness and taught a weary world that its salvation lay not through violence but through non-violence.

Non-violence in its dynamic condition means conscious suffering. It does not mean meek submission to the will of the evildoer, but it means the putting of one's whole soul against the will of the tyrant. Working under this law of our being, it is possible for a single individual to defy the whole might of an unjust empire to save his honor, his religion, his soul, and lay the foundation for that empire's fall or regeneration.

And so I am not pleading for India to practice non-violence because it is weak. I want her to practice non-violence being conscious of her strength and power. . . . I want India to recognize that she has a soul that cannot perish, and that can rise triumphant above any physical weakness and defy the physical combination of a whole world. . . .

I isolate this non-cooperation from Sinn Feinism, for it is so conceived as to be incapable of being offered side by side with violence. But I invite even the school of violence to give this peaceful non-cooperation a trial. It will not fail through its inherent weakness. It may fail because of poverty of response. Then will be the time for real danger. The high-souled men, who are unable to suffer national humiliation any longer, will want to vent their wrath. They will take to violence. So far as I know, they must perish without delivering themselves or their country from the wrong. If India takes up the doctrine of the sword, she may gain momentary victory. Then India will cease to be the pride of my heart. I am wedded to India because I owe my all to her. I believe absolutely that she has a mission for the world.[2]

What makes these words so much the rhetoric of Gandhi's crisis is the extent to which he has pried apart the gates of his soul, so as to expose himself to the harshest standards of the tenets of these concepts. Gandhi was forever the litmus for his own laws; he held no expectations for others that he was not prepared to try and meet.

Another concept Gandhi attempted to express was about democracy. To this Hindu, such a governmental concept did not have anything to do with suffrage, or numerical majorities. Rather, his "democrat" was someone who gave equally of himself for the benefit of everyone:

Let us recognize the fact that the [Indian National] Congress enjoys the prestige of a democratic character and influence not by the number of delegates and visitors it has drawn to its annual function, but by an ever increasing amount of service it has rendered. Western democracy is on its trial, if it has not already proved a failure. May it be reserved to India to evolve the true science of democracy by giving a visible demonstration of its success.

Corruption and hypocrisy ought not to be the inevitable products of democracy, as they undoubtedly are today. Nor is bulk a true test of democracy. True democracy is not inconsistent with a few persons representing the spirit, the hope, and the aspirations of those whom they claim to represent. I hold that democracy cannot be evolved by forcible methods. The spirit of democracy cannot be imposed from without; it has to come from within.[3]

The power one can feel from Gandhi's words comes from the calm with which they are delivered. This is no diatribe, no "argument" in the sense of rhetorical intention. The coolness and even conversational manner with which he expresses his ideas provide insight by themselves for the appeal of these ideals to the sought-after social imperative of a Jane Addams, or to the intelligent scientific applications of an Alice Hamilton, or, as we will find later, to the urgency of the search for effective palliation of society's angers undertaken by Dr. King. Tranquillity of spirit is signaled by the calm of expression. (Calmness can be sinister, as well; the effectiveness of this technique has been used in theatrical presentations for years, and was even recommended by William Shirer's boss Ed Murrow to his radio writers twenty years after Gandhi's Indian National Congress difficulties.)

Gandhi sought with energy for those who came into his sphere to find in his examples the wherewithal to lead integrated lives. It was the fractured life, the organism of disparate energies, the creature of isolated cells of experience, which was doomed. But the focused, integrated existence is characteristic of an organism who can vibrate sympathetically with his fellows; the whole of a "species" consisting of such organisms can move to common music. Thus, the vegetarian who does not practice *ahimsa* is not a being governed by truth; and the citizen who does not lend his muscle to the rope-pull of all the citizens is unsynchronized, fossilized, isolated. This isolate will inevitably die. And this is the fate of anyone who moves in counterrhythm to the pulse of people.

Gandhi's tools of persuasion were more than the rhetoric in his exquisite language. His use of all opportunities, all faculties, was ingenious as well as effective. The simple repetition of the surface elements in his techniques to combat the domination by the interventionist and imperialist country that was fighting India's self-rule was amazing: If you want to object, you lose weight (and health) in a fast. If you desire to express true independence, you get your salt from the sea, not from the foreign merchant with his conditional enslavements. If you have been deprived of cloth for your back, then you learn to spin your own cloth. Self-reliance, as so many social reformers have known, is indivisible from self-respect. And the ability to act, and impart meaningful consequence to the movement of one's life, is inextricably bound to the personal regard one holds for one's own worth—which, by Gandhi's "democratic" meaning, is the worth of the community, and its respect for its own reason for existing and right to exist.

In the 1930s, the Gandhian tactics displayed their creator's ingenuity in a

number of campaigns: notably, the refusal to accept the tax on salt, and the
nondependence on Britain for textile goods, which campaign resulted in Gandhi's resort to daily spinning of wool from flax.[4] During this time, Gandhi wrote
several well-circulated letters to the English viceroy and other influential Britons
in India, articulating cogently his posture on these and other subjects.

The letter to the viceroy is considered the opening effort in the elevation of
swaraj (self-rule) to the level of a determinant in the success or failure of future
relations between India and Britain:

> It is not without a pang that I return the Kaisar-i-Hind Gold Medal granted
> to me by your predecessor for my humanitarian work in South Africa, for
> my services as officer-in-charge of the Indian Volunteer Ambulance Corps
> in 1896, and the Boer War Medal for my services as assistant superinten-
> dent of the Indian Volunteer Stretcher-bearer Corps during the Boer War
> of 1900. I venture to return these medals in pursuance of the scheme of
> Non-Co-operation inaugurated today in connection with the Khilafat
> movement. Valuable as these honours have been to me, I cannot wear
> them with an easy conscience so long as my Mussalman countrymen have
> to labour under a wrong done to their religious sentiment. . . . [Gandhi
> catalogues the "shameful acts" and the "wanton cruelty and inhumanity
> almost unparalled in modern times."]
>
> In my humble opinion the ordinary method of agitation by way of
> petitions, deputations, and the like is no remedy for moving to repentance
> a Government so hopelessly indifferent to the welfare of its charge as the
> Government of India has proved to be. In European countries condonation
> of such grievous wrongs as the Khilafat and the Punjab would have re-
> sulted in a bloody revolution by the people. . . . But half of India is too
> weak to offer violent resistance, and the other half is unwilling to do so.
> I have, therefore, ventured to suggest the remedy of Non-Co-operation,
> which enables those who wish to do so to disassociate themselves from
> the Government, and which, if it is unattended by violence and undertaken
> in an orderly manner, must compel it to retrace its steps and undo the
> wrongs committed.[5]

Gandhi concluded his letter by requesting that the viceroy call a conference
for reparations. At the same time, he wrote to other Englishmen of influence,
to describe the movement he was a part of, and to explain why the English rule
was one he regarded as "evil":

> Dear Friend,—
> . . . . In my humble opinion no Indian has co-operated with the British
> Government more than I have for an unbroken period of twenty-nine years
> of public life in the face of circumstances that might well have turned any
> other man into a rebel. . . . I put my life in peril four times for the sake

of the Empire. . . . So last December I pleaded hard for a trustful co-operation. I fully believed that Mr. Lloyd George would redeem his promise to the Mussalmans, and that the revelations of the official atrocities in the Punjab would secure full reparation for the Punjabis. But the treachery of Mr. Lloyd George and its appreciation by you, and the condonation of the Punjab atrocities, have completely shattered my faith in the good intentions of the Government and the nation which is supporting it.

Gandhi then lists eight repugnant truths demonstrating "what the British Empire means to India":

1. Exploitation of India's resources for the benefit of Great Britain.
2. An ever-increasing military expenditure and a Civil Service the most expensive in the world.
3. Extravagant working of every Department in utter disregard of India's poverty.
4. Disarmament and therefore emasculation of a whole nation lest an armed nation might imperil the lives of a handful of you in our midst.
5. Traffic in intoxicating drugs and liquors for the purpose of maintaining a top-heavy administration.
6. Progressively repressive legislation in order to suppress an ever-growing agitation seeking to express a nation's agony.
7. Degrading treatment of Indians residing in British Dominions.
8. Total disregard of our feelings by glorifying the Punjab Administration and flouting the Muhammadan sentiment.

I know you would not mind if we could fight and wrest the sceptre from your hands [he wrote]. You know we are powerless to do that; for you have ensured our incapacity to fight in open and honourable battle. Bravery on the battlefield is thus impossible for us. Bravery of the soul still remains open to us.[6]

In another letter, Gandhi outlined his intentions to enlist all possible assistance to Indians in the boycotting of foreign cloth. The discussion of this plan, it should be remembered, followed the General Strike in Britain by only a few years. Yet that strike, carried out by a unanimous force of disgruntled workers, ended in regression for the strikers and total victory for the ruling class of England. Gandhi, in contrast, quietly describes the intention of Indians, an already-impoverished lot, to restrict themselves further, and, moreover, voluntarily.

Dear Friend [he began once more],
. . . . Here in India you [as an Englishman] belong to a system that is vile beyond description. . . . You are as much slaves of the system as we are. . . . It is a degrading spectacle for you and for us. . . . [Therefore] I invite

you to join me in destroying a system that has dragged both you and us down . . . [by asking you] to help us in the boycott of foreign cloth. . . .

The Lancashire cloth, as English historians have shown, was forced upon India, and her own world-famed manufactures were deliberately and systematically ruined. India is therefore at the mercy, not only of Lancashire, but also of Japan, France, and America. Just see what this has meant to India. We send out of India every year sixty crores (more or less) of rupees for cloth. We grow enough cotton for our own cloth. Is it not madness to send cotton outside India, and have it manufactured into cloth there and shipped to us? Was it right to reduce India to such a helpless state?

A hundred and fifty years ago we manufactured all our cloth. Our women spun fine yarn in their own cottages, and supplemented the earnings of their husbands. The village weavers wove that yarn. It was an indispensable part of national economy in a vast agricultural country like ours. It enabled us in a most natural manner to utilize our leisure. To-day our women have lost the cunning of their hands, and the enforced idleness of millions has impoverished the land. Many weavers have become sweepers. Some have taken to the profession of hired soldiers. Half the race of artistic weavers has died out, and the other half is weaving imported foreign yarn for want of finer hand-spun yarn.

You will perhaps now understand what boycott of foreign cloth means to India. It is not devised as a punishment. If the Government were to-day to redress the Khilafat and the Punjab wrongs, and consent to India attaining immediate Swaraj, the boycott movement must still continue. Swaraj means at the least the power to conserve Indian industries that are vital to the economic existence of the nation, and to prohibit such imports as may interfere with such existence. Agriculture and handspinning are the two lungs of the national body. They must be protected against consumption at any cost.[7]

Gandhi's techniques—of shaming through courtesy and of whipping Englishmen with the fear that unless they reverse themselves through positive action, Indians will suffer and it will rest on English consciences—were powerful weapons which, even though predicated on a sort of "action through inactivity," produced demonstrable results. Such self-denial, which was so far-ranging, was a template for all of Gandhi's successful maneuvers to bring Britain to a posture of reconciliation and cooperation.

Finally, Gandhi expended considerable energy on the all-encompassing subject of *swaraj,* or national self-government, for India. This, of course, was the continuous focal point for all of India's leaders during the first four and a half decades of the twentieth century. The Raj, the 200-year-old domination by the British, was coming apart; everyone knew this, from the king on down. For the Indian leadership, which at various times included Nehru, Patel, Muhammad Ali

Jinnah (the fierce spoiler whose brainchild, Pakistan, ultimately caused the tragically consequential division of India), and Gandhi—and, not least, the handful of inordinately wealthy princes who depended upon the status quo for the maintenance of their wealth—it was just a matter of time. For the British—including the ministers concerned with colonial matters, and the viceroy—it came down to resistance, resistance, resistance, which, like most other problems adding to Britain's postwar predicaments, simply represented a stalling for time, while the shock of a fallen empire was allowed to settle in, and a face-saving plan could develop.[8] The British government put this dilemma in the hands of Lord Mountbatten, whose strategic acumen, personable presence, tangential ties to royalty, and "secret weapon" made him the ideal swan song viceroy.[9]

One of Gandhi's techniques for dealing with complicated problems was to complicate them further, perhaps on the basis of two negatives yielding a positive. Thus, in 1940, when Great Britain's ministers had their hands full determining whether they would be able to survive war with Germany, the "seditious fakir" elevated the dialogue relating to the war and the future of a free India along lines of discussion about the question of nonviolence. At this point, India had offered its cooperation to Britain on the war, contingent upon its recognition as an independent nation. This Britain rejected.

Even the All-India Congress Committee was internally disputatious on this point. In an effort to come to an agreement within its ranks on the issue, and also to make progress with Britain's obstinacy, the committee issued a resolution stressing the country's valuable contribution to world peace through *ahimsa,* the central notion so dear to Gandhi. To the ministry in London, this talk of neighbor loving was so much inanity; there followed, for a variety of reasons, the imprisonment of many, including Gandhi, Nehru, and others. And then, in rapid succession, came the war's conclusion, the coming to a head of the India question, the appointment of Mountbatten as viceroy, independence, and Gandhi's murder.

There is an abject sadness in the notion that so much martyrdom has had to accompany the special struggles in the six or seven decades of social consciousness in the world. The Darrows and the Kings of the world and the Kennedys (late to social responsibility, and dear payors for the right to have done their part in redirecting mankind's energies from conflict, manipulation, and combative struggle) are signs that the special gifts of two bright and driving women in the early century are bearing wondrous fruit. And the presence of a Gandhi, once in many lifetimes, is gratifying evidence of the rightness of the actions of those powerfully motivated to engage in efforts of social responsibility.

There is something in the story of "Gandiji" which invokes all the sentiments of the Passion of Christ. The martyrdom, the tears of the masses, the flowers with their blanket of scent, the agony, the burning bier with its peaceful figure: Once a breathing being of extraordinary sensibility, now a sacrificial offering, this Mohandas K. Gandhi was a man who gave the ultimate of pain so that others would learn to love.

And yet, it has not been necessary to deify "Bapu" Gandhi, in order to change him from martyr to example. The very comparisons with Christ give all the more credence to the humanity of this man who became a symbol. As Christ washed the feet of beggars, so Gandhi cleaned the latrines of the untouchables. The Kingdom of God which became synonymous with the acts of Jesus is the invitation to greatness which results from following the teachings of a prophet.

ENDNOTE

In the years since Gandhi's death, the import of his life has come to hold widely divergent meanings for different people. In a sense, the weight of his ideas represents now a sort of touchstone for directing the meanings of the lives of many. Using a modern metaphor, his essence is a kind of satellite, roving the void on its own, but remaining in the heavens as a fixed entity against which to bounce the separate signals of our philosophies, as we attempt to redirect them elsewhere, or even back to ourselves.

No one felt closer to Gandhi than his colleague in the pursuit of India's independence, Jawaharlal Nehru. I found in India's first prime minister a complex man with a range of impulses. His character seemed, from what reading I have given him, to contain even more contradictions, in terms of reconciling himself and India with the West, than his mentor.

In John Kenneth Galbraith's recording of his years as Kennedy's ambassador to India, a small anecdote revealed itself to me which says as much about Gandhi, and about India and the Indias of the world, as all the legends of the great mass movements within the sweep of the Mahatma's life.

Galbraith had made an impromptu visit to the Indian prime minister. On a shelf, next to a photograph of the Mahatma, was one of Nehru with Jacqueline Kennedy. The pair were walking, arm in arm, absorbed in themselves in much the same way as Nehru had on countless occasions been absorbed with another Western leader's wife: Edwina Mountbatten. Somehow, with both women, Nehru put his personal allure to work, in an attempt to establish rapport with the women most closely attached to the figureheads of the West who held such influence over India.

As a touchstone for Nehru, Gandhi represented that which is pure Indian; his beloved Bapu kept him directed on the path of humane values, of virtue. This made it possible for Nehru to retain an abiding "forward march" for India, while keeping touch in little ways with the elements that threatened this attention. He neither wore the Western dress of an Ali Jinnah, nor maintained the Eastern asceticism of the Mahatma. Rather, he was just what he knew he was, a flawed Indian, who plucked a rose each day and put it into his jacket's lapel, and who needed some intimate experience of the women who came, with large eyes and pale skin, as emissaries of their husbands and of their husbands' governments.

Thus, as a natural man, Nehru could be forgiven his indulgence of male appetites. But as a leader of India, he might have been praiseworthy for knowing, instinctively, that these very manifestations of instinct could provide a conduit to him of ways of knowing the West and its leaders wholly unavailable from any other means. What the West would have seen as "cheeky" gestures seemed in these contexts to be acts supremely Eastern.

The point of interest in the new prime minister's functioning in the wake of the spiritual leader's assassination is this: Gandhi was "holy," Nehru secular. Gandhi's cause, therefore, was exalted; Nehru's—and India's—execution of the leader's concepts was dismayingly human, flawed in ways lethal and demoralizing. So much of this duality (the eternal conflict between theoretical and applied ethics) suggests the burden to a public left by rhetorical urgings. It is often hopeless for the reality of living to match the quintessence of the rhetorically expressed dream; what the word warrior and the ones for whom he has gone to battle must always ponder is that the effort is everything. The frowning Mahatma had found his passion, spread his philosophical seed, and expired; the smiling Nehru was forever locked within his purgatorial humanity. These poles form a kind of irresolute Jacob's Ladder, and plague every epoch's inspiring leader and beleagured legatee. Yet without such poles, perhaps the spark cannot rise at all.

NOTES

1. Churchill's biting words, and the incident, are cited by Shirer, *20th Century Journey: A Memoir of a Life and Times—The Nightmare Years: 1930–1940,* Little, Brown, Boston, 1984; Manchester, *The Last Lion: Winston Spencer Churchill, 1932–1940,* Little, Brown, Boston, 1988; and Collins and La Pierre, *Freedom at Midnight,* Simon and Schuster, New York, 1975.

2. Gandhi, Mohandas K. *Gandi's Autobiography.* [Edition undetermined; based upon the 1941 English edition issued by the Navajivan Press], passim.

3. Ibid.

4. This habit remained throughout Gandhi's life, even during periods of fasting.

5. Gandhi. *Autobiography,* passim.

6. Ibid.

7. Ibid.

8. This was a process, as noted earlier, begun before Sarajevo was anything but another easily misspelled Baltic place-name, along with Bosnia and Herzegovina, of which it was the capital city. The flashpoint of the Great War, and the locus for Serbian horror in the 1990s, unexotic Sarajevo's mean existence testifies to the democratic hand of history's geographic arbitrariness.

9. The "secret weapon," about which much controversy still exists, was Lady Mountbatten's intimate association with Jawaharlal Nehru, an allegedly Platonic liaison which lasted until Edwina Mountbatten's death in 1961 (see Endnote).

Chapter Three

Clarence Darrow:
Gold in the Land of Pyrite

I know the future is on my side. You may hang these boys; you may hang them by the neck until they are dead. But in doing it you will turn your face toward the past.

—Clarence Darrow

A lawyer of recent acquaintance revealed in casual conversation that he was becoming adjusted to his new specialty, and did not find the adjustment as difficult as he had first thought. As he was in early middle age, and I knew he had been practicing law for some time, I asked what he meant by a *new* specialty.

"Well," he began slowly, "I've only been doing tax law for about a year."

"I thought tax law was right up there with detailing property descriptions," I ventured.

He smiled, a little sourly. "Yeah. Well, I had a choice: either never sleep at night, when I am supposed to be asleep, or risk going to sleep during the daytime, when I am supposed to be examining IRS schedules."

When I asked him to explain, he told me he had practiced criminal law for twenty years. He said the pressure had been just about to kill him.

"Look," he said, and showed me his thumbnails. There was not much left of them. "Chewed 'em off. Long ago. Clean gone. That's what you do when your client's gonna get the chair. Or not get the chair. Depending on what *you* say!"

I prodded a bit. He'd kept twelve men from California's gas chamber. Two others had said goodbye to him, and went inside the green tank—forever.

"But weren't they killers, or something?"

He nodded. "Vicious murderers. If I told you, you'd never forgive me."

"But—that kind of work sounds so—important!" I said. "Can't *anybody* do a 1040?"

He stopped. We'd been out walking, but now he turned to me, and stared intently into my eyes. It was as if he was looking for the right words. He had a feral look about him now; I'd sent him into some place, an old place, he'd tried hard to keep away from. *Don't ask this of me!* he seemed to be pleading. But still he said nothing.

It was only later—months later—that I had any inkling of what was going on in my friend's mind. It was only then that I had come to realize that all attorneys weren't like the downtown San Francisco crowd—gambling three years of time, some pretty steep debts, and the inconvenience of learning a few Latin words on the road to partnership, certain wealth and property, and a reasonable expectation that by forty, they'd never really have to work again. It was only then that I realized all the lawyer jokes and the shark reputations and the golf games and the old guard clubs and the church affiliations didn't actually mean that *all* lawyers were like this.

What had made the difference in my thinking?

One thing was that I'd read about Clarence Seward Darrow.

He'd of course been a legend for a long time. The crusty old guy with the wry mind who'd wiped out old Bryan in Tennessee. The fellow who had saved Leopold and Loeb from the gallows. But it was not until I read about Darrow that his earlier legal career came to my attention—the fact that he'd had an opportunity, early on, to be a corporate lawyer with great reward, that his skills could guarantee him the fabulous kind of wealth most attorneys today cannot get out of their minds.

It was part of his astonishing record that Darrow had defended more than fifty persons accused of murder, and had only failed to save one from execution (Robert Prendergast), and that one early in his career (1894).

Darrow was a thinker, a reader, and a lover of poetry (Rupert Brooke and Swinburne, who were contemporaneous with him, Shakespeare, Keats, Blake, Burns). He had a strong wit, reinforced by social takers-to-task like Twain and Bertrand Russell. He appreciated new thinking; he knew the various writings of the Huxley family; he took Havelock Ellis seriously. He paid homage to Voltaire, whom he credited with being the father of the French Revolution. How many attorneys have paid homage to Voltaire? Darrow thought about, and wrote about, living and dying, about avoiding confrontation with life's questions by overfilling the day with activity, about avoiding the satisfaction of the moment by always thinking about what isn't here now.

This is the man who thought it worthwhile to defend deadbeats, ne'er-do-wells, sick men and rich spoiled men, and men who treated human life with caprice and scorn and cynicism and mortal disrespect. This was the man who didn't think he knew enough about God to be sure a God was there, but thought he knew enough about man to want man to continue being there. He knew men's minds and hearts and souls the way a surgeon knows his patients' insides. He was a preacher in the courtrooms, but one who had a way of making the sermons come out of the accused and turning juries into choruses, choruses in the Greek tradition of contemplators of morality.

Darrow, like Gandhi, was unsure of himself, not in the sense of having a lack of self-knowledge, but in the sense of being possessed of such humility that he knew it unworthy to make judgments. Today, a lawyer's job is not to search for the truth, but rather to take a lot of time to parcel out responsibility for the consequences of an injury in such a way that the letter of the law is met, and some satisfaction accrues to his client, both of which make his fee justified.

It is doubtful that Darrow cared a whit for this kind of thinking. In all like-lihood, his search was *only* a search for the truth. He wanted to find the truths about life and men, whether those verities could be harnessed as elements to present in a court of law or not; for he felt that fundamentally, in the ways that it should count, the law inevitably failed. The law never *revealed;* it only *settled.* Life just didn't open up that way, for Clarence Darrow.

No; Clarence Seward Darrow was a man without illusions. And the less driven by illusions people seemed to him, the more committed he was to their enlight-enment, their protection, their freedom.

If Clarence Darrow ever chewed his thumbnails to the quick, it is not re-corded. But there were to be no self-imposed sinecures to the tax desk for him. No; he had to stick it out, to the last man.

> Your pity I will not implore,
> For Pity ye hae nane!
> Justice, alas! has gien him o'er,
> And mercy's day is gane.[1]

In 1924, two wealthy young college students from respected Chicago Jewish families abducted a fourteen-year-old boy named Robert Franks, and without malice—or feeling of any kind, really—they murdered him in a brutal and disconnected way.

Chicago was ignited with rage. If ever there was a time when justice should be summary, when justice should be swift—!

When the shock, and the grief, had lifted enough to begin the hard road of unremitting reality which would be their lives from then on, the families of Richard Loeb and Nathan Leopold did one thing: They hired Clarence Darrow to defend their sons.

Darrow did defend Leopold and Loeb. And in 1924—a good year for killing murderers—these two sick, spoiled young men were anointed by Darrow's po-tions, and sentenced to life in prison, protected from society, even if not from themselves. Loeb lasted twelve years until being knifed to death by another prisoner; Leopold served thirty-four years and was paroled; he was then only fifty-two years of age, but a much, much older—and presumably wiser—man.

Clarence Darrow never received his fee for this legal service. It was due; it should have been paid. God (if there was one) *knew* it should have been paid. Two families should have rushed to pay him, with deep gratitude. But he was not paid. Human life does not work like this. There are catches to gratitude. Gratitude, like Darrow's approach to law, was in its own way painfully revealing. This was his mistake—succeeding, being a competent lawyer in the age when shame and transference and denial operated, as they always have, in the human psyche. Only in this case these things operated without being redirected in such a way as to serve justice also upon Clarence Darrow.

It did not matter, truly, to this attorney. A fee was never the reason he stepped into the discomfiting swirl of energies which is the inside of a court of law. Darrow's friend Judge Harry Fisher urged him to "go after them," but the lawyer never pursued this demeaning point.

In a packed Chicago hearing room in 1924, a relatively youthful jurist sits, solemn-faced, behind a high, imposing desk. It is covered with papers, with gooseneck lamps, with other paraphernalia suggesting that the age of streamline has not yet been born.[2]

A man whose skin and flaccid form indicate that he has spent too much time indoors stands before, and below, the bench (a common word meaning "judge's desk" and also a legal term meaning "all that we incorporate herewith when we refer to United States Constitutional Law"). The man is physically below the level of the jurist; this is by design and long custom. But what the man is about to say will have him spiritually soar upward with such towering strength that he will elevate the bench, the desk, the jurist, and all concerns juridical, to an imposing and heretofore unconquered height.

Here—as one glimpse into the contribution of Clarence Seward Darrow to the advancement of civilization—is his plea to the jury in the defense of Nathan Leopold and Richard Loeb:[3]

> Were these boys in their right minds? Here were two boys with good intellect, one eighteen and one nineteen. They had all the prospects that life could hold out for any of the young; one a graduate of Chicago and another of Ann Arbor; one who had passed his examination for the Harvard Law School and was about to take a trip in Europe—another who had passed at Ann Arbor, the youngest in his class, with three thousand dollars in the bank. Boys who never knew what it was to want a dollar; boys who could reach any position that was given to boys of that kind to reach; boys of distinguished and honorable families, families of wealth and position, with all the world before them. And they gave it all up for nothing, nothing! They took a little companion, on a crowded street, and

killed him, for nothing, and sacrificed everything that could be of value in human life upon the crazy scheme of a couple of immature lads.

Now, your Honor, you have been a boy; I have been a boy. And we have known other boys. The best way to understand somebody else is to put yourself in his place.

Is it within the realm of your imagination that a boy who was right, with all the prospects of life before him, who could choose what he wanted, without the slightest reason in the world would lure a young companion to his death, and take his place in the shadow of the gallows? . . . How insane they are I care not, whether medically or legally. They did not reason; they could not reason; they committed the most foolish, most unprovoked, most purposeless, most causeless act that any two boys ever committed, and they put themselves where the rope is dangling above their heads.

There are not physicians enough in the world to convince any thoughtful, fair-minded man that these boys are right. Was their act one of deliberation, of intellect, or were they driven by some force such as Dr. White and Dr. Glueck and Dr. Healy have told this court?

There are only two theories; one is that their diseased brains drove them to it; the other is the old theory of possession by devils, and my friend Marshall could have read you books on that, too, but it has been pretty well given up in Illinois.

That they were intelligent and sane and sound and reasoning is unthinkable. Let me call your Honor's attention to another thing.

Why did they kill little Bobby Franks?

Not for money, not for spite; not for hate. They killed him as they might kill a spider or a fly, for the experience. They killed him because they were made that way. Because somewhere in the infinite processes that go to the making up of the boy or the man something slipped, and those unfortunate lads sit there hated, despised, outcasts, with the community shouting for their blood.

Are they to blame for it? There is no man on earth who can mention any purpose for it all or any reason for it all. It is one of those things that happened; that happened, and it calls not for hate, but for kindness, for charity, for consideration.

I hear the state's attorney talk of mothers.

Mr. Savage is talking for the mothers, and Mr. Crowe is thinking of the mothers, and I am thinking of the mothers. Mr. Savage, with the immaturity of youth and inexperience, says that if we hang them there will be no more killing. This world has been one long slaughter-house from the beginning until today, and killing goes on and on and on, and will forever. Why not read something, why not study something, why not think instead of blindly shouting for death?

Kill them. Will that prevent other senseless boys or other vicious men or vicious women from killing? No!

It will simply call upon every weak minded person to do as they have done. I know how easy it is to talk about mothers when you want to do something cruel. But I am thinking of the mothers, too. I know that any mother might be the mother of a little Bobby Franks, who left his home and went to his school, and who never came back. I know that any mother might be the mother of Richard Loeb and Nathan Leopold, just the same. The trouble is this, that if she is the mother of a Nathan Leopold or of a Richard Loeb, she has to ask herself the question:

"How came my children to be what they are? From what ancestry did they get this strain? How far removed was the poison that destroyed their lives? Was I the bearer of the seed that brings them to death?"

Any mother might be the mother of any of them. But these two are the victims. I remember a little poem by the marvelous poet, Housman, that gives the soliloquy of a boy about to be hanged, a soliloquy such as these boys might make:

"The night my father got me
  His mind was not on me;
He did not plague his fancy
  To muse if I should be
  The son you see.

"The day my mother bore me
  She was a fool and glad,
For all the pain I cost her,
  That she had borne the lad
  That borne she had.

"My father and my mother
  Out of the light they lie;
The warrant would not find them,
  And here, 'tis only I
  Shall hang so high.

"O let not man remember
  The soul that God forgot,
But fetch the county sheriff,
  And noose me in a knot,
  And I will rot.

"And so the game is ended,
  That should not have begun.
My father and my mother
  They had a likely son,
  And I have none."

No one knows what will be the fate of the child he gets or the child she bears; the fate of the child is the last thing they consider. This weary old world goes on, begetting, with birth and with living and with death; and all of it is blind from the beginning to the end. I do not know what it was that made these boys do this mad act, but I do know there is a reason for it. I know they did not beget themselves. I know that any one of an infinite number of causes reaching back to the beginning might be working out in these boys' minds, whom you are asked to hang in malice and in hatred and injustice, because someone in the past has sinned against them.

I am sorry for the fathers as well as the mothers, for the fathers who give their strength and their lives for educating and protecting and creating a fortune for the boys that they love; for the mothers who go down into the shadow of death for their children, who nourish them and care for them, and risk their lives, that they may live, who watch them with tenderness and fondness and longing, and who go down into dishonor and disgrace for the children that they love.

All of these are helpless. We are all helpless. But when you are pitying the father and mother of poor Bobby Franks, what about the fathers and mothers of these two unfortunate boys, and what about the unfortunate boys themselves, and what about all the fathers and all the mothers and all the boys and all the girls who tread a dangerous maze in darkness from birth to death?

Do you think you can cure it by hanging these two? Do you think you can cure the hatreds and the maladjustments of the world by hanging them? You simply show your ignorance and your hate when you say it. You may here and there cure hatred with love and understanding, but you can only add fuel to the flames by cruelty and hate.

What is my friend's idea of justice? He says to this court, whom he says he respects—and I believe he does—your Honor, who sits here patiently, holding the lives of these two boys in your hands:

"Give them the same mercy that they gave to Bobby Franks."

Is that the law? Is that justice? Is this what a court should do? Is this what a state's attorney should do? If the state in which I live is not kinder, more human, more considerate, more intelligent than the mad act of these two boys, I am sorry that I have lived so long.

I am sorry for all fathers and all mothers. The mother who looks into the blue eyes of her little babe cannot help musing over the end of the child, whether it will be crowned with the greatest promises which her mind can image or whether he may meet death upon the scaffold. All she can do is to rear him with love and care, to watch over him, tenderly, to meet life with home and trust and confidence, and to leave the rest with fate. . . .

I could say something about the death penalty that, for some mysterious reason, the state wants in this case. Why do they want it? To vindicate the law? Oh, no. The law can be vindicated without killing anyone else. It might shock the fine sensibilities of the state's counsel that this boy was put into a culvert and left after he was dead, but, your Honor, I can think of a scene that makes this pale into insignificance. I can think, and only think, your Honor, of taking two boys, one eighteen and the other nineteen, irresponsible, weak, diseased, penning them in a cell, checking off the days and the hours and the minutes, until they will be taken out and hanged. Wouldn't it be a glorious day for Chicago? Wouldn't it be a glorious triumph for the state's attorney? Wouldn't it be a glorious triumph for justice in this land? Wouldn't it be a glorious illustration of Christianity and kindness and charity? I can picture them, wakened in the gray light of morning, furnished a suit of clothes by the state, led to the scaffold, their feet tied, black caps drawn over their heads, stood on a trap door, the hangman pressing a spring, so that it gives way under them. I can see them fall through space—and—stopped by the rope around their necks.

This would surely expiate the placing of Bobby Franks in the culvert after he was dead. This would doubtless bring immense satisfaction to some people. It would bring a greater satisfaction because it would be done in the name of justice. I am always suspicious of righteous indignation. To hear young men talk glibly of justice. Well, it would make me smile if it did not make me sad. Who knows what it is? Does Mr. Savage know? Does Mr. Crowe know? Do I know? Does your Honor know? Is there any human machinery for finding it out? Is there any man who can weigh me and say what I deserve? Can your Honor? Let us be honest. Can your Honor appraise yourself, and say what you deserve? Can your Honor appraise these two young men and say what they deserve? Justice must take account of infinite circumstances which a human being cannot understand.

If there is such a thing as justice it could only be administered by one who knew the inmost thoughts of the man to whom he was meting it out. Aye, who knew the father and mother and the grandparents and the infinite number of people back of him. Who knew the origin of every cell that went into the body, who could understand the structure, and how it acted. Who could tell how the emotions that sway the human being affected that particular frail piece of clay. It means more than that. It means that you must appraise every influence that moves men, the civilization where they live, and all society which enters into the making of the child or the man! If your Honor can do it—if you can do it you are wise, and with wisdom goes mercy.

No one with wisdom and with understanding, no one who is honest with himself and with his own life, whoever he may be, no one who has seen himself the prey and the sport and the plaything of the infinite forces that move man, no one who has tried and who has failed—and we have all tried and we have all failed—no one can tell what justice is for someone else or for himself—and the more he tries and the more responsibility he takes the more he clings to mercy as being the one thing which he is sure should control his judgment of men. . . .

I do not know how much salvage there is in these two boys. I hate to say it in their presence, but what is there to look forward to? I do not know but that your Honor would be merciful if you tied a rope around their necks and let them die; merciful to them, but not merciful to civilization, and not merciful to those who would be left behind. To spend the balance of their lives in prison is mighty little to look forward to, if anything. Is it anything? They may have the hope that as the years roll around they might be released. I do not know. I do not know. I will be honest with this court as I have tried to be from the beginning. I know that these boys are not fit to be at large. I believe they will not be until they pass through the next stage of life, at forty-five or fifty. Whether they will be then, I cannot tell. I am sure of this: that I shall not be here to help them. So far as I am concerned, it is over.

I would not tell this court that I do not hope that some time, when life and age have changed their bodies, as it does, and has changed their emotions, as it does—that they may once more return to life. I would be the last person on earth to close the door to any human being that lives, and least of all to my clients. But what have they to look forward to? Nothing. And I think here of the stanza of Housman:

> "Now hollow fires burn out to black,
>   And lights are guttering low:
> Square your shoulders, lift your pack
>   And leave your friends and go.
> O never fear, man, naught's to dread
>   Look not left nor right:
> In all the endless road you tread
>   There's nothing but the night."

I care not, your Honor, whether the march begins at the gallows or when the gates of Joliet close upon them, but there is nothing but the night, and that is little for any human being to expect.

But there are others to consider. Here are these two families, who have led honest lives, who will bear the name that they bear, and future generations must carry it on.

Here is Leopold's father—and this boy was the pride of his life. He watched him, he cared for him, he worked for him; the boy was brilliant and accomplished, he educated him, and he thought that fame and position awaited him, as it should have awaited. It is a hard thing for a father to see his hopes crumble into dust.

Should he be considered? Should his brothers be considered? Will it do society any good or make your life safer, or any human being's life safer, if it should be handed down from generation to generation, that this boy, their kin, died upon the scaffold?

And Loeb, the same. Here is the faithful uncle and brother, who have watched here day by day, while Dickie's father and his mother are too ill to stand this terrific strain, and shall be waiting for a message which means more to them than it can mean to you or me. Shall these be taken into account in this general bereavement?

Have they rights? Is there any reason, your Honor, why their proud names and all the future generations that bear them shall have this bar sinister written across them? How many boys and girls, how many unborn children will feel it? It is bad enough as it is, God knows. It is bad enough, however it is. But it's not yet death on the scaffold. It's not that. And I ask your Honor, in addition to all that I have said, to save two honorable families from a disgrace that never ends, and which could be of no avail to help any human being that lives.

Now, I must say a word more and then I will leave this with you where I should have left it long ago. None of us are unmindful of the public; courts are not, and juries are not. We placed our fate in the hands of a trained court, thinking that he would be more mindful and considerate than a jury. I cannot say how people feel. I have stood here for three months as one might stand at the ocean trying to sweep back the tide. I hope the seas are subsiding and the wind is falling, and I believe they are, but I wish to make no false pretense to this court. The easy thing and the popular thing to do is to hang my clients. I know it. Men and women who do not think will applaud. The cruel and thoughtless will approve. It will be easy today; but in Chicago, and reaching out over the length and breadth of the land, more and more fathers and mothers, the humane, the kind, and the hopeful, who are gaining an understanding and asking questions not only about these poor boys, but about their own,—these will join in no acclaim at the death of my clients. They would ask that the shedding of blood be stopped, and that the normal feelings of man resume their sway. And as the days and the months and the years go on, they will ask it more and more. But, your Honor, what they shall ask may not count. I know the easy way. I know your Honor stands between the future and the past. I know the future is with me, and what I stand for here; not merely for the lives of these two unfortunate lads, but for all boys and all girls; for all of the young, and as far as possible, for all of the old. I am pleading for life, understanding, charity, kindness, and the infinite mercy that considers all. I am pleading that we overcome cruelty with kindness and hatred with love. I know the future is on my side. You may hang these boys; you may hang them by the neck until they are dead. But in doing it you will turn your face toward the past. In doing it you are making it harder for every other boy who in ignorance and darkness must grope his way through the mazes which only childhood knows. In [permitting them to live] you will make it easier for every child that some time may stand where these boys stand. You will make it easier for every human being with an aspiration and a vision and a hope and a fate. I am pleading for the future; I am pleading for a time when hatred and cruelty will not control the hearts of men, when we can learn by reason and judgment and understanding and faith that all life is worth saving, and that mercy is the highest attribute of man.

I feel that I should apologize for the length of time I have taken. This case may not be as important as I think it is, and I am sure I do not need to tell this court, or to tell my friends that I would fight just as hard for the poor as for the rich. If I should succeed in saving these boys' lives and do nothing for the progress of the law, I should feel sad, indeed. If I can succeed, my greatest reward and my greatest hope will be that I have done something for the tens of thousands of other boys, for the countless unfortunates who must tread the same road in blind childhood that these poor boys have trod,—that I have done something to help human understanding, to temper justice with mercy, to overcome hate with love.

I was reading last night of the aspiration of the old Persian poet, Omar Khayyam. It appealed to me as the highest that I can vision. I wish it was in my heart, and I wish it was in the hearts of all.

> So I be written in the book of Love,
> I do not care about that Book above,
> Erase my name or write it as you will,
> So I be written in the Book of Love.

Darrow delivered this summation in 1924, forty-six years after beginning the practice of law, and fifteen years before his death in 1938 at age eighty-one. It is a surprising statement—literally surprising, full of surprises: It is not didactic, not "preachy"; it does not whine, it is not righteous or pious or cynical, or chastising. It is not bullying (a tactic lawyers use when either a paucity of supporting evidence or a paucity of talent obtains, but which Darrow rarely used for any reason). Neither does it grovel, or slink with servility.

It is a statement—a mature statement—of a person who has a sober, ripe understanding of the pathos which is in the human character; a statement of a man who, like most men of his age and experience, no longer expects surprises in human nature; a man who weeps—privately—for a dead adolescent, and two twisted young persons on the threshold of manhood who have murdered their future.

It is a statement, foremost, of a man who takes with full and sober sincerity his role as an officer of the court; and in that stance, he speaks directly to the judge, quoting the Shropshire Housman, and pleads for only one thing: life. Not for his clients' lives, for he sees them as all but gone, sentenced either to swift meetings with eternity or half centuries of a surely Dantesque anguish. Rather, he pleads for the life of compassion, respect, religiosity (and this from an agnostic), love. This is what Darrow sees as the law's responsibility, indeed the law's very essence. And on that day in 1924, the law, in the person of the judge, concurred.

Clarence Darrow died on the threshold of the Second World War. One wonders what he would have had to say, had the God he didn't believe in granted him a decade more time—time in which to book passage to Nuremberg, Germany, on behalf of the most aberrant assortment of human specimens ever to sit, stripped of *Hakenkreuz* and swagger, in the dock of reckoning.

NOTES

1. All verses of poetry appear in the public record of Darrow's summation in the case of *State of Illinois v. Richard Loeb and Nathan Leopold.*

2. Architect Otto Matz's 1893 edifice, resembling by intention a forbidding Romanesque prison, housed the Cook County Criminal Courts. In one of its trial rooms Leopold and Loeb answered society in Grand Jury Indictment General Number 33624, Criminal Court of Cook County, State of Illinois. The youthful judge's face belonged to Hon. John R. Caverly. An evocative photograph memorializing the scene appears in a study of the defense attorney: Tierney, Kevin. *Darrow: A Biography.* Thomas Y. Crowell, New York, 1979, plate 13, facing page 455.

3. The text for Darrow's summation can be found in the Criminal Records, Cook County Courthouse, Chicago, Illinois, for the year 1924. Portions of the trial also appear in the defense attorney's quixotic autobiographical collection of essays, *Infidels and Heretics: An Agnostic's Anthology,* Stratford, Boston, 1929.

Part Two

Voices of the Second World War

Great men are two a penny in wartime. It is not that there are more of them about: just that the public is in the mood for the grand epithet.

—Lord Moran
(Churchill's personal physician)

I have never accepted what many people have kindly said—namely that I inspired the nation. Their will was resolute and remorseless, and as it proved unconquerable. It fell to me to express it, and if I found the right words you must remember that I have always earned my living by my pen and by my tongue. It was the nation and the race dwelling all round the globe that had the lion's heart. I had the luck to be called upon to give the roar.

—Winston Churchill, on his
eightieth birthday

Assay: Allies in the Cause of Righteousness

In recent years growing attention has been paid in the literature to the period of "sleep" in England prior to the September 1939 opening of the war. Several biographical works (Manchester, Gilbert, and others) and historical studies (among them Hynes, Gene Smith, Richard M. Ketchum, and Jonathan Daniel) offer strong support for the contention that the movement toward the Second World War was simply the cresting wave of a swell dating at least from the end of the First World War, and in some ways going back to England's infelicitous Boer War experience, as well as America's equally disputatious aggression in the Spanish-American War of 1898. Whether or not these events were causal of later problems, it would be Churchill (in 1940 as in 1915) who would have to deal with things, just as it would be Franklin Delano Roosevelt, in place of Theodore Roosevelt, who would find his presidency on the line.

Any serious pursuer of answers about England and the war must begin earlier, during the time of the Weimar Republic in Germany. In Great Britain the momentum required to give sufficient acceleration to lead to war was brought to speed with the epoch of the Smart Set, those insouciant, aristocratic, upper-crust English who surrounded the figure of the heir apparent. The period was the story of the demise of a facet of royalty in which the handsome "cover" of Edward VIII's "book" could not disguise the textual vapidity most English cognoscenti long had judged to be within. When George V succumbed on January 20, 1936, and his eldest son "David" prepared for coronation, a monarch of staid and benign manner yielded to an heir apparent glistening with the chevrons of his clique; yet, comely as His New Majesty was to the eye, the man known for so long as the Prince of Wales always had had difficulty hiding his lifelong indifference toward others' forgone expectations of his succession. A foreordained and not surprising fate played out quickly in the ten months of his uncoronated reign.[1]

There is a feeling to that time, the period between the last days when all seemed well and the days when the Munich crisis eradicated all hope for felicitous resolve, that indeed has a sleepy aspect to it: Even though we are referring to an island in the North Sea, in the encroaching September weather there is almost a sweetness, a "body," a tactility to the air of the expiring idyll. Something—a dream, a memory, an image from half slumber, a nation, an empire—something is evanescing; it is doing so in a dreamy, slow way, the way youth slips from the floating form of the young, just before maturity weighs us down.

It had all seemed never-ending: teatime when women's eyes sparkled and young gentlemen posed with their *bons mots* and their fables fashioned of aristocratic humor. The regularity of things, the five postal calls a day in London. The trips to that nearby yet exotic cousin-place called Germany, where the music was rich and the language a thrill and the people so charmingly exacting, and the ruling structure so all-mixed-up with the Victorian diaspora of royalty. Tyrolean yodels, too, in that smoke-departing dream; yodels, and *Lederhosen* . . .

But, to reverse Eliot's famous poetic closure, the dream left not with a whimper, but with the tattoo of jackboots, and the disturbing priapic salute, and the misappropriated Asiatic symbol, and the new sort of Wagnerian "operas" which were an ambitious Austrian's diatribes.

Things across the water were different.

In a sense, America down the line would have a better deal of it. It would all come quickly for this former colony—in an instant, in fact: one day, a peace rustled only by foreign forebodings and domestic isolationist rankling; the next day, torpedoes in the boats' bellies and the congressional leadership arm-in-arm, walking down the aisle in a marriage in which death most certainly would (some of them) part.

The stories of the war have become near apocrypha in the legend-bank of a world fifty years removed from the blowing apart of the battleship *Arizona*. The characters have taken on an almost fictive patina, a glaze like porcelain figurines to replace in more permanent ways the cells of flesh which made up those very real, and very scared, people in the world of 1939. There is the legend of the meek one, with the porcelain doll named Neville; there is the tale of the harrumpher, with the stolid Buddha-figure of the warrior called Winston; there is the bristly, hateful Adolf-doll, with its crude, crazed face of black intention. And, after a time, there is the Delano-doll, with the great grinning head and the spindly afterthought lower limbs.

To these legends are added a swarm of characters, all fitting into the sordid tale of how the great nations of Europe gave away their souls, and how six million unnamed porcelain victim-dolls were ground back into sand.

England, lucky in geography if hapless in forethought, had modesty in many quarters—not a nature best designed to scare off an enemy!—which included the new monarch as well as the prime minister. And England would defend itself in an understated way: by the actions of a contained group of flyers, the "few," who zipped up in little foils and retained so much for so many. (Only later, when the danger was gone, would it fall upon the nation to decide whether one of the few was good enough to mate with a princess; and then never would so many owe such confounding obeisance to such tenacious attitudes of class.)

To many, especially in Great Britain, who look back with an analytical view, the pattern commonly known as the period of sleep, followed by the phony war, followed by the Blitz, followed by alliance, followed by endless struggle, followed by victory, is not synchronized with real time. In actuality, they see the pattern as sleep, followed by the preliminary war of 1939–1945, followed by the endless struggle of 1946 to the present. The battle, for all victims and victors of war, is not in dealing with what is lost, but in dealing with what is retained.

If you don't think this is so, just ask any retired German (if he would only give it thought). And ask any elderly Japanese (if they would but tell you).

And then, if you really want to know whether this is so, just ask an *English* pensioner (who, if you'll put ten pence in the fire's meter, might warm enough to reveal to you the feelings beneath the stoicism).

NOTE

1. As a young British major confessed to writer John Gunther following the Allied invasion of Sicily, "Ribbentrop was right. We *were* decadent. We were soft, we were spoiled. We scoffed at the splendid trait of loyalty; we despised tradition; we lost belief in belief. The rich were rapacious, and the poor were greedy; the banks were full, and the churches empty. All that had *made* England seem lost." (From Gunther's pre–June 6, 1944, book entitled *D-Day,* Harper and Brothers, 1944.)

Chapter Four

Man of Munich (Neville Chamberlain)

The sword is the axis of the world, and greatness cannot be shared.
—General Charles de Gaulle, from his 1934 manifesto *The Army
of the Future* (J. B. Lippincott, New York, 1941, third edition)

There is a photograph of Neville Chamberlain and another man taken at Berchtesgaden during one of the British prime minister's two fateful 1938 visits to the *Reichskanzler*. It is a telling piece of photography.[1]

The two men are posed in front of tall, staunchly florid palm fronds. Chamberlain, the tall British political leader intent upon reaping success from failure, stands on the right. His government, responding to his deep convictions, had advanced the cause of appeasement until it had reached the point of becoming a political fetish; and this trip—his first ever in an airplane—was considered by his followers the ultimate effort to resolve the growing world conflict.

Neville, dressed in cutaway coat, looks as if he's just taken a deep breath to inflate his chest with the hubris he obviously feels. His face is faintly grinning; his eyes twinkle with secret surprise. He is determined to evoke approval by literally putting a good face on things.

On the left, and slightly shorter than the Briton, stands a pudgy man with a comical mustache. He is dressed in a light-colored double-breasted jacket with baggy, dark slacks. He has sloping shoulders which conspire with the bad cut of his clothes to give him the meek, bottom-heavy, nonthreatening shape of a pear. Yet unlike the old-school "hail fellow well met" king's minister twinkling at his left, the shorter man stares at the camera with the coldest eyes. Everything about his mien suggests that he is doing his best to hide his impatience with this charade; that when the flashgun fires, and the grinning fool at his side flies back to the increasingly vulnerable island to the northwest, he can get on with the true business at hand: global conquest. Pear-shaped or not, he is a dictator, a pathological personality, a ruthless murderer; and Hitler does not suffer fools gladly.

When Chamberlain straightaway returned to the United Kingdom, he spoke to the press and the assembled crowd on Heston's Field. Barely concealing his delight (which, in Neville Chamberlain, took the form of a soft grin), he spoke with understatement:

> I received an immense number of letters during all these anxious days— and so has my wife—letters of support and approval and gratitude; I cannot tell you what an encouragement that has been to me. I want to thank the British people for what they have done. Next I want to say that the settlement of the Czechoslovak problem which has now been achieved is, in my view, only a prelude to a larger settlement in which all Europe may find peace.
>
> This morning I had another talk with the German Chancellor, Herr Hitler, and here is a paper which bears his name upon it as well as mine. Some of you perhaps have already heard what it contains, but I would just like to read it to you.
>
> "We, the German Fuhrer and Chancellor and the British Prime Minister, have had a further meeting to-day and are agreed in recognizing that the question of Anglo-German relations is of the first importance for the two countries and for Europe.
>
> "We regard the agreement signed last night and the Anglo-German Naval Agreement as symbolic of the desire of our two peoples never to go to war with one another again.
>
> "We are resolved that the method of consultation shall be the method adopted to deal with any other questions that may concern our two countries, and we are determined to continue our efforts to remove possible sources of difference and thus to contribute to assure the peace of Europe."

Next Mr. Chamberlain went to No. 10 Downing Street to inform his public about the peace mission. There, his presentation of the Berchtesgaden results gave cause for another photo. It shows the prime minister, peering with his wife from a window of his official residence, basking in their relief and admiration. Here it was that the prime minister presented to the gathered crowd the news from Munich (with the words he would regret, and which would haunt him until his death): "My good friends, this is the second time in our history that there has come back from Germany to Downing Street peace with honour."[2] The cheering carried the moment high for a considerable time. At last he continued, and gave himself his own *coup de grace:* "I believe it is peace for our time." Again, the response swelled the scene in the little street in whose principal resident's hands the future of England lay. When the cries of "God bless you!"

subsided at last, Mr. Chamberlain added irony to pathos: "And now I recommend you to go home and sleep quietly in your beds."[3]

The eleventh-hour Downing Street moment is a triumphal scene, the kind of media "happening" which today is so well captured by television, and which, fifty years ago, was the province of the well-placed Speed Graphic press camera: People's bodies are poking out of windows, and expectant citizens are swirling all about the leader like the spokes of a fan radiating from its center.

There was, in fact, excitement on all faces—except those in some of the upper windows, which belonged to members of the Foreign Office staff, who feared with lamentable prescience that "Munich" would become the red herring of appeasement with which Hitler would slap the faces of the world's leaders for a long and terrible time.

All too modern was the swiftness of the turnabout of public acclaim for this quaint, quiet-spoken, sweet but self-absorbed man who had made it to the premier chair in Britain's government. Almost a year later, after dropping the thin veneer of earnestness which he had allowed Chamberlain to believe was there, the German chancellor sent his troops over the Polish border in the first true cataclysm of war. Again, in accordance with his parliamentary duty, Neville Chamberlain spoke to his country's elected representatives, and told them their nation was at war: "Everything that I have worked for, everything that I have hoped for, everything that I have believed in during my public life, has crashed in ruins." Within eight months, this pleasant but arthritic anachronism of a leader had been forcibly (some would say rudely) retired from his position as first minister. His successor, with the astonishing grace he would show in so many occasions for the remaining twenty-five years of his life, gave him a cabinet sinecure. Disappointment, as much as disease, did the rest of history's dirty work on Neville Chamberlain.

Chamberlain died not long after Winston Churchill replaced him, and only a touch over two years after the triumphal photograph at No. 10. Replacing the appeaser with the warrior was an action which was not too little, but which was almost too late. The displaced prime minister must have wept in private, to see his earnest, ministry-long folly backfiring so criminally upon the people whom he tried, genuinely, to lead. His death from cancer a mere few months following this brutal expiration of his Munich hopes could not have been worse to his body than those broken dreams must have been to his spirit.

NOTES

1. Both photographs mentioned in this chapter are reprinted in an excellent resource entitled *A Prime Minister on Prime Ministers.* Book Club Associates, London, 1977), Sir Harold Wilson's illuminating study of his predecessors.

2. Chamberlain, Neville. *In Search of Peace.* G. P. Putnam's Sons, New York, 1939.

3. Reality, in the form of American newsmen, saw things differently: "It took the Big Four just five hours and twenty-five minutes here in Munich today to dispel the

clouds of war and come to an agreement over the partition of Czechoslovakia,'' William Shirer reported at 6:30 p.m. on September 29, 1938. An hour later, Ed Murrow broadcast from England: ''Today in London there has been no lessening of recruiting activities and tomorrow morning's press in London will emphasize that any agreement reached tonight, if it is to be acceptable to the British public, must not be the result of a threat of overwhelming force.''

Chapter Five

Comes the Bully:
Demagoguery as Final Solution
(Adolf Hitler)

[I]n Berlin toward the end of the 1920's my friends among the correspon-
dents and diplomats told me Hitler was a forgotten man. He had, as the
British ambassador put it, "passed into oblivion."
—William L. Shirer, *Twentieth Century Journey: The Nightmare Years*

As a group, the early foreign correspondents from American news media who
settled in the capitals of the world's preeminent cities and filed their dispatches
home in a faithful rendering of the goings-on in those far-off places performed
an illustrious and too often unappreciated service. They were the ones—and
sometimes they alone—who made meaningful to the sitters at home, huddled
by the radio or crouched with the newspaper, the miasma of sounds, images,
and emotion-packed but dismayingly incomprehensible words and feelings of
peoples halfway across the globe.

At about the time the halftone engraving plate became available to the newspaper, with the resultant addition of acceptably rendered news photographs, the
citizens at home were developing an appreciation for the importance of learning
what was "going on"; for they now were beginning to know that what was
happening twelve thousand miles away actually could impinge upon their own
lives.

The ideal correspondent was a young person brimming with energy, imagination, and literary skill, who at will could become an unobserved "fly on the
wall" ready to absorb the events before him, assimilate their meaning, distill
them down to the constraints of time and comprehension, and broadcast or file
the stories back home to the waiting editors.

By such a pattern it was possible for Virginians and Tennesseans and New
Yorkers of 1940 to know more about what was happening in world war-devas-

tated Europe than their forebears in Lincoln's day had been able to know about what was happening in Civil War–devastated Virginia, or Tennessee, or New York.

A correspondent who distinguished himself first in print journalism and later as a pioneer in the early days of radio news—a man who was among the most observant and successful commentators in Europe—was the American correspondent for the *Chicago Tribune,* William L. Shirer. Shirer had unique and incalculably valuable traits: He was an international cosmopolite, familiar with several capital settings in Europe. He was adept both at living in a foreign environment, and in the "art" of getting to know and report on the people of such urbanity. Also, and conversely, he was a homespun boy, reared in the quiet stretches of Iowa, and imbued with a rural Iowan's respect for nature (the open eye and ear), and he had the Midwesterner's possession of an unassuming respect for other people. (His neighbor for years, whom he knew well, was the painter Grant Wood.)

In a discernible way, in the years before the 1930s, the portraits Shirer painted of figures like Mohammad Zahir Khan, Gandhi, and the youthful aviator Lindbergh had the same unrelenting clarity to them which neighbor Wood's art-portrayed Iowa farmers had. There was nothing to be "put over" on the men who tended the soil of the Midwest; but also, there was no reason to treat them in any way but how one saw them, and how one wanted to be treated oneself. (Thus, when the *Spirit of St. Louis* bumped down at Le Bourget in 1927, one of the people massed on the runway, watching Frenchmen rip canvas souvenir patches from the little plane, was William Shirer. In temperament, at this stage of their lives, the two young Americans were much alike.)[1]

In this fashion, the reporter's subjects found in Shirer a man to match their ingenuousness. And all of his subjects up to the early 1930s proved willing to match him for honesty, candor, and fairness. Until, that is, Shirer met the man who had "passed into oblivion," and watched as, for the next thirteen years, this creature made oblivion of millions and millions of lives. For the unsociable painter from Austria would later gather (for Shirer's amazed perusal) the most inexplicable collection of cohorts, to make up the retinue of the burgeoning Hitlerian Reich.

Shirer would become a mainstay American reporting back from this new Germany. For him, objective reporting needed license after a time; no one could relate what was visible and felt in Germany without having strong feelings about it, feelings which such a reporter would feel impelled to transmit. But objectivity—and the later censorship—made Shirer watch his step.

In the early days of the Reich, alas, some sources of communication who were not bound by the fears of censorship or personal harm gave to the *Fuehrer* an inestimable gift of gratuitous objectivity. Foremost among these was that youthful and prominent American flier who could speak with straight face to the American people, at the same time that he could count among his courtiers the quirky Bavarian with the toothbrush mustache and the darting, contemptuous eyes.

What essential personal characteristics distinguished these three men—and, handicapping Adolf Hitler's age by a decade or so, he, Lindbergh, and Shirer were roughly contemporary—which, on the face of it, might have explained their fates?

In many ways, Lindbergh is the hardest to understand. In 1922, the tall flier was a twenty-year-old "kid," beginning his fascination with the little heavier-than-air machines which already had changed the nature of warfare. His daring[2]—and even at that tender age, it *was* daring—manifested itself quickly. Only five years later—five years!—Lindbergh installed a gas tank in front of his face and packed a sack with ham sandwiches and flew thirty-three nonstop hours into fame. Five years after this seminal event, Lindbergh—now a national hero with a military title—was again the subject of the country's attention, but the anxiety now was placed in the effort to find his little kidnapped son. And, again five years later, Lindbergh already had made a visit to Nazi Germany, as the guest of Hermann Goering, whose beaming malevolence charmed the aviator and his poetess wife,[3] and in so doing brought out of the quiet hero a tortured network of nerves and pain.

The consequences, perhaps of those years of unrelieved daring and unde-served personal sorrow, became visited upon the world in the form of Lind-bergh's outspoken isolationism. The shy boy with the great grin had gone willingly into the lair of the devil, and he came back, if not with devil worship, at least with fierce admonitions for his countrymen about the indefatigable ca-pabilities of the devil himself.

Shirer's accomplishments were technically earthbound, but just as stellar in achievement of world import. Within a few months of his concluding time with Gandhi (his subject being in jail), he moved into the European theater and quickly established himself as the correspondent most capable of proximity (even if not intimate contact) with the Nazi elite. Watching the 1934 Nuremberg party conference, Shirer had reason to reflect how little time had elapsed since his friends had declared Hitler evanescent on the world scene, and how much the world now had to fear. Perhaps he was thinking of the flier, whom only a handful of years earlier he'd watched alight at Le Bourget's airfield. Lindbergh now said that Hitler's Germany "held today the intangible eastern border of European civilization."[4] It must have been a horrific whirlwind, first the breath-holding Atlantic flight, then the giddy global reception of a hero, then a quiet beginning to domesticity, then the tragic rupture of dreams. And, finally—all within seven years—the courting by a dictator's handmaidens, and the switch, thrown inside the psyche, to torque one's courage from its straight-line accom-plishment, into an angled defense of what could only be seen by many as the posture of a coward.

Shirer, less public than Lindbergh at any time, but of invaluable influence a generation beyond the flier's sad withdrawal with the outbreak of hostilities between Germany and the United States in 1941, would stay the course with the Nazis, being one of few correspondents, and the only American, whom they permitted to broadcast their goings-on, all the way down to the end of 1937, when staying behind began to mean perhaps not getting out at all.

In an act of courage which he probably would willingly have traded for the safety of a daredevil spin in a one-man airplane, Shirer secreted his diaries in the bottoms of two suitcases, after having duped the Gestapo, through an agent friend of rank, to affix a seal on the two packages, unaware of their contents. Anyone in the world who has read the published portions of these diaries, or Shirer's masterpieces *The Decline and Fall of the Third Reich* (1960) and *The Collapse of the Third Republic* (1969), owes a direct debt to the bravery of a pudgy, pipe-smoking, one-eyed journalist who risked certain death in order that the astonishing, and anguishing, story of what he witnessed could escape the murderous fate of truth in the German wartime reality, and come through the barriers of hate into the light of the New World. Their reading has provided as critical a piece of the struggle for the survival of enlightened thought and personal freedom as any achievement in aeronautical history has meant to modern science. This time, courage not only survived, it lived to a happy and fruitful old age.[5]

Hitler wrote *Mein Kampf* as he sat brooding in Landsberg Prison. As a testament of one man's mind, it is without peer. As a statement, it comes as much from the "heart" as anything might have come from this particular individual. In the intensity of the prison's cloistering, in the depths of self-pity and simmering anger which gave this political inmate his wherewithal to continue, the book is an amazing piece of personal fantasy—not so much fantasy in the sense of being a deliberate fiction, but a fantasy in its use as a concordance of philosophical thought. *Mein Kampf* is as thorough a self-brainwashing as ever a man subjected himself to. It established Hitler not as someone suffering delusions, but rather as the delusionist himself. If Hitler wrote out, in seemingly cogent and rationalized prose, his views of history as he lived it or observed its passage, then this *was* history for him. It *became* history, fact, precedent—truth.

These "truths" could be personal as well as political. Here is his early statement about how he faced the quandary of choosing a livelihood:

> I did not want to become an official. Neither "talking to" nor "serious" argument made any difference to my reluctance. I did not want to be an official and refused to be one. Any attempt, by quoting my father's example, to arouse love or keenness for that calling only had the contrary effect. I hated and was bored by the idea of having to sit tied to an office, of not being master of my own time, of spending the whole of my life filling up forms.[6]

Now, no one could fault a young man, agonizing over his need to choose a profession, for holding in disdain the bureaucratic life of "quiet desperation" which evidently had been the fate of Hitler *père*. The young man was apparently "talked to" in the manner of a lecture by the father which surely would have put him off. And the "serious argument" by an elder whose attempt to persuade his son to embark on some sort of institutional job would hardly have inspired "love or keenness for that calling."

Had Hitler's book ended here, or taken another path than the one it did, it would not merit interest, for precisely the innocuous reasons which stand in such contrast to the virulence which followed this bland, attitudinally rather pubescent introduction. But the author was not some one-of-a-countless-million diarists, penning private grudges over an insufferably uninspiring father; no, the author, after all, was Adolf Hitler; and his very next sentence tells more about his fate in a way our minds might encompass: "Now, when I review the effect on myself of all those years, I see two facts which stand out most conspicuously: (1) I became a Nationalist, and (2) I learned to grasp and understand history in its true sense."[7] Whatever self-deception is going on here, at least he gives a full forewarning of what would occupy his and the world's attention for the next twenty-one years.

Adolf Hitler's polemic, in the first sentences of this first chapter of his manifesto, are clear on one point: He intends fervid nationalism—popular nationalism, as he calls it—to be the central focus of his energies. His *Weltanschauung*—worldview—is of ever-widening concentric circles of influence, with Germany-Austria in the center, and a broadening claim on the periphery. In a sense, Hitler was building a political empire based on the concept of the onion: There was no center, it had no center—or, more exactly, it was to be *all* center. Each layer turned from foreign/despised, to encompassed/no-longer-threatening.

Within this framework of strong antipathy against the outsider or foreign idea lay the passionate feeling for a vague concept of nationalism. It would form the central motif of his political faction and give it its official name (the *Nationalsozialistische Deutsche Arbeiterpartei*, the National Socialist German Workers' Party, or NSDAP) and its popular designation *Nazi*. Like a magneto, this political "engine" worked by polar electrical energy, the hate-love poles discussed above. "[T]he feeling of nationality is in no way identical with dynastic patriotism," he proclaimed at the end of the chapter entitled "My Home." "Even then I perceived the deductions from this realization: intense love for my German-Austrian home and deep hatred against the Austrian State."

Shirer's initial experience of the rhetoric of the Reich—Hitler's own rhetoric, moved by some ten years out of the stages of personal polemic—was in the fora of the huge, orgiastic rallies staged each year at Nuremberg, in which took place the celebrations of the growing historical mythos that was the Nazi Party. The love-hate continued, of course; only now, the love was intensely self-absorbed (with solemn, tearful homage to the Brownshirts who fell in Hitler's abortive 1923 *Putsch* filling the hall with the "love" element), and the hate was clear-cut, and straight out of *Mein Kampf.*

One of Shirer's early notes in observing the 1934 rally touches on Hitler's scapegoating theme:

I had not yet quite realized that in order to keep the German people stirred up Hitler needed enemies to blame for all that had gone wrong before and for all that threatened the new, awakened, authoritarian Reich. . . . The chaos from which he had rescued the country, he said, had been the work of "Jewish intellectualism."

Here is another Hitler quotation from Shirer, followed by the same larval sentiments from the manifesto of Landsberg Prison. First, from the 1934 Nuremberg rally:

The alien life and form of ideas, injected into and forced on nations by Jewish intellectualism, which is racially without a basis, led to an alien, rootless state and internationally to complete chaos in cultural life.

And from *Mein Kampf*:

Judaism suffered a heavy setback in my eyes. . . . Unctuous protestations were no good any more now. One only had to look at [the various art forms of Jewish artists] which one saw commended on them, in order to become permanently hardened. It was pestilence, spiritual pestilence, worse than the Black Death, with which the nation was being inoculated.

Hitler saw himself as having saved Europe, Shirer concluded, "not only from the Bolsheviks but from the Jews, and he wanted his listeners to remember it and be grateful."

What the journalist saw in Hitler's rhetoric was a stress on the concocted fear that the dictator had been able, with great success, to impress upon many discerning minds—including the U.S. ambassador in England, Joseph P. Kennedy, and the tall, sad-eyed Colonel Lindbergh, with even his personal burdens taking a backseat now to this emergency: namely, that the likes of a Hitler, and a Nazidom, were the only things keeping the big bear of Bolshevism at bay. Shirer concludes on his own: "But it was beginning to dawn on me . . . that European civilization, at least in Germany, might not survive Hitler's dictatorship."

The German leader played on this anti-Bolshevist theme to great effect. It was a conceit completely within his control for the balance of the war: It would be his to determine the best use thereof through the nonaggression-guaranteeing Nazi-Soviet pact of August 22, 1939; it would be his to determine when he had gained the best advantage of Stalin; it would be his to decide that on June 22, 1941, the time had come to accept the liabilities of a two-front war, and hence a Russian invasion. It would even be his, albeit in rueful, ironic ways, to control the setting at Yalta, where the victorious Allies took the knife to Europe, and the enfeebled Roosevelt unwittingly conspired with the patient and clever Josef Stalin to give much more room for the Russian bear to wander in than Churchill thought safe and decent, let alone prudent.

But the Nuremberg rallies were the beginning. Into them Hitler's stage managers funneled first one hundred thousand, then two hundred thousand, and finally three hundred thousand Nazi functionaries on three consecutive nights. He made these events pageants, with the color and sensibilities of mysticism and religion.

The reporter made a trenchant observation upon his first view of Hitler. He thought him unimpressive, wooden, "flabby," implying there was a puzzle as to how this fellow, "in his almost modest bearing, in his rather common look," could bring the mobs of thousands to such carotid-pulsating frenzy.

About the perceived fiendishness and culpability of the Jews, Hitler's rally presentations had the ring of certitude, while it took *Mein Kampf* a full twenty-two of those "eight hundred tightly-packed pages"[8] to arrive at conclusions: "The more I contended with the Jews," he wrote, as if giving supportive evidence, "the more I learned to know their dialectical methods. . . ." And after his "researches" into the Jewish arts and political activities, he proclaimed that "[i]t was only now that I thoroughly understood the corrupter of our nation. . . . Now that I realized the Jews as the leaders of Social Democracy[,] scales, as it were, began to fall from my eyes. My long mental struggle was at an end."

Before the 1970s, by which time publishers had changed to a shrewd technique for advertising their wares which consisted of making the "dust jacket" copy read like learned (and laudatory) "reviews" of the book in question, the mainstream American publishers sought the dignity of presentation which accrued from modest, if not objective, introductions to the works on their list. In the instance of Hitler's one and only "literary" work, this faithful "objectivity" was to my mind so pronounced in the introduction to the book as to render the publisher a rival for the diplomatic prize of the year.

Here, quoted in full, is the "Publisher's Note" which introduces a Houghton Mifflin book, copyright 1933, which represented the "authorized edition with the consent of Verlag Frz. Eher Nachf. GmbH. Munchen, Germany." (The *L* in the opening word *Like* is two lines in height, and of "Old German" typeface, in the manner of an ancient rubric; so even as late as the year Hitler's chancellorship commenced, America still saw Europe's political tidal waves with a kind of Hollywood motif.)

Like "New Russia's Primer" Herr Hitler's "My Battle" was written not as propaganda for foreign consumption, but for the instruction and guidance of those already committed to his movement—for those, as he says in the Preface to the first edition, who "belong to it in their hearts." It is a significant historical document, in which the leader of a successful revolution, the actual head of a great European state, tells the story of his

life, traces the growth of his social, economic, and political philosophy,
and states both his aims and his methods.

The writing of the first part was done in 1924, while the author was
under detention in the fortress of Landsberg am Lech, after the unsuc-
cessful Munich uprising of the previous year. Under the title of "Mein
Kampf" it was published in the autumn of the year in which it was written,
and followed by a second part in 1927. The entire work of eight hundred
closely printed pages was re-issued in the spring of the present year, just
after Herr Hitler's accession to the German chancellorship.

The work is here offered to American readers in an English version,
somewhat abridged to omit matter not of general or international interest,
but including, it is believed, all of the sentiments and ideals of government
expressed by the author in the final complete German edition.

For the convenience of the reader there has been included a chronolog-
ical table of the chief events in Herr Hitler's career up to the present time.

This toneless reportage would make a good soporific, if it did not include
one of the most charged names in history. In contrast, another text examined
for the present work, one on Herbert Hoover and the Depression, infuses much
more interest in its subject than that suggested by the American publishers of
"Herr Hitler" in 1933.

To the book: "It stands me in good stead today that Fate decided that Braunau
on the Inn should be my birthplace," *Mein Kampf* begins. "That little town lies
on the frontier between the two German States, the reunion of which we younger
ones regard as a work worthy of accomplishment by all the means in our
power." Here is a disquietude, a fundamental, gnawing injustice suffered by
this young author. He wants his homeland restored to its neighbor!

This is especially interesting inasmuch as the eighth sentence of the first page
of Hitler's tome states that following the attainment of economic security for
the German people, "[t]he plough will then be the sword, and the coming
world's daily bread will be watered by the tears of war." So, within one hundred
words of this caveat, the Austrian has announced that any sanctity implied by
the Armistice and Versailles would hold no importance once his ideas were put
into effect. Moreover, only seven pages later, the author mentions Jews for the
first time.

At first, he is not "hard" on the Jews. He takes some pains to indicate his
objectivity, recounting his initial belief that any "questions" regarding "Jews"
were only matters of religion, and thus came under general notions of "tolerance"; in effect, early on, he is saying, he took no notice of them. But after
continual exposure to Jewish prolificity in the arts, in politics, in commerce, he
began to form an opinion. They were "a foreign race." The more he "contended
with the Jews, the more I learned to know their dialectical methods." Finding
them slippery in discourse, he discovered that "[w]herever one attacked such
apostles, one's hand met foul slime...." "One did not know which to admire

most," he felt, "—their glibness or their artfulness in lying. I gradually began to hate them."

Thus, the experiences described in his "Studies and Struggles in Vienna," which we believe from objective texts to consist of his systematic rejection by art institutions, actually (according to Hitler) were decisive for evaluating his exposure to members of a particular religious group. "It was at this time," he concluded, "that the greatest change took place in me that I was ever to experience. From being a feeble world-citizen [!] I became a fanatical anti-Semite." In summation of his second chapter, Hitler casts the Jew in the role of Marxist, in order to cement the foe's perfidy. "Thus did I now believe that I must act in the sense of the Almighty Creator," he intones; "by defining myself against the Jews, I am fighting for the Lord's work."

The fact that none of this posturing bears the test of logic gives weight to the importance of performance in Hitler's verbal appeals. Shirer bore an inestimable firsthand witness to Hitler's oratorical attributes and accomplishments. Noting that the pattern he had first observed at Nuremberg would remain constant in almost all his speeches over the following six years, Shirer describes this effective style of address:

> He would begin invariably in a low, resonant voice, beautifully modulated, speaking slowly and seeming to measure his words. . . . As he worked toward the inevitable climax of his discourse, the natural voice would reassert itself, the tone rising in scale, and, as the words came tumbling out in a torrent, it would become shrill and he would begin to shriek hysterically and reach . . . an orgasm of sound and fury, followed by an ecstasy such as I had never seen in a speaker, and which the awed listeners seemed to fully share. . . .
>
> At such times the born actor in him would emerge and he would screw up his face and curl his lips like a comedian, rolling his eyes and rolling his "r's" broadly as the Austrians and Bavarians do, manipulating his voice to get the last drop of sarcasm out of it.

From *Mein Kampf* we learn that Hitler understood on an intuitive level the value of oratorical skill for the person embarking on public life. He would practice his skills on whatever audiences he found, starting with the denizens of soup kitchens. These would make ideal beginning points for the mobs at the Nuremberg rallies years hence. The German audience, starving, still shame-ridden from Versailles, soaked up the drama, the invective, the passion, the seeming profundity of Hitler's spiel. Shirer notes that during the years when he had to suffer dozens of such speeches from the *Fuehrer,* he would say to himself: "What utter rubbish! What brazen lies!" But, looking around the audience, he would make the sobering, frightening realization: "His German listeners were lapping up every word as the utter truth."

At *Mein Kampf*'s midpoint, Hitler takes stock. At length the book replays

Germany's involvement in the disastrous world war. Out of the limitless variety of causes of her defeat, the prisoner at Landsberg draws but one conclusion: "Thus, if we review all the causes of the German collapse, the final and decisive one is seen to be the failure to realize the racial problem and, more especially, the Jewish menace."

Hitler concludes his prison manifesto by reciting the speech he gave in his own defense at the 1924 trial for his *Putsch,* which action landed him in the prison to begin with: "Though the judges of this State may be happy in their condemnation of our actions, yet History, the goddess of a higher truth and of a better law, will smile as she tears up this judgment and will declare all of us innocent of blame and the duty of expiation."

To anyone who took the time to study this amazing document, Adolf Hitler's intentions were absolutely clear: Find a scapegoat—blame the Jew. Create the persona of Germany as victim. Declare her reassertion on the international stage of nation-states as the ultimate goal. Vow to enable Germans to relish in their hearts the sweet taste of revenge:

—Revenge on England ("England's permanent desire is to maintain a certain balance of power between the States of Europe among themselves, since that appears to be a necessary condition for British hegemony in the world")

—Revenge on France ("We must be absolutely clear on the fact that France is the permanent and inexorable enemy of the German nation")

—Revenge on Bolshevism, and its influence within Germany ("On the day when Marxism is broken in Germany, its bonds are broken in good truth; for never in our history have we been conquered by the forces of our enemies, but rather by our own depravity and by the enemy in our own camp")

—Revenge on the fiercely independent Prussian states of Westphalia, on the Baltic states, on Pan-Slavic Russia ("The present-day rulers of Russia have no intention of entering into an alliance honourably or of sticking to one. We must not forget that they are low bloodstained criminals")

And the benefit of such revenge taking? Elimination of the "perfidious Jew" and restoration of complete respect for the Reich; for after all, "Fate itself seems to wish to give us our direction."

It is interesting that in 1933, Houghton Mifflin was content to import *Mein Kampf* in the abbreviated form discussed above; the text as published under the English title *My Battle* represented only about 50 percent of the text the imprisoned Nazi leader wrote in 1924. This was still a leader, it seems the publishers reasoned, who had not yet moved from the chancellorship (a position technically subordinate to Germany's leader) into the presidency and the other offices Hindenburg had held. But in the following year, 1934, he would become the full-fledged leader of Germany; within a few more years he had cultivated the comparative handful of soldiers into a massive standing army, with an air force which laughed at all suggestions of a challenge; and the several annual

Nuremberg rallies had demonstrated without doubt Hitler's control, and his nation's dedication, by the millions, to rearmament and apparent conquest. There was still Munich, in the future; and from there, the invasions of Poland, and beyond. But the *Anschluss* of Austria had happened; the sunshine of peace was dimming, and the world knew it. The king and queen of England would prepare to visit the United States before war got under way; in their kingdom, shortly, the children would prepare to evacuate the cities, to go to the country. Europe was shuddering with anticipation of events whose tenor they had felt before.

In 1939, only six years after publication of Houghton Mifflin's tamer version, Reynal & Hitchcock brought out a new book, entitled *Mein Kampf*—"complete and unabridged, and fully annotated"—with the note that "any abridgment must necessarily fail, in proportion to the degree of its condensation, to give the full flavor of the author's mind." In other words, the world was beginning not to dismiss Hitler; now, readers *needed* to know more. It was no longer the entertainment of a buffoon of the 1920s; it was, moreover, no longer even an intellectual exercise, a political theory lesson. Now, more to the point, people were plainly scared. The growth of Hitler's power could easily make far-off America a target, as well. No, Americans said in effect: Print the whole book, please. We *need* it.

And so now the Introduction in an American edition of Hitler's exegesis took on a much more sobering tone:

> This is an accurate translation of a book which is likely to remain the most important political tract of our time.
> . . . .
> The Austrian and Czecho-Slovakian crises of last year . . . have awakened the American public as never before to the seriousness to the world and to themselves of the Nazi program.
> . . . .
> *Mein Kampf* is, above all, a book of feeling.
> . . . .
> *Mein Kampf* is a propagandistic essay by a violent partisan. As such it often warps historical truth and sometimes ignores it completely.
> . . . .
> One point in particular may need emphasis. Large portions of *Mein Kampf* are devoted to the question of race as a substructure on which to erect an anti-Semitic policy.
> . . . .
> The engines of industry now spin round in trepidation, and the engines of war are piled giddily in higher and higher pyramids. . . .

And the Introduction concludes, in dramatic departure from the quaintness of the 1933 version, with a stand-taking:

It is our profound conviction that as soon as enough people have seen
through this book, lived with it until the facts they behold are so startlingly
vivid that all else is obscure by comparison, the tide will begin to turn.

And what of Lindbergh, with his "aw-shucks" grin and his undeniable daring, and—that most precious possession—the rapt attention of a nation?

The "America First" movement in the United States was the work of grim
"hardball" fellows, and one of them was Colonel Lindbergh, who had been
Goering's guest, and had been convinced of the Luftwaffe's superiority, even
at a time (1936) when the Nazis so skillfully hid the fact that this was not yet
so. Lindbergh, who with his wife Anne Morrow had occupied the country cot-
tage of Harold Nicolson and Vita Sackville-West during the Americans' stay in
England, had spoken disparagingly to Nicolson of England's aerial chances, and
suggested a treaty before they were tested.[9] Despite Lindbergh's reputation for
thrilling many statesmen with his negativity, his host told it as it was, finding
the flier's views biased, according to Mosley, and "all tied up with his hatred
of degeneracy and his hatred of democracy as represented by the free press and
the American public." Nicolson, a writer, thinker, statesman, and patriot of great
distinction, may be trusted for the veracity of his reportage, and admired for his
honest conclusions about a friend's deviant patterns, as anyone who has read
his collected diaries will attest.

So much of Hitler's behavior had the ring of adolescence to it that it can be
posited that his development was arrested at the point of pubescence. His behavior exhibited many adolescent preoccupations, and some distortions peculiar
to him alone: the striving for attention, the fantasy life which centered first upon
his own desired art career and Wagnerian music, the Germanic mythos of Romantic tragedy, the mountain symbology of Teutonic exaltation. Then, his fix-
ations turned toward his perceived exclusivity and celebrated difference, the idea
of personal salvation through discovery of a "calling," the needs of rebelling
against his father's ways and his family's stressing of average behavior and
anonymity. Lastly, he suffused his mind with the burgeoning of the NSDAP
into an actual entity of strength, the cult attractions for which the Party was
ideal.

Much later, when Germany had fallen into advanced stages of decay and the
war was effectively lost, Hitler behaved in ways which again reflected that his
level of development had been frozen at pubescence: He expended increasing
resources, and his and others' own personal energy, on the epic propaganda
films which represented egregious flings into disarray and unreality for his with-
ering military forces. Moreover, these forces themselves took on the full aspect
of youthfulness, for as early as 1944, mid-teens and younger boys were being
conscripted and sent by this aged and mentally infirm "teen" to the cold killing
grounds of a bitter infantry existence.

At the eleventh hour of madness and imminent defeat (acknowledgment of
which Hitler never gave), the *Fuehrer* created the greatest fantasy of all: his

elevation into adulthood. In the last hour of his life, as virtually his last deed, he married the doomed Eva Braun in a sordid wedding ceremony which had almost no witnesses save his police dogs. Then, the way another groom might light candles to welcome future wedded bliss, Hitler shot the dogs, murdered his bride, and sent, for good measure, both a bullet and a cyanide capsule into the being he had become and from whom, by this act, he now stood aloof.

This bullet, which Hitler intended to fire originally from his Browning revolver in 1923 while retreating from capture and being hidden by Helene Hanfstaengl, was (metaphorically) twenty-two years too late in reaching him; he brought about the deaths of upwards of ten million human beings before it smashed into his skull, releasing from its corporeal incarceration whatever kind of spirit had settled long ago into a grim-faced, sad-eyed child of Austria.

So it was that the man who had "passed into oblivion" took advantage of a temporary measure of societal incapacity, to devise through one form of rhetoric the means by which to garner attention long enough to use another form of rhetoric; and through his claim upon the living soul of the mass, this one man, an "oaf," a "flabby," "oblivious" fanatic, was able in the course of sixty-nine months of declared war, to alter national outlines of the globe and the guideposts of the politics of mankind to such an extent that only firestorm, fission, and millions of human deaths could impede, and finally destroy, its power.

How can we learn from this rhetoric of hate? I believe it to be a hard reality—perhaps the hardest—that the only way to have it be "never again" is to do the most courageous thing imaginable with respect to Adolf Hitler: that is, to view him in the most human terms possible.

The description of Hitler as an arrested adolescent fits the evidence well. He gave off the teenager's less desirable characteristics in abundance: weakness, fearfulness, vulnerability; the schizoid aspects of the adolescent period, when one burgeoning selfhood emerges to fight another, while the true "stages" of the self lock horns for the right to achieve personal union and spiritual fecundity. We must strive to see him in a sympathetic light, in order to keep *ourselves* from killing, from becoming, like him, people divorced from feeling, people whose ends justify the means. We must, in essence, place ourselves in the role of his parents, ask ourselves the old parental cliché "Where did we go wrong?" and then ask ourselves also, "What can—and must—we do about it now?" Only then will we have any right to hope that this epoch will not reappear before us—or our children.

Does Hitlerism live today? Is intolerance a problem on the global level, and something more ominous than a few rocks thrown through synagogue windows in cities already steeped in many indefinable turmoils? Can an outbreak of genocidal violence happen again? The growing anger of millions of ordinary, anonymous people suggests that it can. Hatred so deeply rooted can quickly assume fearsome social dimensions, and is abetted all the more by those who stand aside in indifference.

NOTES

1. There are portraits of Lindbergh which have a curious ring, considering his later prewar isolationism: The tall boy with the shy smile had been a test flier, who some mornings crashed the little "Jennies" then in use and would be in the air in other craft later that same day, with nary a word of emotion or exclamation.

Similarly, Shirer, whose rounding middle, thinning hair, twinkling face, and puffing pipe gave him the air of a youthful Santa Claus, quietly reared a small family and enjoyed ski trips to the Alps, while he nightly moved into the Nazis' den, and, later, got by rooftop to the German broadcast studio so as to dodge bullets.

2. Any doubts of Lindbergh's daring can be dispelled by the recommendation that now, sixty-four technically advanced years after the first transatlantic flight, the reader put down this book, find his way to a small airport, and pay for a flight in a canvas-wood-and-glue craft which has amazing resistance to wind currents, but crumples like a drifting sheet of newsprint upon impact with the earth.

3. Anne Morrow Lindbergh's verse is a fixture of American poetry. Her father was Dwight Morrow, the American diplomat whose life was recorded in a critically praised 1935 biography by Harold Nicolson. (The Nicolson home in Kent was a later base for the Lindberghs' highly criticized trips to Nazi Germany.)

4. Nicolson, Harold. *Diaries and Letters: 1930–1939.* Atheneum, New York, 1966, pp. 272, 343.

5. William Shirer lived to see Germany struggle again—this time with reunification—and died in 1994 at age eighty-nine.

6. Hitler, Adolf. *My Battle (Mein Kampf).* Abridged and translated by E. T. S. Dugdale. Houghton Mifflin, Boston, 1933.

7. Ibid.

8. A boastful, if truthful, enticement offered by Hitler's American publishers.

9. This well-known friendship, and the resultant negative attitudes expressed by Lindbergh, are well documented in the literature about England's slide toward war, but never as intriguingly as in Leonard Mosley's fine book *On Borrowed Time: How World War II Began.* Random House, New York, 1969. In it, he relates the conversation between the two men as reconstructed by Harold Nicolson in his diary entry of September 8, 1936; but apparently, Lindbergh, embarrassed by his prewar sentiments in the hindsight of 1969, when Mosley wanted to publish them, refused permission. Mosley gallantly cites the passages in Nicolson's diaries, demonstrating that a thirty-three-year-late utterance of an unseemly truth is more palatable than an unsavory fact with a three-decade history of being hidden.

Chapter Six

"In Their Righteous Might!"

WINSTON CHURCHILL: THE RIGHT HONORABLE DEMOSTHENES

The Battle of France is over. I expect that the Battle of Britain is about to begin. Upon this battle depends the survival of Christian civilisation. Upon it depends our own British life, and the long continuity of our institutions and our Empire. The whole fury and might of the enemy must very soon be turned on us. Hitler knows that he will have to break us in this Island or lose the war. If we can stand up to him, all Europe may be free and the life of the world may move forward into broad, sunlit uplands. But if we fail, then the whole world, including the United States, including all that we have known and cared for, will sink into the abyss of a new Dark Age, made more sinister and perhaps more protracted by the lights of perverted science. Let us therefore brace ourselves to our duties, and so bear ourselves that, if the British Empire and its Commonwealth last for a thousand years, men will still say, "This was their finest hour."

—Winston Churchill
After Dunkirk, 1940[1]

He often avoided the formal dress that was regular fare for members of the government; in three-quarter top hat and tails, he looked like nothing as much as a backwater carney boss. His preferred footwear items included a pair of zip-up oxfords; and once, visiting the battlefront, he was seen in balletmaster slip-ons. He always strolled with a cane, which conspired with the top hat to Chaplinize his walk. On cold days he donned an overcoat, but buttoned it by the top button only, so that the heavy wool hung, A-frame fashion, like a tent over the corpulence below.

His face was ruddy, pudgy, and bumpy—a great balloon with a little of the air gone out, leaving creases like latex delineating the basic blimp. His manner was often brusque and contemptuous.

Huge cigars were a normal (and frequent) part of his daily life. Some people felt him rude, some comical; a few considered him the meanest man alive. He was a fact of life in England for the last years of the nineteenth century, and for the whole of the first four decades of the twentieth century. For a long time, most of his countrymen dismissed him, until dismissing him was no longer possible. In 1939, he was an annoying autumnal disturbance, a gadfly whose daily buzzing distracted the stolid drones in Neville Chamberlain's government.

But barely four months into 1940, at age sixty-five—the point when most men retire—this ornery, long-suffered, and long-suffering advocate of opposition had become the one fact of life without which England could not survive. Winston Leonard Spencer Churchill did more than anyone else to create a way out of the unfathomable morass into which the entire world was steadily sinking. His was, surely, a faith that could move mountains.

Why was this man such a phenonemon? Why was he the ideal choice to lead Britain through its trial?

He was a soldier with formidable battle experience. (A onetime cavalry officer and excellent rider, he also was, with Swinton and Hankey, credited with inventing the tank.)

He was a military strategist of the first order. (His prediction of the advent and outcome of the First World War, made many years before that war had even begun, proved to have been exact down to the dates, personnel, and materiel figures involved.)

He was an executive with unflagging energies and keen intuitions about how to run an organization. His list of government positions included the offices of president of the Board of Trade and secretary for war and air after Versailles, in which capacity he established the Royal Air Force. At various times he had also been undersecretary for the colonies, home secretary, and first lord of the Admiralty. He became full colonial secretary, founding the nations of Iraq and Jordan, and planning the state of Israel. In later governments, he was Baldwin's chancellor of the Exchequer and first lord of the Admiralty again under Neville Chamberlain. All told, he served in the governments of Campbell-Bannerman, Asquith, Lloyd George, Baldwin, and Chamberlain.

He was a writer and historian, with a writer's and historian's grasp of world events. (His bibliography includes three major works written *before* the turn of the century.) He followed these with his three-volume biography of his ancestor the first duke of Marlborough (*Marlborough*), a six-volume history of the First World War (*The World Crisis*), and others. William Manchester has written: "During Churchill's long spell as a backbencher [1929–1939, when he was completely out of power], he wrote and published nine million words."[2] He was a man who knew how to use the time which was on his hands. It made him self-sustaining by his pen, and it bought him his home, Chartwell, which he built largely by himself, and which was his planned retirement dwelling.

He was a man whose knowledge of his country, and whose command of the language to express that knowledge, were without peer. (*The History of the English-speaking Peoples* was nearing completion as the first bombs fell on London in 1940; its publication was delayed until after 1945, when Churchill received the cheering accolades from those grateful English speakers below Buckingham Palace's balcony.)

And, finally, he was a diplomat whose instincts were refined for work with a national government. Chamberlain's severest critic for years prior to his own appointment as leader of the government, Churchill maintained his predecessor's friendship and respect in ways which put to shame common patterns of partisan meanness.[3]

These are among the many reasons why the man who had all these credentials was the only one who could save Britain. And like it or not, Britain knew it.

In the same manner as his predecessor, Winston Churchill developed memorable phrases in his rhetorical presentations to the world. But unlike Chamberlain's paltry and culpable words, Churchill's verbal communications to his parliament (and through them, his constituency, his public, his enemies, the world at large, and posterity) were proclamations of oratorical genius; they brought hope, courage, and fortitude to a people who rightly sensed aloneness, consuming fear, and demonstrably certain doom. Many feel that his speeches alone, made when he was war leader, and their resultant effect upon the English people and their allies, saved mankind from the "merciless degradation" he had foreseen and, until 1940, had urged in vain that England heed. It is for this unmatched achievement that he is widely felt to have been the greatest Englishman of all time; and this accolade can be justified because his gifts were carried through his oratory to the world's ears.

How could Churchill's words do so much? Why (to paraphrase some of them) did so many people owe so much to such a small number of one man's utterances?[4] The answer has to do with the peculiarly vital and creative quality of his thinking processes, the exact and apt choice of language to convey those processes, and the serendipitous readiness of the right moment in history to deliver them.

This chapter will refer to a number of his speeches. Many are among the best-known of his wartime messages, and surely their brilliant fulfillment of the three rhetorical requirements of this text is reason for their continued fame and accounts for their inclusion in this or anybody's study of Churchill's contributions. But presented here will be only one speech—the Chamberlain valediction. It is little known in comparison with "blood, toil, tears and sweat" or "Some chicken; some neck!"; but it is quintessential Churchill. It reveals in full measure the qualities of a leader who might savage the ideas of an opponent (as he certainly did, remorselessly, with Neville Chamberlain), but who would rather be shot than be said to have given personal offense. (In this practice, he had much in common with a certain "seditious half-naked fakir.")

For a literate man, a speech is an occasion for oral literacy. To a dramatic man, a speech is an occasion for literate elocution. To a Churchill, the most literate of literate men, and the most emotionally dramatic of men who lived lives of drama, speeches were occasions for flinging brilliant thoughts into the hearts and minds of his people, and doing it with style and pace. His acuity of mind and dynamism of spirit turned each of his most literate of speeches into a separate whisper for the heart.

Every aspect of Churchill's activity became funneled into the wartime task at hand. Each element of his work as prime minister became harnessed to pull the weight of his messages through the foils of the microphone and out to the ears of his listeners. Here was a man of limitless resources, who knew how to use them.

Having expended so much energy in the task of writing during his long governmental "sabbatical" in the 1930s, he carried the power of the pen with him back into government. Writing became a style of his leadership, for from the moment of recommencement of his ministerial responsibilities, he wrote short directives, or "minutes," to convey orders or notions to his staff. He wrote numerous ones daily; his apical post was a great gymnasium for the speaker. It allowed him to think with the pen, to refine his communicative tools on a many-times-a-day basis. By war's end, these communications would number in the thousands. While by definition they do not contain his elevated phrases, the heightened language he reserved for the resonant chambers of the House, their recording provided a catalogue of the thoughts, plans, and actions of the Allies' primary individual during the entirety of the war.[5]

A full six months before the first meeting off the coast of Newfoundland of the British prime minister and the American president (which meeting produced the Atlantic Charter of August 1941), and throughout the early years of the war, Churchill's greatest anxiety came not from Hitler, but from not knowing how to create that initial impetus to get America "off the dime." He knew from Harry Hopkins, Roosevelt's unofficial liaison, and from FDR's communications directly, that the American leader was fully in support of Great Britain's courageous and lonely stand against the Axis. But there was nothing tangible behind the sentiment of encouragement, from that "never again" stranglehold on Congress which the isolationists held.

Until incredibly late in the game (and "late" for Great Britain was every minute of every hour of every day of the entirety of 1940 and 1941, up to the attack on Pearl Harbor on December 7), the isolationist voice in the United States held great sway. The average citizen, who remembered all too well going off to war in 1917, and now faced the fact that the "gathering storm" was clouding out the sun's rays for his own sons as well, listened with heartfelt earnestness to the broadcasts of Father Coughlin and Colonel Lindbergh, and Wendell Willkie, and swore under his breath at the president with his cape and his big smile and his love of the pudgy prime minister who was courting him from England.

At last, the lend-lease idea was conceived, and a palpable commitment was put together by the administration which could pass the congressional muster without too great a cry of dissent.[6] On March 11, 1941, the Congress passed the Lend-Lease Act, which touted itself as "An Act to Promote the Defense of the United States." The act proposed to accomplish this "by authorizing the President . . . [t]o sell, transfer title to, exchange, lease, lend, or otherwise dispose of, to any such government any defense article. . . ."

By this means did Winston Churchill procure for his exposed island fifty rusting ships of the sort which in other circumstances would have made better sunken hatcheries than bulwarks of freedom's defense. But the prime minister would have accepted with glad heart the very garden hose of FDR's metaphor,[7] if its transfer had signified the willingness of the new English-speaking people to come to the defense of the old.

Thus, on March 12, 1941, when news of the previous day's congressional vote reached Churchill, the prime minister stood in the House of Commons, and reported, with admirable restraint, perhaps the best news he'd received since the beginning of hostilities:

The Lend Lease Bill became law yesterday, when it received the signature of the President. I am sure the House would wish me to express on their behalf, and on behalf of the nation, our deep and respectful appreciation of this monument of generous and far-seeing statesmanship.

The most powerful democracy has, in effect, declared in solemn Statute that they will devote their overwhelming industrial and financial strength to ensuring the defeat of Nazism in order that nations, great and small, may live in security, tolerance and freedom. By so doing, the Government and people of the United States have in fact written a new Magna Carta, which not only has regard to the rights and laws upon which a healthy and advancing civilization can alone be erected, but also proclaims by precept and example the duty of free men and free nations, wherever they may be, to share the responsibility and burden of enforcing them.

In the name of His Majesty's Government and speaking, I am sure for Parliament and for the whole country, and indeed, in the name of all freedom-loving peoples, I offer to the United States our gratitude for her inspiring act of faith.[8]

When the time came for such a speech in the lower House of Parliament, or for a radio address, the words presented themselves with dispatch. Only toward the end of his second prime ministerial term, in the mid-1950s, did Churchill allow anyone else to pen words which he would use in an address; and these few ghostwritten efforts came from John Colville, the British Foreign Office's congenial and bright secretarial figure in Churchill's official entourage.[9] After nine years of intimate experience with the Churchill idiom, Colville felt he could come close enough to "pinch-hit," but never to replace, his principal's expression.[10]

In family matters, one must be forgiven one's loyalties and resentments. Churchill's career, at first in major part, and latterly in a spirit of acknowledgment, honored his father's image. But this image of Lord Randolph Churchill (1849–1895) favored color over substance: the audacious and thrilling voice of a once-imposing young M.P. with the American beauty Jennie Jerome on his arm. It seems a nod to the bombastic, rather than the substantive, side of Churchill *père*'s oratory.

Winston Churchill's career far outdistanced his father's, as did, apace, his oratory. Indeed, reaching the age of ninety, he lived almost exactly twice as long as Lord Randolph. Being no rake, and living into the age of penicillin, Winston never stood a chance of meeting the fate of his father;[11] but the blue polka-dot bow tie which he wore to the end symbolized his courtesy to his father's "certain splendid memory." This was long after Lord Randolph's public words were encased in the modest frame history correctly has used to display them.

As has been pointed out, the ten years from the late 1920s until the late 1930s found Churchill in the political wilderness. During that time, his was the sole voice for rearmament, arguing from the back benches of the House of Commons that Germany was violating the Versailles agreements in virtually every sphere, and was itself rearming to the point where a conflict was imminent. His advice was ignored totally, being benignly neglected by some, and caustically rebutted by others.

At last, feeling the great international political strains of Hitler's irresistible drive, Neville Chamberlain in 1939 invited Churchill back into the government. Winston occupied his old seat as first lord of the Admiralty, initially occupied by him in 1911; and on the first day back in Whitehall, he began the long uphill battle to rectify the imbalances of might between the old antagonists, Germany and England.[12]

Churchill's first speeches out from the "wilderness" were in this position of limited authority. He was first lord from September 3, 1939; in April 1940 he was appointed president of the Military Coordination Committee, in addition to his Admiralty responsibilities. This provided him more of an official persona, and aided him in his vociferous calls for action, via the radio waves. Inevitably, with the Munich crisis of 1938 having cast disfavor upon Chamberlain's leadership, in May 1940 the great appeaser's government fell. Because of his efforts to rebuild the Admiralty, guide the War Council, and communicate with the common people of Great Britain, Churchill was anointed to replace Chamberlain as prime minister, being chosen over the royally favored foreign secretary, Lord Halifax.[13]

Even while in such circumscribed capacities as the subordinate cabinet positions, Churchill blossomed as an exalted harbinger, and made the famous broadcasts of early 1940.[14] His expressed views in these radio messages were a godsend to many Britons. Yet, eloquent though they may have been, his words were received by some as anything from cheeky to scandalous. Lord Halifax, in his role as Chamberlain's foreign secretary, had to reprimand Churchill (in the thickly polite language used between His Majesty's government ministers). But from the start, the first lord's eloquence had its intended effect, even if not spoken from the highest rank.

Some felt Churchill was "pushy," elbowing his way around the war cabinet by co-opting all major war counsel decisions for himself. It was hard for some to face the fact that he was simply more energetic, far-seeing, enthusiastic, and resourceful than anybody else about the conduct of the war.[15] In effect, he was seen by his detractors as exercising a kind of divine right of Churchills. This assumption—in both senses—had brought him to ministerial rank before the ten-year exile; it now reasserted itself with a vengeance. Within eight months of being invited back into the government by Chamberlain, he had replaced him.

The truth is he had more vision than anyone else, had more drive, and more and better ideas. He had a chess master's "if-then" perspicacity, and could move the main events on the map of his mind with greater accuracy than any other ministerial figure. Moreover—and it is our focus on this giant of oratorical history—he could state all this to the anxious citizenry with vastly superior expression. He had a fanatical patriot's zeal, a chess master's skill, a leader's genius, a writer's eloquence.

It might be deemed, in facile argument, that he was at the right place at the right time. In fact, by his own hard work and sincere concern, Churchill had *made* himself the right man. Now he had arrived at the right place; the time, if anything, was overripe by years.

As one might imagine, because of his singular and stellar place in history, there is a wealth of material already written on myriad aspects of Churchill. But only one book is dedicated to the study of the man as orator. This volume is James Humes' *Churchill: Speaker of the Century* (New York: Stein and Day, 1980).

A biography, and short as Churchill biographies go, this book was written with loving care by a former speechwriter of Richard Nixon's. It advances an historical picture of the young parliamentarian, and his intention to make his way as a politician by being a communicator of superlative skill. Churchill's greatest gift as a young man was his writing ability, which gave him his two acclaimed volumes of war-experience narrative before he was thirty. Thus, Humes argues, Churchill the writer emerged from Churchill the warrior, and Churchill the orator emerged out of Churchill the writer. Humes pinpoints the formative influences upon the rising young Commons member, of which there were four: his father, Lord Randolph Churchill, and the American Bourke Cochran influenced his speaking ability (with the barbed-epithet style acknowledging his father, and substantive eloquence giving the nod to Cochran); the Victorian

Macaulay and the earlier Gibbon, both of whose works Churchill had scrutinized and even memorized far back into his youth, influenced his writing style.

With any accomplished orator, refinement of expression must become second nature, so that virtually any utterances, or writing, have a richness to them which are not of ordinary aspect.[16] This explains the care with which Churchill as war leader penned those thousands of daily "minutes" he sent to his underlings and other ministers.[17] Some are droll, or masterpieces of invective, worthy of Lord Randolph. Some are informational, and served as early soundings for later statements of public policy. All minute-directives of moment are a part of the Churchill canon which he created during the Attlee Labour government from 1945 to 1951, the period of peaceful amnesia seeking which Britons bestowed upon themselves, while bestowing upon Winston the time to write his indispensable memoirs of the war.[18] (And, Churchill became the only surviving wartime helmsman who documented the experience.)

One of Humes' greatest contributions in his book is to show the lineage of some of Churchill's most memorable phrases, back to oratorical concepts early in his career. Winston developed some staples of expression, and they appear throughout his life. Inasmuch as this exemplary life is well-known for the oratory it produced, it is moving to remember that much of Churchill's splendor of language, the language which gave heart in the blackest hour, was created in his underground "cell" in Whitehall's war rooms. This chamber, not very different from an actual prison cell, enabled its occupant to grab ten-minute naps, after which he hastily wrote some of the parliamentary speeches and radio addresses which have lasted fifty years without tarnish. Even more humbling than the picture of the prime minister of England sitting on a cot in a room decorated with steam pipes is the memory of his maiden parliamentary address, during the last days of Victoria's life. Still taunted for his rasping lisp, and ever aware of the likely comparison with the dashing and resonant Randolph, the young Winston memorized his speech, and in its delivery lost his way. Mortified, he flung his hands up to cover his face, and left the podium in a horridly personal infliction of humiliation. Perhaps the road which led him to invigorate his countrymen's spirits on their way to their "finest hour" began half a lifetime before, in almost the same spot, with his own most mortifying moments.

What can be said, then, about this story of two prime ministers, really, and their words—of the wretchedly personal sadness of a Chamberlain, who thought that with "trying, trying again" he could appease a Hitler, at the very moment when his nation needed someone who could truly take a madman's measure, and give back in kind?

With Chamberlain, English reserve held forth; the war-as-a-gentlemen's game idea persisted, despite the First World War's savagery, which is why a policy of appeasement had such sway with Parliament; surely, Germany had its gentlemen, didn't it? Negotiate! That was sufficient, despite the sour wag Winston's whining about rearmament violations of Versailles.

In this atmosphere, from 1933 until September 1939, Churchill's vocal objection gave the impression to Parliament's power brokers of having the cast of the shouts of a paranoid, instead of what it was: the prescience of a brilliant strategist and candid realist. During this long period, when, violating numerous tenets of the Versailles treaty, an increasingly daring and boastful Germany rearmed and then—systematically and unopposed—invaded its neighbors one by one, even rhetoric as skillful as Churchill's caught no one's ear.

This awful predicament showed how much oratory's effect depends upon the receptivity of the listener. Until the Munich charade, the quiet Chamberlain was the embodiment of England's character: methodical, courteous, marked by old-boy honor. By the time the imperial island realized its errors, no rhetorical pronouncement was louder than the collective sudden-sucked breath of a people duped.

In May of 1940 the new prime minister made two wise decisions about the future use of his rhetoric. First, Churchill did not afflict Parliament, or Neville Chamberlain, with any "I-told-you-so!" talk whatsoever. Indeed, to the dis-credited Chamberlain, he remained friendly, inviting him into the new war cab-inet, and treating him with great affection and respect. And second, with regard to the German *Fuehrer,* he avoided any direct, brow-furrowing dialectical dis-cussion. Instead of formal refutation of the madman's aggressive assertions, Churchill only responded to his ravings with irony; at an angle. The defender of the threatened British Empire gave no due to the dictator that was not laced with sarcasm, and the effect was gratifying. Gone was the Chamberlainite "may it please the court" proffering of courtesies. In their place came the "To hell with you!" countercharge from the fearless Omdurman cavalry officer, done in such a way as to convey that, though unprepared, England would be no sup-plicating victim, shaking with foreboding.

The effect in England of this new strength and candor was electrifying. The nation's latent outrage became galvanized and expressed; in short order after May 1940 the bitten lips gave way to "we can take it!"; and by September 1940, with the RAF fighter planes defending the skies against Goering's fighter planes, "We can take it!" was replaced by "We can dish it out!" Hitler's dagger-threat invasion was delayed, and its possibility atrophied with each day's passage.

Syllable by syllable, Churchill defended his island, against impossible odds, by language which—men will still say—was its finest, because it had to be.

SPEECH DELIVERED TO THE HOUSE OF COMMONS
NOVEMBER 12, 1940:
TRIBUTE TO NEVILLE CHAMBERLAIN

Since we last met, the House has suffered a very grievous loss in the death of one of its most distinguished Members, and of a statesman and public servant who, during the best part of three memorable years, was first Minister of the Crown.

The fierce and bitter controversies which hung around him in recent times were hushed by the news of his illness and are silenced by his death. In paying a tribute of respect and of regard to an eminent man who has been taken from us, no one is obliged to alter the opinions which he has formed or expressed upon issues which have become a part of history; but at the Lychgate we may all pass our own conduct and our own judgments under a searching review. It is not given to human beings, happily for them, for otherwise life would be intolerable, to foresee or to predict to any large extent the unfolding course of events. In one phase men seem to have been right, in another they seem to have been wrong. Then again, a few years later, when the perspective of time has lengthened, all stands in a different setting. There is a new proportion. There is another scale of values. History with its flickering lamp stumbles along the trail of the past, trying to reconstruct its scenes, to revive its echoes, and kindle with pale gleams the passion of former days. What is the worth of all this? The only guide to a man is his conscience; the only shield to his memory is the rectitude and sincerity of his actions. It is very imprudent to walk through life without this shield, because we are so often mocked by the failure of our hopes and the upsetting of our calculations; but with this shield, however the fates may play, we march always in the ranks of honour.

It fell to Neville Chamberlain in one of the supreme crises of the world to be contradicted by events, to be disappointed in his hopes, and to be deceived and cheated by a wicked man. But what were these hopes in which he was disappointed? What were these wishes in which he was frustrated? What was that faith that was abused? They were surely among the most noble and benevolent instincts of the human heart—the love of peace, the toil for peace, the strife for peace, the pursuit of peace, even at great peril, and certainly to the utter disdain of popularity or clamour. Whatever else history may or may not say about these terrible, tremendous years, we can be sure that Neville Chamberlain acted with perfect sincerity according to his lights and strove to the utmost of his capacity and authority, which were powerful, to save the world from the awful, devastating struggle in which we are now engaged. This alone will stand him in good stead as far as what is called the verdict of history is concerned.

But it is also a help to our country and to our whole Empire, and to our decent faithful way of living that, however long the struggle may last, or however dark may be the clouds which overhang our path, no future generation of

English-speaking folks—for that is the tribunal to which we appeal—will doubt that, even at a great cost to ourselves in technical preparation, we were guiltless of the bloodshed, terror and misery which have engulfed so many lands and peoples, and yet seek new victims still. Herr Hitler protests with frantic words and gestures that he has only desired peace. What do these ravings and outpourings count before the silence of Neville Chamberlain's tomb? Long, hard, and hazardous years lie before us, but at least we entered upon them united and with clean hearts.

I do not propose to give an appreciation of Neville Chamberlain's life and character, but there were certain qualities always admired in these Islands which he possessed in an altogether exceptional degree. He had a physical and moral toughness of fibre which enabled him all through his varied career to endure misfortune and disappointment without being unduly discouraged or wearied. He had a precision of mind and an aptitude for business which raised him far above the ordinary levels of our generation. He had a firmness of spirit which was not often elated by success, seldom downcast by failure, and never swayed by panic. When, contrary to all his hopes, beliefs and exertions, the war came upon him, and when, as he himself said, all that he had worked for was shattered, there was no man more resolved to pursue the unsought quarrel to the death. The same qualities which made him one of the last to enter the war, made him one of the last who would quit it before the full victory of a righteous cause was won.

I had the singular experience of passing in a day from being one of his most prominent opponents and critics to being one of his principal lieutenants, and on another day of passing from serving under him to become the head of a Government of which, with perfect loyalty, he was content to be a member. Such relationships are unusual in our public life. I have before told the House how on the morrow of the Debate which in the early days of May challenged his position, he declared to me and a few other friends that only a National Government could face the storm about to break upon us, and that if he were an obstacle to the formation of such a Government, he would instantly retire. Thereafter, he acted with that singleness of purpose and simplicity of conduct which at all times, and especially in great times, ought to be the ideal of us all.

When he returned to duty a few weeks after a most severe operation, the bombardment of London and of the seat of Government had begun. I was a witness during that fortnight of his fortitude under the most grievous and painful bodily afflictions, and I can testify that, although physically only the wreck of a man, his nerve was unshaken and his remarkable mental faculties unimpaired.

After he left the Government he refused all honours. He would die like his father, plain Mr. Chamberlain. I sought permission of the King, however, to have him supplied with the Cabinet papers, and until a few days of his death he followed our affairs with keenness, interest and tenacity. He met the approach of death with a steady eye. If he grieved at all, it was that he could not be a spectator of our victory; but I think he died with the comfort of knowing that his country had, at least, turned the corner.

At this time our thoughts must pass to the gracious and charming lady who shared his days of triumph and adversity with a courage and quality the equal of his own. He was, like his father and his brother Austen before him, a famous Member of the House of Commons, and we here assembled this morning, Members of all parties, without a single exception, feel that we do ourselves and our country honour in saluting the memory of one whom Disraeli would have called an "English worthy."

NOTES

1. Churchill, Winston. *The Second World War.* Vol. II: *Their Finest Hour.* Houghton Mifflin, Boston, 1949.

2. Churchill's years of political nonpersonhood are told movingly in Manchester's *The Last Lion: Winston Spencer Churchill 1932–1940.* Little, Brown, Boston, 1988.

3. Prime Minister Churchill's eulogy to the man whom he credited with almost giving away the empire follows this section; it illustrates not only its author's sure grasp of language, but his magnanimity as a man.

4. "Never in the history of human conflict have so many owed so much to so few," he said to the House of Commons on August 20, 1940, referring to the brave RAF pilots who parried the aerial thrust of Hitler's Fokkers in the Battle of Britain.

5. The foremost scholar of the Second World War to use this invaluable resource was—Winston Churchill. The whole of his astonishingly thorough six-volume history of the war draws heavily upon the minutes for their continuity, particularity, and consequence.

6. The present work's ensuing treatment of Roosevelt will delineate the wording by which the presidential rhetoric solved this problem.

7. Discussed by Churchill in *The Unrelenting Struggle: War Speeches by Winston S. Churchill.* Little, Brown, Boston, 1942.

8. Recordings of Churchill's addresses in the House of Commons include the "Hear, hear!" responses of the parliamentary body. Such remarks as this one of Winston's noted a veritable turning point in Britain's war chances; yet the verbal reception is muted, in that British manner. Only a more encompassing sense of British character would find in these utterances what is truly there: the deep feelings of the members of this governmental organ at that time.

9. Strikingly unassuming for a man in his position, Colville's geniality kept him as a Churchill favorite throughout most of the years of both Churchillian prime ministerships. That geniality also won for Colville the hand in marriage of Lady Margaret Egerton, who was until 1948 then-Princess Elizabeth's senior lady-in-waiting.

10. Colville, John. *The Fringes of Power: 10 Downing Street Diaries 1939–1955.* W. W. Norton, New York, 1985. Colville kept a clandestine (and improprietous) diary throughout his tenure as Churchill's aide. It serves as an excellent guide to Churchill's journey as prime minister. An example is his entry for Thursday, August 15, 1940, on the matter which the following year became codified as the lend-lease statute: "The President has sent a message to the effect that he can persuade Congress to let us have

our fifty destroyers if we give him an assurance, not necessarily for publication, that we will not allow the British fleet to be scuttled or surrendered. . . . In his reply Winston says he is cheered by this information and continues: 'You will, I am sure, send us everything you can, for you know well that the worth of every destroyer you can spare to us is measured in rubies.' "

11. Lord Randolph died painfully, in the last years of the Victorian century, of tertiary syphilis. The son who adored him was not yet twenty-one years of age.

12. The full extent of Chamberlain's ostrich-stance policies came home to Churchill on his first day back at the Admiralty: His office, the very one he had left in disgrace after Gallipoli in 1915, still had on the walls the same maps he had placed there.

13. Halifax, a nobleman, had been King George VI's choice, perhaps because of his nobility, or perhaps because the monarch remembered Churchill's steadfast support of Edward VIII's right to marry Wallis Simpson. In the interview with the king, with both "candidates" present, Churchill used the quintessential choice of words for the occasion—which were none at all. The silence was ultimately filled by Halifax's diplomatic withdrawal.

14. These magnificent addresses are as much an essential part of the English language as anything in its history. This text acknowledges their ubiquitous reproduction, and omits them here, in deference to one not as well-known.

15. FDR, in an admiring description of Churchill to someone who doubted the Britisher's qualities, said that Winston had about a hundred ideas a day, four of which were good ones. (Even if both figures were extreme, taken at that rate Churchill would have produced 8,000 good ideas throughout the war.)

16. In researching a later section of the present work, the author came upon an anecdote in John G. Adams' book *Without Precedent,* wherein he questions lawyer Joseph Welch's "spontaneity" in his riposte to Joe McCarthy during the final moments of the Army-McCarthy hearings. Adams cites a Churchillian response to a query about what the great statesman did during his spare moments. Churchill's answer, reportedly, was: "I rehearse my extemporaneous speeches."

17. James Humes estimates that by war's end, these minutes numbered one million.

18. The memoirs formed Churchill's six-volume masterwork *The Second World War,* Houghton Mifflin, Boston, 1948–1953.

FRANKLIN DELANO ROOSEVELT: CHATS FROM THE FIRESIDE, WORDS FROM THE HEART

There is a description of Winston Churchill and Franklin Delano Roosevelt which never fails to evoke from me an emotional response. It is detailed in Joseph Lash's fine work, *Roosevelt and Churchill, 1939–1941: The Partnership That Saved the West*. During Churchill's December 1941 visit to Washington, he solidified the warm feelings which always had accompanied his correspondence with the U.S. president; and he was invited to stay in the White House, where he took his meals with FDR, almost as would a family member. Before dinner, Churchill and FDR would talk privately (the president, no doubt, mixing the drinks himself), and then the British prime minister would push the American President, who sat in a wheelchair, into the dining room.

That image, of that era's two most important human beings in the Western world silently rolling along the carpet into dinner, tells more than any position paper or reading of *Parliamentary Debates* or the *Congressional Record* about why the Grand Alliance worked. These two men understood each other keenly. That understanding cut through formality and preliminary, and right through to essence.

Each needed the leadership of the other, guidance from the other. Frances Perkins, a formidable figure as secretary of labor under Roosevelt and close to him, spoke of their swift bond. Churchill, she said, became a real friend of Roosevelt's. "Their friendship grew out of mutual need and a common ability to appreciate the drama of history, as well as out of the burdens of those who must make the history." FDR, for his part, "teased Churchill unmercifully," Perkins continued; "but that was a sign of his being 'in the family.' " The friendly teasing no doubt broke tensions, and Roosevelt is described as expecting to get as good as he gave. More telling, perhaps, is Mrs. Perkins' familiarity with Winston, whom, it happens, she had known well and long.[1] "When he was a young man he could cast a spell over people," she observed.

This spellbinding quality, felt by an American in the presence of the famous Briton, had its royal reciprocal. Churchill was careful, throughout his contacts with the American president, to be aware that the latter was not only the country's political leader, but also its head of state. In a mind as formalistic as this prime minister's, such a circumstance required honorifics befitting a king. It is thus telling that in 1939 when George VI and Queen Elizabeth visited the Roosevelts, the British monarch was able to feel for himself the spellbinding magic from this foremost American: "Why don't my Ministers talk to me as the President did tonight?" King George wrote after an evening in Roosevelt's company. "I feel exactly as though a father were giving me his most careful and wise advice."

Churchill's personality was so alive and so active that it is not at all difficult to envision it as a full, founding partner of the Grand Alliance. But there were two leaders, representing their two countries, in this beginning structure of the Allied forces. Unimaginable as it may seem, there would need to be a force of leadership, a personality fully up to the measure of Churchill's, in order for there to be a balance in the Allied effort; else, it would have been as doomed to failure as were so many where one partner was strong, and one not up to the other's strength. (One thinks of de Gaulle, of Stalin, of Hitler himself; these were not men meant for "Gemini" colleagues.) In the American president, Winston Churchill found his balancing side. And never had yin been such a match for yang.

FDR: PHENOMENON

It is almost impossible to contemplate it today: a single individual, elected willingly by the people, to be allowed to spend sixteen years in the White House. It is equally difficult to conceive that even with the abridgment of death, that individual man ended up spending over twelve years in the White House. The electorate who every fourth November provide a person truly not well-known to them with a $200,000-a-year job for four years, with a follow-up lifetime of comfort, security, protection, and renown, might, by April, have tired of their chosen leader; by August, they might be incensed at his inability to grasp or act decisively on the great issues of the day. Many champ at the bit for three years, jumping at every chance to discredit this fellow whom once the majority adored.

Indeed, two presidents have faced impeachment. One was forced to resign. Several could not get reelected. Several decided not to seek second terms, fearing the vindictive forces of a disillusioned electorate. Even the slick media candidate Reagan, who cultivated the astonishingly inappropriate sobriquet of "The Great Communicator," appears in his retirement to be in the process of being placed by history back on the dusty shelf of B-movie ranks, from which simplicity he emerged, and, with the aid of public relations experts, was catapulted into world authority.

How then, with an electorate so shrewd and disdainful, could there ever be someone handed four successive terms at the task which has so overwhelmed its incumbents that few have left office with anywhere near the public regard which ushered them into it? The answer came in the form of an individual so uniquely suited to the task of the presidency that his achievements on almost any front would have served as formidable credits for any other president. Yet, only Franklin Delano Roosevelt could, at his death, have been credited with the following:

—Revamping the American banking system

—Establishing the system for supporting the citizenry in their old age or infirmity

—Using the available media (press, radio, film) to bring the people their president in regular, informative, and human ways

—Reversing the financial chaos which entrenched the American economy in the worst failure of the country's history

—Developing governmentally supported financial nourishment for every institutional aspect of the life of its citizens, so that Americans could hope for a positive future

—Facing the threat of a rising, unchallenged world conquerer and inaugurating America's participation in the concept of a world community

—Mobilizing the nation so successfully that, in partnership with its allies, it suffocated an international virulence and restored peace and productive living to the home citizenry and the world community

Roosevelt's enemies resented his aristocratic background, his Hyde Park speaking style, his arch, Eastern U.S. posture as a member of a moneyed family with presidential celebrity already in its past. There were so many troublesome things to contend with in having this man as their president: There was the very eloquence which forms the key to the interest this book finds in this individual, off-putting to the everyday man who took such sounds for pretense or plutocracy. There was this man's absolute grasp of and control over world-shaking events. Worse, there was the fact that the country's very continuity out of despair and stasis had been in his hands since the March 1933 assumption of his responsibilities, and that he had leapt to the task of their correction. And there was the damnable knowledge that his personal strength of character, so evident in his victory over the hellish pain and unbelievable rehabilitative agenda necessary to conquer a near-fatal and crippling disease, was indefatigable and winsome.

Roosevelt's biographers carefully depict the many impedimenta against the kind of assumed easy success which is suggested by the cheerfulness with which he tackled his job. He had formidable congressional opposition; he had drawn the straw of president at perhaps the worst time of anyone since Lincoln faced a civil schism; and, of course, he faced the drudgery, minute by minute every day of his life from the age of thirty-nine, of dealing with the inert lower half of a once tall and muscular frame.

Many of the public addresses which the president delivered during his second term in the years leading to war represent some of the strategic ways in which Franklin Roosevelt crafted his words to bring fruition to his desire that public enrichment emanate from his presidential life. Even during the intense isolationist debate, FDR insinuated (and later, stated more directly) that America would be duty-bound, by honored custom and bald self-defense, to involve itself in the growing malaise.

The length confines of a book of this nature do not accommodate reproduction of even a representative sampling of FDR's verbal legacy. But highly recommended among them for the reader's perusal is a presidential speech, carried live over radio by the Columbia Broadcasting System on September 26, 1938 (an appeal during the Munich crisis which the American leader intended as a direct address to Adolf Hitler).[2] In many ways it is the first interjection of FDR into the international sphere; and with this initiative he bore the responsibility of defining the character of American expectations (as well as, and he knew it, of defining for the German chancellor his own strength of character as an American leader, and—despite the descriptions of neutrality—as a potential foe).

Next, from that fateful year 1941, came his "Four Freedoms" speech to the Congress. Apart from its moving aspect, and its strength as an expression, it is a roadmap of the country's leader's thinking at a crucial moment *before* American involvement in the war.

Reproduction space will be given here, however, to the Atlantic Charter statement (August of the same year), released in tandem with Prime Minister Churchill. Following this statement come the brief addresses delivered yet later that year by the president when "the cat was out of the bag": The first of these is the terse, emotion-laden statement of indignation and outrage delivered to Congress almost exactly eleven months after the "Four Freedoms" speech, on the morning following the sobering tragedy of Pearl Harbor. This well-remembered statement is followed by one as consequent from the declarations of war—the United States' upon Japan and Germany's upon the United States—as the last stage of maternal labor is consequent from delivery of the newborn: the declaration of war upon Germany.

If these key rhetorical documents stand on their own—and they stand well—the body of this chapter's discussion is important for the opportunity to consider another quality of this remarkable leader's expressiveness. It is worthwhile to feel Roosevelt's rhetoric in the more informal and even more intimate ways by which he made available to Americans his humanness, and his sensitive awareness of their humanness, through the Fireside Chats. In many ways, it can be said that these broadcast "conversations" introduced informality to the interchange of an American leader with his constituency. And in the same spirit of these "chats" (if more in the spirit of jousting) is an example of Roosevelt's communication with the members of the press.[3] It was in the course of one such communication that Roosevelt ripened his thinking and expression on the issue of open assistance to Great Britain.

In the predicament over American entry into the war, perhaps as with no other leadership quandary in this book—save the dilemmas facing Churchill during the Battle of Britain—we find a leader in crisis who needed to summon the most incisive rhetoric available to the mind, pen, and tongue. The ways in which he succeeded at these tasks also have no parallel, save the eloquence of the British "bulldog," as evidence of the capacity for individuals to alter the directions of forces of world tumult.

FDR FROM DEPRESSION TO WAR: THE RHETORICIAN
STEPS ONTO THE WORLD STAGE

To feel the full measure of the rhetorical import of the words of Franklin Delano Roosevelt, it must be remembered how we defined that import at the beginning of this book. It was pointed out that "an orator's first task is to convey the colors of his own feelings to others, using the most moving verbal means available to him."

"Moving," of course, means stirring, effective words which by their power strike the emotional receptors of the listener, and alter his sensibilities. With this president, "moving" also meant changing thinking, enlisting allegiance. All Roosevelt's language was put forth in the act of persuasion: if not to convince lawmakers to face a certain issue, then to show the opposing sides of a domestic dispute in such a way that his point of view was not merely unassailable but *attractive.* When there were no particulars at stake, FDR felt the need to apply all means and circumstances of his oratory toward the task of making his public familiar with him, and, once familiar, trusting of him.

In this light, and for these purposes, his Fireside Chats came into being. Short radio addresses which usually reached entire families, they offered, through his fine vocal range, well-chosen vocabulary and language construction, a tone of warmth and intimacy, opportunities for those cold toward him to "warm up" a bit, and chances for those uncertain of his ideas or his style to come over onto his side. To be sure—and he knew this—no amount of verbal cleverness, or even eloquence, would change the attitudes of those who found him repugnant (and, of course, his enemies hated him with as much, if opposite, fervor as those who held him in adulation).[4] But, he felt, if fair play was given a chance, people who listened to him and really understood him would likely come around to his point of view.

In this vein, his Fireside Chats became articles of persuasion, or (as those who were not among his friendlier constituents would say), "selling" sessions. Frances Perkins explains that the radio contacts were more than persuasion, they were sharing experiences, for both Roosevelt and his audience. She describes how the President would visualize his audience, and go through gestures and facial expressions he would have used had people been there in *his* living room. These moments were, writes James MacGregor Burns in *Roosevelt: The Soldier of Freedom,* Roosevelt's most important link with the people.

As the war progressed, an issue developed which would generate the same feeling—and indeed, reverberated with much the same arguments—as the original debates over the American involvement in any part of the conflict. This was the argument over aid to Britain, which only later became known as lend-lease, that policy proposed first to FDR by Churchill. Knowing how difficult a time Roosevelt was having with the dominant view of isolationism, by means of this new program the prime minister hoped to acquire some armaments from the

United States without further infuriating American congressmen who adhered to the neutralist position.

Roosevelt discussed the notion with his Treasury secretary, Henry Morgenthau. In the conversation, Morgenthau acknowledged the importance of helping Britain in this way, but advised Roosevelt to be careful when it came to Congress. From this exchange, FDR carried the idea into a press conference later the same afternoon, December 17, 1940. In the meeting with reporters, Roosevelt used an analogy to neighborliness, which he had devised after the casual conversation with his secretary of the Treasury.

Searching for a way to make the case for U.S. involvement *without* "any" U.S. involvement, he used the "neighbor's house on fire" idea, and in his skillful fashion for making things personal, wove around it a parable for national self-interest:

> Suppose my neighbor's home catches fire, and I have got a length of garden hose four or five hundred feet away; but, my heaven, if he can take my garden hose and connect it up with his hydrant, I may help him to put out his fire. . . . I don't say to him before that operation, "Neighbor, my garden hose cost me $15; you have got to pay me $15 for it." . . . I don't want $15—I want my garden hose back after the fire is over.[5]

It was moments like this one which most effectively persuaded domestic listeners of the wisdom or efficacy of whatever issue was being presented in the press conference.

What it did in far greater measure than could be appreciated was to show, indirectly, to Prime Minister Churchill that he had an ally in Washington on whom Britain truly could count. That despite the isolationists, the parochialists, the right wing, and the meaner Republican members of Congress, it was Franklin Delano Roosevelt who was in control, it was Roosevelt who believed passionately in the British cause, and it was Roosevelt who would come through for the embattled island nation.

Such gifts of support and confidence meant as much, in the end, to Churchill as the fiscal or materiel contributions which ultimately resulted from this inspired radio presentation. These "promises," in effect, operated in the fashion of businesspeople initialing an early form of a proposed contract. It was a statement of good faith from the U.S. president to the British prime minister, at a time when Churchill had precious little else upon which he could count.

If England could hang on, with such small, unofficial, private, and indirect expressions of intention as the meanings deciphered from the president's radio messages, then it could hang on through anything. Churchill the optimist *did* hang on; it was not the fifty old battleships eventually "loaned" which mattered. It was the confident expressions of faith from the Americans. There is good reason to believe that of all the billions of dollars and pounds and francs and other currencies spent by the Allies to defeat the Axis over a period of six years, the determination of victory came by the end of August 1941, and that the first efforts toward that eventual victory were made by the "few" hundred tiny single-engine British Spitfire planes, and a handful of old, rusting relics of a decades-past conflict.

The booty of fifty corroded barges in mothballs from 1919 was worth nothing in comparison to the infinite number of words of propaganda value from this first, undeclared American incursion into the Second World War. And the first of these words came forth for reporters that December 17, 1940, in the thin yet reassuring Yankee tones of the man in the White House, meeting the members of his people's presses.[6]

FDR: LITERARY LODE AND HISTORICAL FOCUS

The books which were used in the research for Roosevelt's appearance in this volume reflect his many facets. There is the adulation of James MacGregor Burns and Frances Perkins, the respect and scholarly exactitude of Robert E. Sherwood, the intimacy and family comfort of Joseph Lash. There is the focus upon the weight of his accomplishments in the undistinguished but factually impressive treatments of a great number of other biographers. (FDR is in all likelihood the most chronicled president.) Lastly, there is the gratitude and deep love of his colleague across the ocean, the cosignatory of the Atlantic Charter and the one man who deserved to toast victory with Frank Delano Roosevelt but was denied the opportunity. Each of these admirers frames a variant of the image of FDR; each saw within this complicated and thoughtful man the scope of human potentiality, and, in every real sense, the hope of the free world.

On the deck of the *Augusta* back in 1941, at the religious service held by the men of that ship and those of the British *Prince of Wales,* there sat among them, wrapped respectively in coat and cloak, the two souls on whom millions placed the confidence that civilization would endure. The military band played "Onward Christian Soldiers." The two leaders, as with so many everyday persons occupying places in the pews of the churches of the world, sang the lyrics of the venerable hymn with the forgettable untrained voices of average fellows. But for the man from Whitehall, who had crossed dangerous waters to come thousands of miles for his first meeting with the leader of the United States, momentous thoughts arose (he later wrote) while the stirring verses of musical encouragement coursed:

When I looked upon that densely packed congregation of the fighting men of the same language, of the same faith, of the same ideals and to a large extent, of the same interests and certainly in different degrees facing the same dangers, it swept across me that here was the only hope but also the sure hope of saving the world from merciless degradation.[7]

The hope was, indeed, sure; but only one leader of the chorus singing "Onward Christian Soldiers" that morning would remain to envision the sunlit uplands at battle's end. The finality of war's weight, age, and the niggling but inexorable effects of partial paralysis conspired to seize the bountiful quarry of Franklin Delano Roosevelt in April 1945 when a cerebral hemorrhage put an end to the president's life. The country mourned, profoundly stunned by its shock; for many, the only leader of their lives had died.

In London, the pall in Churchill's quarters settled in hard, and earned the prime minister's resentment that his colleague had not been permitted to see the war to its imminent conclusion. In Berlin, Hitler convulsed with his cohorts in gleeful celebration. And in Washington, the first lady, presented with solicitous comments from her husband's successor in deference to her feelings, answered with irony (and no little laconic twist) about *his* situation: "No, Harry," Eleanor Roosevelt said, refusing the offer of consolation. *"You're* the one who's in trouble now."[8]

THE ATLANTIC CHARTER
AUGUST 14, 1941

[The scene on board the ships in the Newfoundland harbor, for the maiden meeting of the century's most portentous defense-counsel strategy session, has been described. Aware of all constituents—and factions—who awaited the meeting's outcome, the participants put forth a statement.

We know—from King George VI—what regard the British royal family had for the American president. Now it was the prime minister's turn to assay by personal contact the measure of the one man who could help Britain reclaim the life of Europe. The prime minister was not disappointed. "Winston was greatly taken by him," the king wrote after a post-Newfoundland session with his first minister. Perhaps the "dream" piece of rhetoric would be one created by Winston Churchill and Franklin Delano Roosevelt. Whether "dream" or not, there is one of their joint creation. Here it is.]

The President of the United States of America and the Prime Minister, Mr. Churchill, representing His Majesty's Government in the United Kingdom, being met together, deem it right to make known certain common principles in the national policies of their respective countries on which they base their hopes for a better future for the world.

First, their countries seek no aggrandizement, territorial or other;

Second, they desire to see no territorial changes that do not accord with the freely expressed wishes of the peoples concerned;

Third, they respect the right of all peoples to choose the form of government under which they will live; and they wish to see sovereign rights and self government restored to those who have been forcibly deprived of them;

Fourth, they will endeavor with due respect for their existing obligations, to further the enjoyment by all States, great or small, victor or vanquished, of access, on equal terms, to the trade and to the raw materials of the world which are needed for their economic prosperity;

Fifth, they desire to bring about the fullest collaboration between all nations in the economic field with the object of securing, for all, improved labor standards, economic advancement and social security;

Sixth, after the final destruction of the Nazi tyranny, they hope to see established a peace which will afford to all nations the means of dwelling in safety within their own boundaries, and which will afford assurance that all the men in all the lands may live out their lives in freedom from fear and want;

Seventh, such a peace should enable all men to traverse the high seas and oceans without hindrance;

Eighth, they believe that all of the nations of the world, for realistic as well as spiritual reasons must come to the abandonment of the use of force. Since no future peace can be maintained if land, sea or air armaments continue to be employed by nations which threaten, or may threaten, aggression outside of their frontiers, they believe, pending the establishment of a wider and permanent system of general security, that the disarmament of such nations is essential. They will likewise aid and encourage all other practicable measures which will lighten for peace-loving peoples the crushing burden of armaments.

Franklin Delano Roosevelt
Winston S. Churchill

THE PRESIDENT'S EMERGENCY MESSAGE
TO CONGRESS
DECEMBER 8, 1941

[Of all the words of rhetoric in this volume, and of all the rhetorical words which selectivity left latent, none which emerged from the American leadership of the Second World War have registered the psychological and emotional impress of the announcement from the lips of the president of the United States that the Japanese had—with ineffable violence—ruptured the remaining membranes of goodwill and international civility.

Almost equally moving as the rhetoric summoned by FDR to convey received insult and consequent determination is the image of the nation's leadership mounting the podium to announce the global despond. With this one event, this one public moment, the United States of America stepped forever away from the distractions of adolescence, and reached firmly forward to the altar of maturity.

The congressional leadership, arms locked together, with smiling faces, moved between the partisan aisles and toward the dais; all divisiveness disappeared. And then, the man in the steel supports made his way to the prominence in this Congress of unity. And yet as heavy a speaking burden as this was, no statement has ever been made as effortlessly as that made to this company from the pinnacle by the one person who could command their attention now.

Gone now into ancient archive was Czechoslovakia's desperation. Long gone, even, the rendezvous off the Atlantic coast. As dry as the calcium leavings of dinosaurs now, the uplift of the Four Freedoms. Now, the world was at bottom, *au fond*. It would be easier now, ironically; for it would all be *up* from this place.

Franklin Delano Roosevelt, thirty-second president of the United States— throat atomizer-sprayed, eyes grave—inspired the breath, the long breath, which would have to give him vocal expression for the length of the evening, the length of the conflict, the length of the age.]

Yesterday, December 7, 1941—a date which will live in infamy—the United States of America was suddenly and deliberately attacked by naval and air forces of the Empire of Japan.

The United States was at peace with that nation and, at the solicitation of Japan, was still in conversation with its Government and its Emperor looking toward the maintenance of peace in the Pacific. Indeed, one hour after Japanese air squadrons had commenced bombing in the American island of Oahu, the Japanese Ambassador to the United States and his colleague delivered to our Secretary of State a formal reply to a recent American message. And while this reply stated that it seemed useless to continue the existing diplomatic negotiations, it contained no threat or hint of war or of armed attack.

It will be recorded that the distance of Hawaii from Japan makes it obvious that the attack was deliberately planned many days or even weeks ago. During the intervening time the Japanese Government has deliberately sought to deceive the United States by false statements and expressions of hope for continued peace.

The attack yesterday on the Hawaiian Islands has caused severe damage to American naval and military forces. I regret to tell you that very many American lives have been lost. In addition American ships have been reported torpedoed on the high seas between San Francisco and Honolulu.

Yesterday the Japanese Government also launched an attack against Malaya. Last night Japanese forces attacked Hong Kong. Last night Japanese forces attacked Guam. Last night Japanese forces attacked the Philippine Islands. Last night the Japanese attacked Wake Island. And this morning the Japanese attacked Midway Island.

Japan has, therefore, undertaken a surprise offensive extending throughout the Pacific areas. The facts of yesterday and today speak for themselves. The people of the United States have already formed their opinions and well understand the implications to the very life and safety of our nation.

As Commander-in-Chief of the Army and Navy, I have directed that all measures be taken for our defense.

But always will our whole nation remember the character of the onslaught against us.

No matter how long it may take us to overcome this premeditated invasion, the American people in their righteous might will win through to absolute victory.

I believe that I interpret the will of the Congress and of the people when I assert that we will not only defend ourselves to the uttermost but will make it very certain that this form of treachery shall never again endanger us.

Hostilities exist. There is no blinking at the fact that our people, our territory and our interests are in grave danger.

With confidence in our armed forces—with the unbounding determination of our people—we will gain the inevitable triumph—so help us God.

I ask that the Congress declare that since the unprovoked and dastardly attack by Japan on Sunday, December seventh, 1941, a state of war has existed between the United States and the Japanese Empire.

A PRESIDENTIAL REQUEST OF THE CONGRESS
TO DECLARE WAR UPON GERMANY
DECEMBER 11, 1941

On the morning of December 11 the Government of Germany, pursuing its course of world conquest, declared war against the United States.

The long-known and the long-expected has thus taken place. The forces endeavoring to enslave the entire world now are moving toward this hemisphere.

Never before has there been a greater challenge to life, liberty and civilization.

Delay invites great danger. Rapid and united effort by all of the peoples of the world who are determined to remain free will insure a world victory of the forces of justice and of righteousness over the forces of savagery and of barbarism.

Italy also has declared war against the United States.

I therefore request the Congress to recognize a state of war between the United States and Germany, and between the United States and Italy.

Franklin D. Roosevelt

THE WAR RESOLUTION

Declaring that a state of war exists between the Government of Germany and the government and the people of the United States and making provision to prosecute the same.

Whereas the Government of Germany has formally declared war against the government and the people of the United States of America:

Therefore, be it

Resolved by the Senate and the House of Representatives of the United States of America in Congress assembled, that the state of war between the United States and the Government of Germany which has thus been thrust upon the United States is hereby formally declared; and the President is hereby authorized and directed to employ the entire naval and military forces of the United States and the resources of the government to carry on war against the Government of Germany; and, to bring the conflict to a successful termination, all of the resources of the country are hereby pledged by the Congress of the United States.

AFTERWORD ON FDR

"If my neighbor's house catches fire, and I lend him my garden hose . . ."

" . . . all of the resources of the country are hereby pledged . . ."

Between the neighborly analogy for the newsmen, and the war resolution of Congress, exactly 362 days had passed. Little doubt that in his Whitehall basement cell, with the cot and the water pipes and the notebook for his notions, Winston slept the sleep of the angels.

NOTES

1. It was his labor secretary, Frances Perkins, to whom the president first turned to get his initial sense of the Churchillian flavor, when the Atlantic meeting was being planned.

2. The instrumentality of wireless communications did not shorten this second global conflagration, but it did make it the first conflict to be brought instantaneously into the homes of radio listeners worldwide. Through the ingenuity and leadership of the most illustrious figure of broadcasting, in that era and since, in the person of Ed Murrow, a network of commentators stationed strategically throughout European capitals was linked with the Washington and New York facilities of the Columbia Broadcasting System. These first "World News Roundups," as Murrow called them, enabled the compelling agony of the Second World War's overture—the Munich crisis—to be carried everywhere.

When the machinations of the minister with the umbrella and the *Reichskanzler* were heating up, Hitler (as was his pattern) singled out a single person, in this case Edward Benes, the leader of Czeckoslovakia, for special torment. At about the time the *Fuehrer* was addressing his minions in the Sport-Palast in Berlin, the American president was preparing to lend his large (and to that time untapped) prestige to the world stage in the call for peace.

It betrays a bit of naiveté—even for FDR—that he made this statement. Yet, on the other hand, having done so helped measurably to build the counterweight of legitimacy to the position the president was forced to take, by the time the crisis had moved into the later stages of the next two years.

3. The importance FDR placed on press conferences, in comparison with his successors, says much about the wartime president's regard for, and sense of responsibility to, his constituency: In three terms and one month in office, FDR held two shy of 1,000 press conferences. Truman's record was 324 in seven years. Eisenhower held less than 200 in the full eight years. JFK held 64 in his three years. LBJ held 126 in six years. And Nixon, in six full years, held only 38. (Statistics from Minow et al; *Presidential Television: A Twentieth Century Fund Report,* Basic Books, New York, 1973.)

4. "No slander is too vile, no canard too preposterous, to find voice among those who regard the President as their mortal enemy," Marquis Childs wrote in the September 14, 1938, issue of *The New Republic.* This was when the president was approaching the time to decide whether to run for a third term.

5. Joseph Lash credits Harold Ickes with the original concept of the garden-hose-seeking neighbor; the concept was underscored in FDR's thinking in later discussion with Ambassador William C. Bullitt. Then in December 1940 it emerged in the press conference, from the president's storehouse of unconsciously absorbed expressions.

6. By the beginning of 1941, with Britain engaged for more than a year in the first of many critical phases of survival strategy and war management, any notions of the conflict's going away through diplomacy and eloquent calls for peace had all but vanished. Still (as he would point out later), negotiations between America and the strident leaders in Japan lay ahead; and the early discussions with Churchill over what would evolve into the lend-lease proposition were not yet one month old.

In the inevitable congressional address on the topic of lend-lease delivered by the end of 1941, the president's obligations far exceeded merely honoring his constitutional responsibility of annual reportage. In coming this close to a United States war commitment, FDR felt not a sense of victory, but a vexing, ubiquitous query: What would America do? This was a question any young man, and any parent of any young man, and any relative of any young man, asked daily. These troubled citizens asked this question of themselves, of each other, of their president. Franklin Delano Roosevelt faced his anxious constituency, and answered them.

7. Churchill, Winston. *The Second World War.* Vol. I: *The Gathering Storm.* Houghton Mifflin, Boston, 1948.

8. Asbell, Bernard. *When F.D.R. Died.* Holt, Rinehart and Winston, New York, 1961.

Part Three

Postwar Panic

Come; let us reason together.

—Isaiah

Assay: Fear and Public Policy, and Voices of Rejoinder

No person shall be held to answer for a capital, or otherwise infamous crime, unless on a presentment or indictment of a Grand Jury, except in cases arising in the land or naval forces, or in the Militia, when in actual service in time of War or public danger; nor shall any person be subject for the same offence to be twice put in jeopardy of life or limb; nor shall be compelled in any criminal case to be a witness against himself, nor be deprived of life, liberty, or property, without due process of law; nor shall private property be taken for public use, without just compensation.[1]

There are some curious connections between one of the principal persons involved in the eleventh-hour attempts at resolution of the North-South divisions during the Civil War, and one of the figures featured in this section. Given the ninety years which separate Mr. Lincoln's travails of 1864 from those of the political leaders of 1950s America, these ironic commonalities might seem merely to be oddities of passing interest.

Perhaps they are not.

A public person of wide repute during the cabinet organization period for Abraham Lincoln was the journalist Horace Greeley. Lincoln had considered naming him postmaster general, a not inconsequential appointment for a man of the press—in fact, a high-profile platform of the day. But Greeley was passed over, for the innocent reason that another New Yorker figured in Lincoln's cabinet, and the president needed geographical distribution for the governmental circle. Later, in 1864, Greeley attempted to act as a kind of go-between in a Canadian-sponsored effort at Northern-Confederate negotiations for peace. He initiated, and kept afloat, a lengthy correspondence with Lincoln; but the events in question, and Greeley and Lincoln's discussion of them in correspondence, ultimately led to mishap and misunderstanding.

The part Greeley played in this episode, and the character of his motivations, are not fully understood, for Lincoln would not permit the full publication of their letters because of what the president considered certain easily misunderstood sections which might have proved embarrassing to the process, and Greeley would not consent to their expurgated release. However, there is some reason to feel that Greeley (perhaps bitter over the cabinet matter?) made an ambitious event of the ostensibly selfless function of intermediary. It had been known at the time of Gettysburg that Greeley wanted Lincoln replaced in 1864; so, his designs appear somewhat murky and suspect.

Greeley was a person whose public utterances were many, but few were of the kind of lasting note which warrants inclusion here. However, Greeley's connection with mid-twentieth-century America does stem from one of his remarks; to be precise, it was his most famous utterance. Back before Lincoln's time—all the way back to the 1840s—there was an occasion when Greeley ran into a young theologian named Josiah Bushnell Grinnell, who had sought the newspaperman's advice about where in the country lay promise for settlement. The theologian had abolitionist feelings (Grinnell had been the first minister in Washington, D.C., to sermonize against slavery) and wanted room to expand his philosophical, as well as geographical, horizons.

"Go west, young man!" Greeley told Grinnell.

The young man took the advice, traveled to what we now call the Midwest, and made a settlement in central Iowa. He founded an educational institution which he called Grinnell University, halfway between Des Moines and Iowa City, in the cornfield flatlands east of the town of Maytag. Originally a church school, some years later the institution became more secularized and joined forces with the city of Davenport's Iowa Band of missionaries, who then moved to the community of Grinnell and changed the "university's" name to Grinnell College.

In later years, J. B. Grinnell was to become friendly with Lincoln, and have a certain influence on politics in the seat of national government; but now he considered home the little town which bore his own name—the name of the man who had taken Horace Greeley's advice to heart.

A little less than fifty years after Greeley's *contretemps* with Lincoln over the Canada peace talks, in the early years of the second decade of the 1900s, the now thriving and highly reputed Grinnell College attracted two young men to its doors. They entered, matriculated, became fixtures, and left.

How well they knew each other, I have not been able to determine. They were a year or two apart in their dates of attendance. One of them was Harry Hopkins; we already have encountered his name, and intimated his contribution to world rhetoric by his inestimably valuable services to Franklin Delano Roosevelt.[2]

The other student was Joseph Nye Welch. And, ninety years after Horace Greeley was creating political machinations involving the attempts to heal a nation split into civil factions, this earnest student of the college begun by Josiah

B. Grinnell found himself—in a posture strident, public, and adversarial—clashing with arguably the greatest force for national schism since the Civil War: another Joseph, one Joseph McCarthy of Wisconsin.

The influence of one's collegiate experience being what it is, especially in such an academic place and at such a time, it cannot be ignored that two persons—one President Franklin Roosevelt's most effective transatlantic *alter ego,* and the other Joseph McCarthy's most crucial public challenger—took matriculatory dips in the same obscure but formative pool of academic ideas.

Another commonality which might have more to do with all these curious connections, and the energies which seemed to vibrate around all these men, is a notion mentioned by Allan Nevins in a small edition of collected essays on Lincoln he compiled with Irving Stone. Nevins perceptively sees that the land toward which Greeley advised Grinnell to head, the great midwestern states, was native soil to all these individuals. This is the land of Lincoln: the broad fields whose loam nourished the sixteenth president, and accepted the transplanted J. B. Grinnell, and gave rise to Hopkins *and* Welch *and* McCarthy. This is the place—as was the Founding Fathers' Pennsylvania—where Amish chose to settle, with simple word and faithful deed.

It is little wonder that a Lincoln can emerge from this soil, or that the earthly rhythm of seasons, with their counterpoint in human contentment, can bring forth a Harry Hopkins and a Joe Welch; but what derelict moment of godly labor created a McCarthy?

The question is, I regret to say, "rhetorical"; what was done was done. But it would take the strains of many—including all the earnest, Grinnell-College-bred skill of Counselor Welch, to deal with this raging demagogue.

NOTES

1. Article V, Bill of Rights, United States Constitution [Fifth Amendment to the Constitution of the United States].

2. Hopkins, a man with a liberal reputation and FDR's WPA relief administrator, was politically unpopular from the earliest New Deal drafting of social legislation. Roosevelt then wisely moved Hopkins to the position of secretary of commerce, and began using his cabinet officer as an advisor. When the war came along, the president chose to send the physically frail and neurasthenically thin Hopkins on a string of transatlantic voyages to meet and confer with Winston Churchill. In effect, and in FDR's own words, "Harry is my legs" when it came to conveying the president's thoughts to the prime minister.

Very quickly, the confidence in Hopkins was reciprocated by the attentive Winston; and Grinnell College's wry, lean-faced graduate created a unique and invaluable role for himself and his country throughout the war effort.

Chapter Seven

The Goat-Song of Joseph Raymond McCarthy: The One-Word Harangue as Chorus

Somewhere in McCarthy was buried the true tragedy of American conservatives: a total incomprehension of their own cause.

—Theodore H. White

I do no man's bidding.

—Horace Greeley

He was an illiterate chicken farmer, whose worst problem was finding time to do double duty as a gas station attendant. Once, when he became ill, he had to entrust the care of the chickens to friends, and the animals all died. A crisis befell him: Now was the time to *do* something, to make something of himself. He knew this meant only one thing; he had to do what he had avoided doing until then—go to school. He needn't have worried, all those years which made him quite senior to his fellow freshmen beginning high school: It turned out he had the gift of an astonishing memory, and a driving will. He finished all four high school years in one year. He leapt through college, and then finished off law school.

Four years removed from the dead chickens, he was a member of the judiciary. Only seven years later, he was a United States senator. Four years after that, he was infamous, a household word, the scourge of presidents: hated with passion, loved with passion. Another four years, and, discredited, he had become a bellowing inmate in an institution for treatment of mental disorder and alcoholism. Two years later, he was dead. Joseph Raymond McCarthy, in a brief white heat of demagoguery, had forever changed the American political template. In so changing it, he—more than any other force before or since—threatened to bring its institutions down.

His speech had an upswing to it, a phrasing of the word *Communist* ("KOMM-monist!")[1] which had a gilding of emotionalism to it, the way a murder victim's wife pronounces the name of her husband's assailant. That one word leapt out of sentences he used in public, with its own special acridity and contempt. It was to the demagogue from Wisconsin what the word *Jew* was to Germany's mad *Reichskanzler*. In fact, it is not stretching the point to suggest that his keynote, oft-repeated, trisyllabic utterance was this political opportunist's sole oratorical contribution. But drone though it was, it was sufficient to garner him quick and fearful renown.

Joseph McCarthy's story is fantastic, an incredible tale of Horatio-Alger-cum-evil proportions. Even forty years after his demise (at age forty-seven, a cirrhotic fragment of his once bilious presence, unrepentant and hounded by mentally hatched voices of outrage from the scenes of his many crimes), the episode of McCarthy defies reality.

That an illiterate chicken farmer of the 1930s could lift himself into a law career and a judgeship by the 1940s, and by the beginning of the next decade could become the singular force of reckoning in the United States Senate, were events which alone lent him credence to begin and maintain his crusade. He gave his name to an age and an "ism," and devoted his life to the gaining of publicity by mass, indiscriminate character assassination. His goal was to "rid the country of the evils of Communism"; instead, he tore at the fabric of the nation's public trust until suspicion and fear infested every corner and extinguished many careers. In ways whose brutality and illegality matched Hitler's (excepting murder, but including driving people to suicide), this demagogue showed for all time that the greatest public nuisance is an adventurous man so devoid of scruples that he fits the legal definition of insanity: the inability to tell right from wrong.

How could such a thing happen? How could it begin? As a relatively new junior senator from Wisconsin, McCarthy was searching for a source of publicity. He'd had periodic attention in the fight to remove postwar sugar quotas, and the several ramifications of public housing issues. Then, on February 9, 1950, McCarthy flew to West Virginia to give one of several mundane speeches in honor of Lincoln's Birthday. This stop was at the Ohio County Republican Women's Club in Wheeling, West Virginia. McCarthy had had prepared two different speeches by two different writers; one covered the merits of one of those housing issues currently creating mild attention. The other speech concerned another issue which was receiving some attention, but, like the housing issue, it was an issue which still had not found its constituency. So, Wisconsin's junior senator asked a former GOP congressman, Francis J. Love, who had come to give him a ride to the meeting, which speech he should yank out and get into: housing, or Communism?

Before Love answered, it might have occurred to McCarthy that this conversation had taken place before. He had asked for advice about a new issue to "jump onto." Someone then had suggested the housing problem again. No;

he'd already done that. Another suggested issues surrounding the St. Lawrence Seaway. McCarthy frowned: "Not sexy enough." Then another person had suggested the question of Communists in government.

Francis J. Love, in his turn, answered. "Communism," he suggested.[2] McCarthy smiled. He was off and running.

A witness can plead the "Fifth." A person can defend himself, protect himself. But how does a government face the virus of implication? How does an army clear its name? How does a president immunize himself? How does a country do these things?

Alan Wolfe views the McCarthy experience as an issue of power. In a compelling book about the forces of repression, his thesis is that the energies exerted by those in leadership roles, and those whose lives are being led, are often in a dynamic conflict. In its healthy form, this conflict is a driving force, through which the beneficial works from a symbiosis come about. In its unhealthy form, the governing body seeks to repress the will of the mass, which, in turn, seeks to do in the threatening leadership, and eradicate its virulence by removing its base of power.

Resentment is a motivating factor in this diseased form of leader-led activity. When the people feel threatened by their officeholders, they revolt, or at least, exert pressure on the elite to conform to the wishes of the many. When both groups are feeling powerless, misguided movements can develop. This, says Wolfe, is what happened to allow for the development of a movement like that given life by the issue- and publicity-seeking Wisconsin junior senator. "McCarthyism can be more realistically seen," Wolfe asserts, "as the outpourings of a middle-level group of officeholders protesting the existence of an even higher level of nongovernmental power."[3]

As Edward R. Murrow later would put it, McCarthy did not begin repressive and censorious activity; he merely took advantage of it. And indeed, the restrictive impulses of the Truman administration provided the carpet of continuity for Joe McCarthy. Much, in fact, of his early effort appeared during the period when he was just another committee head doing the work pioneered by the House Committee on Un-American Activities ("HUAC") as early as 1947. Wolfe cites Athan Theoharis' work on the Truman Administration,[4] reflecting that anyone intent upon doing so could construct the plausible argument that it was not forces of reaction but *liberal* forces which were passionately concerned with national security, subversion, and the dangers inherent in too lenient acceptance of vocal criticism.

In furtherance of his thesis, Wolfe draws a table, tracing in block fashion the forms of violent repression from 1919 to 1969 in broad groupings. The years of the 1920s reflected repression from criminal syndicalist laws; the 1930s featured labor repression; the war years dealt with Japanese-American loyalty (or its "lack") and conscientious objection; the "swing" postwar years of the late 1940s concentrated upon a certain amount of national security legislation; and,

of course, by 1950 and through the first two years of the Eisenhower administration, repression was almost the exclusive province of McCarthyism. (Later
efforts saw the civil rights clampdown in the 1960s, and toward the end of that
decade, the direct confrontations with groups such as the Black Panthers.)

It is interesting how the scapegoat is so clearly defined in the earlier groupings; a syndicate "boss," or a corrupt labor leader (and, indeed, an alien during
wartime) are clear-cut fantasies or projections (or realities?) of evil, whose energies need the corralling of community action to dispel. But by the advent of
McCarthy, and his nod to Mr. Love's supportive endorsement of Communism
as a vehicle for publicity, the enemy had become unclear (nonexistent?), re-
quiring a constant underscoring by the "champions" of such causes like Mc-
Carthy. Others, such as Richard Nixon, had planned equally virulent attacks
upon such overrated enemies. But, fortuitously for the ladder-scaling Nixon
(whose own climb was impressive—from congressman to U.S. senator to vice
president within six years!), the strident, adolescent emotionalism of the Wisconsin senator allowed the Nixonian type of red-baiter to appear sober, senior,
and above the fray—a more exalted type, a philosopher-theoretician rather than
the "thumb-breaker" persona of McCarthy.

Even though Dwight Eisenhower strove to remain above the dogfighting level
of McCarthy (a remove which the new president studiously sought, having
learned from an ill-advised appearance with the senator in preelection days), his
mixed-character administration fell into the trap of wanting to appear on the
side of the prevailing "righteousness" of the early 1950s, which was to say,
with McCarthy. Thus, members of his cabinet and inner staff were placed constantly in positions of appeasement and mollification of the brutish and increasingly accusatory crusader. Without realizing it, some administration members—
such as the army's hapless secretary, Robert Stevens—indeed became toadies;
fearing wrecked careers from pointless stands of bravado, they kowtowed to
McCarthy and as a result lost not only position, but ultimately respect from
those whose faith in them had been so badly placed. That the reputations of
such high-level Eisenhower appointments as C. D. Jackson, John Adams, and
Sherman Adams should have had to endure the obscene and adolescent fulmi-
nations of Roy Cohn, McCarthy's youthful committee counsel, and that the life
of one of the most earnest presidents should have been made so difficult, is as
amazing and indefensible as any other aspect of McCarthyism.

As with every change of leadership in Washington bureaucracies, the connections between the administrations of FDR and Truman, and between those
of Eisenhower and Nixon (though separated by eight years), reflect threads in
the form of certain personalities. And it is painful to realize that some of the
most trusted and honorable of elected leaders during the years of the 1950s,
1960s, and even beyond were men and women who considered Joseph Raymond
McCarthy a friend.

The most surprising for many to learn about were the members of the Kennedy family, all of whom welcomed McCarthy frequently to their homes in

Boston and Hyannisport. The Wisconsin senatorial fighter was a "natural" for the Kennedy touch football games, and he lent his roughness to them in—for once—a harmless use of his bullying drive.

Another of these McCarthy friends was William P. Rogers, first undersecretary of state under Eisenhower, and later a full secretary of state in his own right serving Richard Nixon (until Nixon began undercutting his secretary by sending Henry Kissinger out on secret diplomatic missions, forcing Rogers' ultimate withdrawal). Rogers, an unashamed friend of McCarthy's during the rising years of 1950 and after, nonetheless perceived his friend's grave shortcomings, and begged him to stop being deceptive, stop tearing at people, stop lying. "Yeah, I'll be different from now on," the senator would intone; but the words would go unhonored.

No matter what the issue, and no matter how cooperative McCarthy announced to his friends he would be on that issue, he would end up seizing on his friends' good intentions, or his adversaries' missteps, and using these against them. "McCarthy always preferred an impediment to an olive branch," Rogers once said of the senator, as quoted by historian William Ewald. "Out of an impediment, he could make something."[5]

What was McCarthyism to those who were personally affected by it?

For most, McCarthyism was a defining event, like Pearl Harbor, or the death of a president. Who were some of them?

For Donald Marcus, a biophysicist in Oak Ridge, Tennessee, it was the creeping pain of being "listed" for having had the ill luck years before of pushing a pesky petition-signing solicitor out of his laboratory with a dollar bill to buy the fellow off.

For Henry Luce, a magazine publisher in New York City, McCarthyism was America's chance to solidify a strong stand regarding China, the looming monolith rising above Generalissimo Chiang's frail, infinitesimal Taiwan.

For Elizabeth Birnbaum, a former psychiatric social worker and physician's wife in Oklahoma City, McCarthyism was a woman at a neighborhood "welcome wagon" tea in 1953, leaning close for a swift, stolen moment, and whispering, between immobile lips, "I'm a Democrat, too!"

And for Joseph N. Welch, Esquire, a quiet lawyer close to retirement from Boston, Massachusetts, it was ten weeks of hard-slogging legal contest, followed by several moments of painful enduring of the boorish headline-grabber's attempt to slander Welch's associate, Frederick Fisher, followed in turn by two minutes of the most eloquently expressed indignation in the memory of the Senate chamber's habitués.

When Welch had turned on his heel, he left behind not a demagogue who made men tremble, not a phenomenon of cunning and intrepid self-aggrandizement, but a sheepish, slack-jawed bully-become-bested who had overstepped his bounds and put his foot in it.

From Welch's "Your forgiveness will have to come from someone other than me'' to McCarthy's terminal cirrhosis was an astonishingly short thirty-six months. The Boston lawyer's honest rhetorical nugget was a moment of ethical perfection; and it was as precious to his country's political future as a victory in the Pacific was to ending the war a decade previously, for it saved many reputations, as many claimed Truman's decision to bomb Hiroshima shortened the war and saved many lives.

A FASHIONABLE BRAVERY

In a land of ironies, which is what the democratic union of the United States of America constantly proves itself to be, those ironical events occur, almost by definition, in unlikely places. One of those ironies is that a person can rise to his own potential level of achievement. This simple notion has caused millions of foreign-born persons to abandon all comfort and geographical familiarity, and to endure travel of thousands of sea miles, in order to settle uncomfortably into a country whose language, habits, and welcome may all be totally alien to them. Some who arrive, ironically, give it a ''go,'' and turn on their heels after a time to return to their ''Old World,'' their mission failed. Some who arrive make a ''graft which takes''; and of these, many become materially successful. A few make it into the ranks of millionaires.

Another irony, seemingly on a smaller scale than immigrant opportunity, but in fact even more ironical and amazing, is that the American face in the crowd of 250 million faces is anonymous. Our senators and administrative leaders have constituencies in the millions, drawn from those very faces which they would not recognize individually, but merely for their collective earnestness or questioning, or complaining. But when one of those faces is in the witness chair at a congressional hearing, the immigrant/constituent/witness becomes an individual, a clear multidimensional person, whom a United States senator then not only cannot and does not ignore, but of whom he may implore communication considered vital to the intentions of the hearing.

On the morning of June 17, 1954, in the Congressional Hearing Room of the nation's capital, in the high point of the flame of the era of Joseph McCarthy, this kind of encounter happened between an unknown American and her nation's leaders. The encounter bore not only the irony implied by the meeting, but many more ironies besides. Such a communication, from such an individual, came from Annie Lee Moss, a Black woman from the District of Columbia.

Mrs. Moss worked for the Army Signal Corps. To Senator McCarthy (that is to say, judging from his attempted assertion, that Mrs. Moss had worked as a coding agent for the Communists), she was a dangerous woman who had made serious efforts to compromise national security. To the army, however, she was pretty much just what she claimed to be—a cafeteria worker who did not even know who was meant in a reference at the hearings to Karl Marx. At the end of McCarthy's grilling of this witness, Senator Stuart Symington spoke out against the unnecessary time, cost, and inquisition of such an individual, by offering her a job if the events of the hearing caused her to lose the one she had.

Sometimes, there is a final irony in this wonderful meeting between the mighty and the modest; and it happened in Mrs. Moss's case. Often, despite the strategizing of aides and the posturing of highly visible leaders, it is the directness of the words of such persons as Mrs. Moss which can undo the efforts of the great. When McCarthy could not get Mrs. Moss to admit to nefarious Communist connections (because there were none, and because she had no calculating network of defenses over which to trip and fall), he could not add her assassinated character to his belt of victims; instead, her clearly apparent goodness, strong on its own and stronger as an example of the good character of thousands who had been injured under the Senator's villainy, helped to bring McCarthy down.

In a world of increasingly diminishing examples of justice, this one sent out pealing waves of victory's song. The unlikely Mrs. Moss had done her part to bring the giant to his knees. But it was not the last moment for either injustice *or* justice, in the period of American life known as the Army-McCarthy hearings.

NOTES

1. For purposes of this book, of the uncountable words uttered by him during the six years of his virulence, McCarthy's record as a rhetorician boils down to this single, and singular word. Its introduction to the lexicon of an age not only carries with it haunting associations for thousands of people (many of whose destroyed careers represent "notches" on McCarthy's belt), but it is in turn responsible for some of the most striking and significant rhetoric to emerge from Middle America in mid-century. Much of that rhetoric has been portrayed here already; more will be found in the succeeding chapters of this section on the country's wrenching struggle with its conscience as it came of political age.

2. Reeves, Thomas C. *The Life and Times of Joe McCarthy.* Stein and Day, New York, 1982.

3. Wolfe, Alan. *The Seamy Side of Democracy: Repression in America.* David McKay, New York, 1973.

4. From Theoharis' essay "The Rhetoric of Politics: Foreign Policy, Internal Security and Domestic Politics in the Truman Era, 1945–50," which appeared in *Politics and Policies of the Truman Administration,* edited by Barton J. Bernstein (Chicago: Quadrangle Books, 1970). These and other works deal in depth with the issues of repression and the subversion of loyalty questions.

5. Adams, John G. *Without Precedent: The Story of the Death of McCarthyism.* W. W. Norton, New York, 1983.

Chapter Eight

Joseph N. Welch:
Indignation in Triumph

In a book covering an important event in the life of a country beginning to realize it is in the grip of fascism,[1] a photograph depicts a figure of a man of some corpulence, standing in a crowded room; his arm is raised high, for he is about to take an oath. At his right, two men in military uniform sit; one is turned away; one has a smirk on his face, and appears to be looking at another man in military dress, who is sitting to the left of the oath taker. Immediately in front of the oath taker, a second photographer is captured by the image, in the act of seeking a vantage point, his great flashgun set to record for posterity the "solemnity" of the moment.

A civilian—a middle-aged man in a business suit—seated to the left of the oath taker holds fingers to forehead; a look of incredulity has swept over his face; his brows are knit with the vigor of his own disbelief.

Something about the oath taker, on the other hand, lends him an air which could be taken for that of a southern bigot; but this is no southern backwater justice; it is the hearing room of the United States Senate, in Washington, D.C. The military men are high-ranking officers of the United States Army; the corpulent arm raiser (and photo grabber) is the junior senator from Wisconsin, Joseph Raymond McCarthy. And the knit brows and expression of fingerssteadied astonishment, which sit atop this "pixie's" bow tie, belong to another Joseph, Joseph Nye Welch, a senior partner from the Boston law firm of Hale and Dorr.

These are the Army-McCarthy hearings, and they will change the fundamental questions of the postwar era.

How did these men come to be there? How did our *country* come to be there?

In William Ewald, Jr.'s thorough and sensitive book *Who Killed Joe McCarthy?* (New York: Simon and Schuster, 1984), the energy of the Senate's self-appointed knight errant is seen throughout his adult life as, in Welch's term, the efforts of a reckless man. "From source [of alleged Communists in the State Department] to speech [the one at Wheeling, West Virginia, he would make on Lincoln's Birthday in Francis J. Love's company, discussed above], McCarthy and his ghosts had made a leap":

> The boxer had thrown a haymaker. The gambler had stayed in the game with not even a pair of deuces. The Marine lieutenant who converted a freak accidental chemical burn into a wound of war, the Marquette debater who made up his evidence as he went along, the law student who never learned to question, sort, use a scalpel, divide and distinguish, analyze, or reflect had made his assertion [that there were 205 State Department Communists], doubtless without knowing or caring about its implications. And now he stood back.
>
> The reverberations shook the earth. For with that leap McCarthy took the Communist-in-government issue across a boundary—the boundary that divided fact from speculation, certainty from conjecture.[2]

The apparent truth about Joe McCarthy's character is not that he was a man full of evil, or full of anything else. He was, in fact, just the opposite: an *empty* man, a man without personal ethics, an opportunist of the first water who had an uncanny innate barometer for other human beings' weaknesses, and a driving, relentless energy. In the 1940s and 1950s, these qualities made an almost unbeatable combination; and, as we have seen, Joe McCarthy was that—almost unbeatable. But then came the other Joe.

McCarthy's career was neither the target nor the goal of Joe Welch. But the senator's brand of bigotry, with its styles of political assassination, character defamation, and self-serving hysterics was indeed the focus of the Boston lawyer's sense of what was fair game for any attorney who believed in the rule book and went by it.

How did a lawyer like Welch work, and how can the utterances of such a relatively unknown man claim such influence?

A senior partner in an established law firm is in a singular, if parochial, position of power. His word controls the fate of every firm attorney junior to him, and often the fate of his firm peers as well. His experience brings breadth and focus to the firm; his contacts assure its fortunes. His reputation and presence bring guidance; his legal expertise can instill case law precedent and alter the direction of jurisprudence itself. Yet, as all-pervasive as his presence is in his firm, and as influential and visible as his personage may be in the greater legal community, his is nonetheless usually a parochial kingdom. Rarely do his utterances send ripples out from his familiar forensic pond and into the legal oceans at large.

But on this one occasion, the utterances of one lawyer, Joe Welch, did ripple rings into the wider world. These words—which barely cover a couple of printed pages—were encapsulated in one impromptu speech which was itself an "aside" during a congressional hearing. The effect of the words of Hale and Dorr's senior partner was to bring down the blackest of black knights, the father of fear, in the black-night era of fear of the 1950s. These few hundred words, and their creator, deserve a look, and an homage.

It seems almost preposterous to believe that this lawyer who was responsible in large measure for the undoing of Joseph McCarthy was not among the sophisticated and experienced counsel in the White House, or the Senate, or in any department of government. The one lawyer without whom the results of the army's contest with the senator might have taken much longer, in the sense of the resultant eclipse of McCarthy and McCarthyism, was "the youngest and newest of the Juniors in the firm" of Hale and Dorr of Boston: Mr. Frederick G. Fisher.[3]

Fred Fisher's story of how Welch called upon him and his associate, James St. Clair,[4] has all the earmarks of a spy tale. Bugged telephones in the Pentagon, attorneys getting off airplanes wearing boutonnieres for easy identification by a "contact" man, and whispered strategy sessions designed to anticipate the hearing moves of the senator, all seemed bewildering to this young lawyer whose ostensible task was to do for Welch the odd legal "legwork" which would materialize during the course of the hearing. Welch asked his younger associates if any shadowy event from their pasts could emerge and do damage to their client's case. Fisher explained that he had been a member of the Lawyer's Guild, an association felt to have some Communist-tinged members among its far greater body of simply energetic and idealistic new attorneys-at-law. It was decided in this truth-telling session that Welch would meet with equal indignation any impertinence of McCarthy's toward Fisher's youthful Guild membership. What followed was a drama of extraordinary proportions, a meta-drama, in a quasi-judicial setting, with outsized combatants whose subcontextual quarrel was, in truth, not at all about the ostensible subject of favors granted to one Army private David Schine. The quarrel, in fact, was between the desperado from the Senate and his country's constituency of fear-weary citizens.

Schine, like his intimate fellow McCarthy assistant Roy Cohn, had extravagant tastes; and together the two assistants roamed far, wide, and high on the hog in alleged pursuit of information for McCarthy. When drafted, Schine mounted a campaign of delay, and, when finally inducted, took outrageous advantage of his privileged position and continued working for McCarthy with Cohn.

In the hearing room, Welch had forced the senator into a corner over his coercive involvement in Schine's patently (and outrageously) favorable treatment. Later that day, with the Fisher question still, by agreement, undisclosed, and with Roy Cohn on the witness stand being skillfully (and almost laconically) interrogated by Welch, McCarthy must have felt the instinct—erring, this time—

to silence his opposing counsel with deep embarrassment. He raised the subject of Fisher.

Realizing that his boss had succumbed to the impetuous urge, Cohn scribbled a note to McCarthy: "This is the subject which I have committed to Welch we would not go into. Please respect our agreement as an agreement, because this is not going to do any good." McCarthy shrugged the note off, and charged ahead. In doing so, he pushed the trial to its climax. "[I]n view of Mr. Welch's request that the information be given once we know of anyone who might be performing any work for the Communist Party," McCarthy suddenly intoned with his nasal, feigned sincerity,

I think we should tell him that he has in his law firm a young man named Fisher whom he recommended, incidentally, to do work on this committee, who has been for a number of years a member of an organization which was named, oh, years and years ago, as the legal bulwark of the Communist party, an organization which always swings to the defense of anyone who dares to expose Communists. I certainly assume that Mr. Welch did not know of this young man at the time he recommended him as the assistant counsel for this committee, but he has such terror and such a great desire to know where anyone is located who may be serving the Communist cause, Mr. Welch, that I thought we should just call to your attention the fact that your Mr. Fisher, who is still in your law firm today, whom you asked to have down here looking over the secret and classified material, is a member of an organization, not named by me but named by various committees, named by the Attorney General, as I recall, and I think I quote this verbatim, as "the legal bulwark of the Communist party."

I am not asking you at this time to explain why you tried to foist him on this committee. Whether you knew he was a member of that Communist organization or not, I don't know. I assume you did not, Mr. Welch, because I get the impression that, while you are quite an actor, you play for a laugh, I don't think you have any conception of the danger of the Communist party.

At this point, the committee chair, Karl Mundt of Indiana, interjected that Welch had not put forth Fisher's name as a subcommittee counsel. McCarthy added a touch more to his virulently false charge, and then stopped, a smug smile on his face.

Welch—who was of course the man in the photograph mentioned above with the agonized look on his face—turned that tired face, and his quiet manner, toward the Wisconsin lawmaker:

Until this moment, Senator, I think I never really gauged your cruelty or your recklessness. Fred Fisher is a young man who went to the Harvard

Law School and came into my firm and is starting what looks to be a brilliant career with us.

When I decided to work for this committee I asked Jim St. Clair, who sits on my right, to be my first assistant. I said to Jim, "Pick somebody in the firm who works under you that you would like." He chose Fred Fisher and they came down on an afternoon plane. That night, when he had taken a little stab at trying to see what the case was about, Fred Fisher and Jim St. Clair and I went to dinner together. I then said to these two young men, "Boys, I don't know anything about you except I have always liked you, but if there is anything funny in the life of either of you that would hurt anybody in this case you speak up quick."

Fred Fisher said, "Mr. Welch, when I was in law school and for a period of months after, I belonged to the Lawyers Guild," as you have suggested, Senator. He went on to say, "I am secretary of the Young Republicans League in Newton with the son of Massachusetts' governor, and I have the respect and admiration of my community and I am sure I have the respect and admiration of the twenty-five lawyers or so in Hale & Dorr."

I said, "Fred, I just don't think I am going to ask you to work on the case. If I do, one of these days that will come out and go over national television and it will just hurt like the dickens."

So, Senator, I asked him to go back to Boston.

Little did I dream you could be so reckless and so cruel as to do an injury to that lad. It is true he is still with Hale & Dorr. It is true that he will continue to be with Hale & Dorr. It is, I regret to say, equally true that I fear he shall always bear a scar needlessly inflicted by you. If it were in my power to forgive you for your reckless cruelty, I would do so. I like to think I am a gentleman, but your forgiveness will have to come from someone other than me.

Rather than feeling the weight of this chastisement, McCarthy tried to pick up the attack on the young Fisher. Welch stopped him:

Senator, may we not drop this? We know he belonged to the Lawyers Guild, and Mr. Cohn nods his head at me. I did you, I think, no personal injury, Mr. Cohn?

Cohn answered that this was so. Welch went on, in his courtly fashion:

I meant to do you no personal injury, and if I did, I beg your pardon.

Let us not assassinate this lad further, Senator. You have done enough. Have you no sense of decency, sir, at long last? Have you left no sense of decency?

Still McCarthy attempted the slander. Welch bore down:

> Mr. McCarthy, I will not discuss this with you further. You have sat within
> six feet of me and could have asked me about Fred Fisher. You have
> brought it out. If there is a God in heaven, it will do neither you nor your
> cause any good. I will not discuss it further. I will not ask Mr. Cohn any
> more questions. You, Mr. Chairman, may, if you will, call the next wit-
> ness.[5]

And—just like that—it was over. The hearing, for all practical purposes, was
over. The nightmare, for all practical purposes, was over. The brief advent of
an empty man with a talent for hurting which set the nation to merciless flame
for a time, was now, mercifully, over.

And what of Joe Welch? This scene reflects what is meant by a man being
the totality of his past, the sum of his parts. This is what Churchill meant when
he became prime minister in 1940, and said all his life had taken place as it
had to prepare him for that moment. And this is what the corn country of Iowa,
the sober earnestness of Grinnell College's teaching, the personal balance maintained with wit, and the experience in law holding people's feelings and pains
in his hands had produced—this statement, this two minutes out of Joseph
Welch's sixty-three years, a moment by which any man would be proud to be
measured. "[He] is one of the most amazing men I have ever met: He believes
in a moral universe that requires him to stake out the high ground and stay
there," a scholar said recently of a Baltic leader.[6] But it could have been said
without hesitation about Joe Welch that June day in the year of our country's
trial, 1954.

How are these events seen in recent times by the individual whose name
figured so briefly but so importantly around the Senate Hearing Room's counsel's table? Fisher's retelling of what happened is a textbook example of two
lawyers concerned with the law, and not with the flare of attention:

> Toward the end of the hearings, while Joe Welch was questioning Roy
> Cohn of Senator McCarthy's staff, the Senator broke in and took, as Joe
> [Welch] later told me, the one weapon from the arsenal that all had agreed
> he (the Senator) should not use. He charged that Joe Welch had brought
> to Washington to look at secret Government files a communist lawyer.
>
> The retort of Joe Welch is history, and there are many who say that his
> eloquence was not only the turning point of the hearings, but of the move-
> ment headed by Senator McCarthy. When Joe returned to Boston, he was
> the first to say that as a lawyer he had not proved his case.[7]

It is entirely probable that Welch anticipated the attack from McCarthy toward his associate. It is also possible—as another well-known lawyer has charged—that Welch could have rehearsed a retort for such an occurrence. (Certainly, he had embellished Fisher's explanations, with Welch placing his own respect for Fisher in terms as if quoted of the younger man.) But the look of anguish on Welch's face as recorded by that photographer during McCarthy's accusations toward Fisher leaves no doubt that anticipation of an event gives no preparation for the shock of disbelief when such an event occurs. The reasons for not attacking Fisher, a calculated reticence which came from the senator's own colleagues, is not often discussed in the historical record;[8] but there is no mistaking, in films of the hearing and of these crucial moments of confrontation, the desperate and fear-filled attempts of the usually cocky Roy Cohn to divert and silence his boss, the senator. Joe McCarthy's usually unerring instinct for the jugular-plunge at just the moment of an opponent's loss of balance failed him badly on this occasion. He paid the price for this small mistake, and for the unending stream of misprisions, errors of judgment, "cruelties," and wrongs which he had perpetrated upon his nation and its citizens for the entirety of his concocted stance of outrage over the vastly overrated red scare.

The drama in the hearing room, between the misstepping master demagogue and the Iowa-bred attorney in the bow tie, has in common with Edward Murrow's CBS television program of June 19, 1954, something besides the subject matter of McCarthy's methods. For at both points—seen now with history's acute vision—the subtle passage of McCarthy's momentum over the fulcrum of a crest had taken place already. Welch's indignation, and Murrow's brave and surgical reportage, were not quite denouements to McCarthy's career; but in a large measure they simply functioned as catalysts for the real actors on the stage (toward whom Murrow had alluded): the American public. The people's cry of outrage, so long stifled in the throat, needed the double kick of two men's courage to loose its own voice, and to urge it toward the inevitable remonstrance.

It is clear not only from Fred Fisher's loving narrative, but from the powerful and direct evidence of the hearing in 1954, that Joe Welch's character was constructed of fibers of unusual solidity. The strength to confront evil was there when it was needed; wit was set aside; and courtesy—so hard to dispense with for Welch—instead was corralled, and transmuted into weaponry as well.

Fisher's manuscript of reminiscence provides a wonderful insight into an aspect of Welch's professional life which suggests the "poetic justice" inherent in his being chosen to defend the army, and especially when his defense came to be given as it had. Fisher's narrative concludes with reference to a statement Welch created for the people in his firm not long before he died.

"I have lived my whole professional life in an office free from grief, envy, and jealousy," Welch wrote. "Few lawyers have been so blessed in their associations continually all through life. For the serenely happy life I have had with all of you, I say a simple and inadequate thank you."

To any who have worked in a law office, such an atmosphere of trust and love seems a gift from Heaven which could not possibly have been donated more than once. If there was indeed such an ambience, and if it could only have been given once, then there is much to be said regarding the absolute rightness that it should have been given to the working realm which nourished, and was nourished by, Joseph Nye Welch.

NOTES

1. William Ewald, Jr.'s book, cited below, on the Army-McCarthy hearings chooses carefully the photographic images to represent the times. One such photograph is described here.

2. Ewald, William Bragg, Jr. *Who Killed Joe McCarthy?* Simon and Schuster, New York, 1984.

3. I am greatly indebted to the late Frederick Fisher for sharing with me his unpublished memoir of his senior partner, Joseph N. Welch. Its characteristics of warmth, modesty, and wit clearly reflect the influence of his mentor Welch when the younger man began the practice of law in the 1950s.

4. Mr. St. Clair would have the unenviable distinction of representing yet another side under attack in a case which endured the most severe public scrutiny, when he represented Mr. Nixon during the American crucible of Watergate, a mere twenty years after the McCarthy brushfire.

5. Army-McCarthy Hearings testimony, Senate Hearing Room, Washington, D.C., June 1954.

6. Said of President Landsbergis of Lithuania on National Public Radio, January 11, 1992, by Paul Goebel, of the Carnegie Endowment for Peace.

7. Fisher, as cited above.

8. This does not surprise historians of the incident. A few days before the hearing, Cohn, with McCarthy's consent, had effected an agreement with Welch that the McCarthy side would not mention Fisher in exchange for Welch's promise not to introduce the fact that Cohn had flunked the entrance examination to West Point. However self-served by the agreement Cohn was, to him a bargain was a bargain. Breaking it, Cohn seemed instinctively to realize, would bring into play from Welch an outrage far more consequential than the tame finger-pointing about one fellow's "blown" West Point entrance exam.

Chapter Nine

Postwar Panic—A Postscript: Resolution and Retribution—The Rhetoric of Righteous Indignation

If the United States Senate had been as punctilious and determined to catalogue the truth about Senator Joseph Raymond McCarthy during his reign of terror as it was during the time when it sought to censure him, the American political landscape would be a far different terrain today. Alas, such care, itself the victim of that nightmare period, was not available even to a Senate led by such stalwarts as Lyndon Baines Johnson, a House under the leadership of a man of massive strength, Sam Rayburn, or an executive branch with the hero of D-Day at its helm.

The chief executive mentioned above notwithstanding (and his contributions to McCarthy's downfall were more than many believed), most of the hard work and risk taking in the seemingly impossible task of demystifying McCarthy fell upon a handful of journalists; upon Mr. Murrow and Mr. Welch, as described; and, lastly, upon the president of the United States. At the end of May 1954, the month before Joseph Welch gave his astonishingly effective public rebuke to the Wisconsin senator ("Have you left no decency, sir?"), Eisenhower finally broke his own silence. Speaking on the evening of the last day of May before the National Bicentennial Dinner of Columbia University, on the theme "Man's Right to Knowledge and the Free Use Thereof," the president's rhetorical skills soared, as he allowed himself at last the privilege of addressing the issues of demagoguery, even if he still did not name the nemesis outright:

Whenever, and for whatever alleged reason, people attempt to crush ideas, to mask their convictions, to view every neighbor as a possible enemy, to seek some kind of divining rod by which to test for conformity, a free society is in danger. Whenever man's right to knowledge and the use thereof is restricted, man's freedom in the same measure disappears.

Here in America we are descended in blood and in spirit from revolutionaries and rebels—men and women who dared to dissent from accepted doctrine. As their heirs, may we never confuse honest dissent with disloyal subversion.

Without exhaustive debate—even heated debate—of ideas and programs, free government would weaken and wither. But if we allow ourselves to be persuaded that every individual, or party, that takes issue with our own convictions is necessarily wicked or treasonous—then indeed we are approaching the end of freedom's road. . . .

As [the Founding Fathers] roused in mankind the determination to win political freedom from dynastic tyranny, we can ignite in mankind the will to win intellectual freedom from the false propaganda and enforced ignorance of Communist tyranny. Through knowledge and understanding, we will drive from the temple of freedom all who seek to establish over us thought control—whether they be agents of a foreign state or demagogues thirsty for personal power and public notice.

A bare two months after this rousing speech, the Senate voted for Resolution 301—a resolution of censure. Written in cold bureaucratese, it began:

On August 2 (legislative day, July 2), 1954, Senate Resolution 301, to censure the Senator from Wisconsin, Mr. McCarthy, submitted by Senator Flanders on July 30, and amendments proposed thereto, was referred to a select committee to be composed of 3 Republicans and 3 Democrats and named by the Vice President.

Thus the reader of this resolution, Vice President Nixon, in the manner suggested by Arthur Schlesinger,[1] was able to select one of his many faces—this time, the McCarthy-rebuking face—and exchange it for the one he had worn for so long, the McCarthy-aiding-and-abetting face. However, in choosing his "3 Republicans and 3 Democrats" Mr. Nixon did manage to include the senator from North Carolina, Sam J. Ervin, Jr.[2] The select committee also included Arthur V. Watkins of Utah, its chairman; Edwin C. Johnson of Colorado (vice-chairman); John C. Stennis, Mississippi's perennial public servant; Frank Carlson of Kansas; and Francis Case of South Dakota. The Senate drew up "some forty-and-odd alleged instances of misconduct on the part of Senator McCarthy."

The record was as orderly and governmentally exact as any hearing in the history of the country's judicial bodies. There was no hint—except for the emotional tenor of the very content of the charges—that this case was anything other than a rural township's easement dispute. In the matter of this resolution, the United States Senate was as sober and guided by probity as would have been the elders of Mr. Watkins' church in Utah.

Their reported concerns included the many instances of the Wisconsinite's opprobrious conduct, including questionable handling of funds; exploitive behavior with respect to the use of the time of judicially deliberative bodies; badgering of witnesses, including the insulting and harassing treatment of distinguished senior officers of the United States Army;[3] mishandling or fraudulent reference to official documents, including denial of access to such documents by officials of the Court and members of Congress. The list did not exhaust itself until the sixty-seventh page of the report.

At last, in the same somber spirit of rectitude, the people's representatives presented their resolutions:

VIII. Recommendations of Select Committee Under Senate Order Pursuant to Senate Resolution 301.

For the reasons and on the facts found in this report, the select committee recommends:

1. That on the charges in the category of "Incidents of Contempt of the Senate or a Senatorial Committee," the Senator from Wisconsin, Mr. McCarthy, should be censured.

2. That the charges in the category of "Incidents of Encouragement of United States Employees To Violate the Law and Their Oaths of Office or Executive Orders," do not, under all the evidence, justify a resolution of censure.

3. That the charges in the category of "Incidents Involving Receipt or Use of Confidential or Classified or Other Confidential Information From Executive Files," do not, under all the evidence, justify a resolution of censure.

4. That the charges in the category of "Incidents Involving Abuse of Colleagues in the Senate," except as to those dealt with in the first category, do not, under all the evidence, justify a resolution of censure.

5. That on the charges in the category of "Incident Relating to Ralph W. Zwicker, a general officer of the Army of the United States," the Senator from Wisconsin, Mr. McCarthy, should be censured.

6. That with reference to the amendment to Senate Resolution 301 offered by the Senator from New Jersey, Mr. Smith, this report and the recommendations herein be regarded as having met the purposes of said amendment.

7. That with reference to the amendment to Senate Resolution 301 offered by the Senator from Connecticut, Mr. Bush, that an amendment to the Senate Rules be adopted in accord with the language proposed in part VII of this report.

The chairman of the select committee is authorized in behalf of the committee to present to the Senate appropriate resolutions to give effect to the foregoing recommendations.

One can almost hear the gavel come down, and echo about the room. It is all very businesslike, these sixty-eight tightly printed pages from the United States Government Printing Office. Probably as many charges, in as many Senate reports, cover misuse of coffee-kitty funds, or inferior quality of paint used in governmental offices. However, in the rhetoric of this particular style of narrative, there is a rightness peculiarly appropriate in the matter of Senator Joseph R. McCarthy. After all the "flash"; all the press; all the oaths, and vituperation, and charges and scandal and ruined lives and tears shed and jobs lost and health destroyed and bodies hurled by despair out of windows; the government answered in the only way it could: This is a country of laws. We will listen to the call for resolution; we will hear the charges; we will sit in judgment; we will judge. And when we have discharged our duties, with a comportment befitting our station as the duly elected representatives of the people, and the leaders of the government of the United States of America, we shall act upon our decision, and then ask that it be printed in the record.

This is most fitting, the restorative quiet, a soothing rhetoric of rectitude after the turbulent words of outrage. This is just as fitting as restoring the dignity of a United States Army general who was humiliated for no apparent reason—but only when another (former) general was willing to go on record and give some clue to the torment and violence done his principles of conduct.

As the report says, with magnificent understatement, within the body of the text (on the matter of a subpoena for Senator McCarthy): "The matters against Senator McCarthy under investigation . . . were of a serious nature." When a man under the scrutiny of the Senate declines to cooperate, the Senate will haul him up there any way it can. "This must be the rule," the report concludes on this point, "if the dignity, honor, authority, and powers of the Senate are to be respected and maintained. . . ."

Nowhere, except in parenthetical passings, is the word *Communist* used. Nowhere, even when it is used, are emotions attached to it. We do not hear, as we did for so painfully long, a lachrymose "KOMM-monist!" coming from anyone. The days of hitting the fist into the hand, and screwing up the face, and yelling "KOMM-monist!" (or "*Juden!*" or "Liberal!") are, it is earnestly to be hoped, dead as a fallen Reich, or a dusty report in the bowels of the nation's proud archives. The only problem with the Senate's belated rebuke is that sometimes poetic justice comes so late that the poetry has withered a bit. And after McCarthy, much convalescence was needed before our words could become lyrical once more.

NOTES

1. "The key to Nixon is provided by the word to which he has been so long devoted—the word 'image.' A serious man does not spend time fussing about the image he presents to the public. He knows that, for better or for worse, he is what he is. His identity is secure. He can't transform himself, and he can't hope to persuade others that he is different from what he is. The 'other-directed' man, however, has no sure sense of his own identity: he is real, even for himself, only as he sees himself reflected in the eyes of others; he thus perceives himself, not as an individual, but as an image." (From *Kennedy or Nixon: Does It Make Any Difference?* Macmillan, New York; 1960.)

2. Ervin was then in his early years in the legislative body, and of course could not

predict that the instrumentality of his judicious mind, his personality of witty understatement, and his constitutional expertise, all of which no doubt contributed to his selection by Richard Milhous Nixon to help censure Joseph McCarthy, would twenty years later have made it attractive to bring his expertise to bear upon another subject of censure—the task before the Senate Watergate Committee.

3. McCarthy's belittling and berating treatment of General Zwicker was the last straw even for many conservative "fence-sitters."

Part Four

The Modern Epoch

Assay: Greatness Right There in the Living Room

Much of what would become public policy in 1950s America would be determined in some measure by how the country's leaders would learn to use the medium of television. The early use of this means of mass communication contained the component of rhetoric; and by the time the postwar era was in full swing, rhetoric and television had begun to operate in service of politics. Almost immediately—with the first national political use of television in the 1952 presidential election—the medium lost some of its innocence.

School children viewing television for the first time as America geared up for the presidential election of 1952 had many advantages over each preceding generation. One advantage was opportunity for perception of the candidates, by word and now image, through means which narrowed sharply the candidates' permissible use of inflated verbiage. From now on, rhetoric would have to be reasoned, carefully carved, equally carefully conveyed. While the idea of the politician's "image" had not yet emerged in so cogent a concept, what he represented certainly came to be understood through his manner.

Not surprisingly, within 1952's victorious executive team were embodied all the traits of the age they would rule. In Ike, blandness, the new quiet on the Western front, grandfatherly beneficence, a presiding over family values, the goodness of golf, the dutiful and loving Mamie. And in Nixon, the studied mendacity, the duplicitous character, the issue-dodging craftiness. Eisenhower privately may have felt stuck with this other fellow; but as a foil, Nixon was superb, and the general must have realized this. Ike never looked better than when next to Nixon.

Young people generally require resoluteness and clarity of purpose in their leaders. Like parents, national leaders become models for behavior, but the "Ike can do no wrong" manner of their president began to change. With him, issues

couldn't be dealt with on the merits; Ike never seemed to say anything of substance. Worse, there was much to talk about, for these were the McCarthy years,
the beginning years of civil rights matters, the years of Suez and Sputnik. But
Ike seemed—well, not slick, certainly, but—slippery.

Democratic partisans drew distinctions between Republicans and Democrats,
complaining that Eisenhower seemed to *respond* to issues, rather than to initiate
them. In the early Eisenhower years, the issues which surfaced in discussions
of the chief executive were ancillary at best: matters of presidential health; the
rising red tide perceived seemingly everywhere; the importance of relaxing on
the links. Political dialectics were becoming flaccid, decidedly lacking the buoy-
ancy and snap of the days preceding November 1952. (Could anyone imagine
Eisenhower remarking of a general's speech, as Ike's predecessor earlier had
said of MacArthur's swan song speech before Congress, that it was "nothing
but a bunch of bull shit"?)[1]

The Eisenhower experience for America was certainly not without its rhetoric,
however. In fact, it began with one of Republicanism's classic examples of it.
Even before that first term got under way, an issue emerged from the vice
presidential candidate's camp. Richard Milhous Nixon had run into some trouble, and he took to the television airwaves to use words to get himself out of
trouble.

It was amazing. For sheer fascination, Nixon's pyrotechnics far outstripped
his words. His head moved. His hands gestured. His jowls did a lateral dance.
His voice, a fine baritone, moved up and down importantly. He drew his points
to a warbling climax by talking about a little dog and a cloth coat.

However transparent to some, it had been this base rhetoric, this emotional
pandering, which had won for Nixon the right to remain at the war hero's side.
Even children had understood that a man had used words to persuade people of
the importance of an idea, or a program, or himself.

So, here they were: the leaders of our country. Eisenhower, the historical.
Nixon, the rhetorical. Many clues about leader's thoughts lay in the *rhetoric*
they used to describe their deeds, as well as the deeds themselves. It takes much
more rhetorical skill to be a liar than to tell the truth; and that was why Nixon
was such a clever speaker, and Eisenhower such an apparent bumbler.

When Stevenson lost the first election to Ike, he told the anecdote about the
little boy who stubbed his toe ("It hurt too much to laugh, but not enough to
cry"), borrowed from his Illinois compatriot Mr. Lincoln. With the elevation of
the hero of D-Day to his country's highest civil post, it was America which had
stubbed its toe and would have much recourse to yelling "ouch!"—recourse
which Eisenhower himself would address in one of his few claims to eloquence,
his too-little-too-late swan song speech on the alarming control accorded the
military-industrial complex in the rapidly changing nation.

The first subject to follow this assay, however, is not the former president
but his adversary in both elections. During a brief period in American history—
from Truman's departure until the Watts riots in Los Angeles—Americans had

a chance to see and feel among them a man of profound greatness, supreme intellect, sublime insight, and unremitting bad luck.

NOTE

1. Truman's verbatim remark upon hearing Douglas MacArthur's farewell address before the joint Houses of Congress, April 19, 1951.

Chapter Ten

Polity, Poetry, and Caveat

ADLAI EWING STEVENSON:
ELOQUENCE OFFERS ITS NECK

This section of the chapter, about one of this book's most thoughtful souls, is also the story of one of its saddest souls. In it, a great man attempts to bring enlightenment to a society which eschews light: Better, the people of the postwar United States feel, to be in the safety of shadows than in the sulphuric flare of the antipersonnel bomb's light. This is what postwar America is all about: inversion. Hiding our outsides inside; and hiding the insides even more inside.

This was the country to which Adlai Ewing Stevenson found it incumbent upon himself to appeal with his mission. In two monumental exertions he offers them his fineness; in two predictable remonstrances, they decline. Their acceptance of the mediocre makes him feel doubts; and his doubts weaken his resolve. By the time America sees its way again to the party which claimed Stevenson, its leadership role is filled instead by a bright but brash boy; true intellectuality, in the form of Adlai, is ultimately dispensed with, sent for sinecure to the UN General Assembly.

It is a very American story; it is about the chance of becoming president. And it reminds many that as late as 1956, America had a chance to take the same cloth to form its cloak of leadership as formed the cloak which seemed to perish with Lincoln. Already in his fifties, Adlai Stevenson will summon all his strengths, and make supreme efforts to don this cloak.

Like Lincoln, Illinois-born Adlai Stevenson was a thinker whose intellect was capable of meeting far greater tasks than those laid before him. Suddenly, with the 1952 appearance on the national scene of the first-term governor of Illinois, the missing new voice for American enlightment seemed for the moment to be found. Balances seemed capable of redress. If a bumbling incident occurred, Governor Stevenson found just the right word with which to defuse it. Here was someone so identified with intelligence that to his mentation the coinage of a sardonic new word for intellectual would be attributed. Thus was brought into prominence, as a match for the popular hero of Normandy, the egghead of Illinois.

When Adlai Stevenson ran for president the first time, he wanted the best things to happen to America, and he felt the obligation to help in that elevation process. When he addressed a group as part of campaigning, his speeches avoided the platitudes, homilies, party cheerleading, and other energetic but empty forms of expression. Stevenson *was* an intellectual. Letters written during that period—naturally for campaign purposes, but also maintaining contact with friends—exemplified the kinds of communities this man wanted to reach and involve in the political process. In the collection of Stevenson's papers edited by Johnson, Evans, and Sears,[1] most of his campaign or campaign-era speeches are interwoven with selections from his correspondence. Inasmuch as the Stevenson canon is profound, and any one address not only difficult to choose but too lengthy for inclusion, our attention is turned to those items of correspondence. And, in a manner and style evoking a grander, more epistolary age, the Stevenson letters capture the personalities of the letter writer and recipient, the emotions and issues of the time. They also captivate the modern reader in a way most people outside the Stevensonian circle of the 1950s would not have been capable of feeling. History, the great changer and the last survivor, smiles in triumph, even if alone.

If our focus is upon his letters, one of their first revealed truths is that nowhere is there a better gauge of a public figure's depth and breadth from his general output of rhetoric than in these quickly dashed missives. Many of his correspondents held this opinion.

Notes are sent to Mrs. Roosevelt, Averell Harriman, Malcolm MacDonald, and Arthur Schlesinger; to Dean Acheson, Brooks Atkinson, Norman Cousins, Bernard Baruch, Einstein, Eve Curie, Archibald MacLeish, and Carl Sandburg, of course. And most of these bore personal salutations. Stevenson, in the vernacular of his time, was a "heavyweight."

After he lost the election of 1952, Adlai Stevenson received this note from General George C. Marshall:

I send you my sympathy over the results of the campaign. You fought a great fight. *Your political speeches reached a new high in statesmanship.* You deserved far better of the electorate, but you will be recognized increasingly as a truly great American. [Emphasis added.][2]

Some of Stevenson's letters lend historical insights into his character as well. After the initial press furor over the Nixon "slush fund" revelations immediately preceding the 1952 campaign, Stevenson wrote, on Biltmore Hotel stationery, revealingly of his feelings:

I have been repeatedly pressed for comment in the matter of Senator Nixon.

From what I have heard about it, the questions seem to be: who gave the money, was it given to influence the Senator's position in public questions, and have any laws been violated?

I am sure the great Republican party will ascertain these facts, will make them public, and act in accordance with our best traditions and with due respect for the second most important position in the land.

Condemnation without all the evidence, a practice all too familiar to us, would be wrong.[3]

There is range and economy in this one short note: Stevenson has (1) been magnanimous, (2) given backhanded compliments to the opposing party and to its candidate, (3) implied that the Republican vice presidential candidate ought be chosen as one with an unblemished record, and (4) upheld the dignity and fairness of American jurisprudence, all the while signaling his repugnance for the tactics of one "familiar to us" at the time, undoubtedly referring to the junior senator from Wisconsin.

To John Kennedy, following the Democratic convention in which both figured, he wrote on August 26, 1956:

My Dear Jack:

I had hoped to see you before you left Chicago, and left, may I say, a much bigger man than you arrived! If there was a hero, it was you, and if there has been a new gallantry on our horizon in recent years, it is yourself. I say with confidence that you couldn't have been half as disappointed about the Vice Presidency as my children were, and I *know* that they reflect the view of many.

The news about your wife's misfortune [Jacqueline Kennedy recently had miscarried] has just come to me and I am heartsick. I wish there was something I could say that would help either you or her—aside from the fact that I was honored beyond measure to have you nominate me, and so beautifully, and to have had your support and encouragement in this trying task.[4]

A compelling explanation of the continuing force and power of Stevenson's writings—more fully exemplified in his addresses, but in trenchant and incisive ways in the letters as well—is to see them as the natural descendants of the Puritan concept of the sermon. These sermons were "passionate appeals for conversion. They stressed a process of self-examination by which the inner corruption of the soul could be exposed and for which God, at his own pleasure, might forgive the penitent sinner."[5]

Two notions emerge from this possibility of Puritan inheritance. First, there are given elements of salvation incipient in the listener; careful digesting and use of the sermon's message can act as absolute salvation (saving the sinner, revealing God). But some action is required on the part of the listener. ("No one can do it for you; you've got to get there by yourself.") Thus, despite the manifest liability of the sinner/listener, a good can still come of his mess. Second (and in a way denying the first point), the power is in the listener's hands! He is already blessed, for he is in control of his fate, and can effect it just by altering his attitude, changing his behavior.

Politics clearly has co-opted Puritanism's effective use of the sermon. The people have lost control of their destiny, the candidate declares; somehow, ambitious and even ruthless leaders have taken over, and have almost cost the electorate their freedoms. But—there is a saving grace: They are still, after all, the electorate! Fate still is in their hands. They can "throw the bums out!" They can "clean house!" They can rectify; they can be saved.

There is sometimes a confusion as to who is the savior, and who the saved; who the supplicant, and who the redeemer. Politicians like it that way; the more malleable the people (the more flexible the vote seeker's argument), the easier it is always to seem right.

Adlai Stevenson used the sermon, too. He used it better than most. But Stevenson never hit people over the head with his ideas; vote getting ("soul saving") was not his intent. Discussion of ideas was his intent. In this respect, the intellectual from Illinois was more in the Sophist tradition, more an adherent of the elliptical wisdom of Talmudic inquiry.[6] Unfortunately, in the contest which variously might be named Eisenhower versus the Sophist, or Ike versus the Talmudic twinkler, the outcome in America was not a great mystery. Argument for argument's sake, questions leading to more questions, these postures are anathema to the politician. He wants to seem to be providing answers, because he wants his potential vote givers to seem to be asking questions to which only he and his schemes can give answers. Stevenson, in the respected fashion of exponents of the school of the inquiring mind, wanted questioning to rip apart the ludicrous confines of facile Republicanisms, such as the handy, alliterative Nixonian catchphrases about Communism.

In a sense, Stevenson (who, like Eisenhower and Joseph Welch and Jack Kennedy and other heroes of moderation, was required to make his own statements about the need to contain Bolshevism-socialism's menacing offspring) was interpolating Churchill's verbal jigsaw about China, and inverting it. If China (and Communism, and the threat of nuclear war, and other angst creators of the postwar period) were puzzles inside enigmas wrapped in mysteries, then the resolutions of these problems could only come about by positing more questions when questioning: World Problem X was a quandary covered by a postulate, over which was the umbrella of hypothesis, on which rained the rain of conjecture.

But in a Puritan world, the Socratic questioner does not fare well. We know Stevenson's fate. And, in a curious way, his fate was bound up with the fate of Puritanism. "By the beginning of the eighteenth century," Foner and Garraty conclude, "Puritanism had both declined and shown its tenacity. Every New England generation, especially through the characteristic rhetoric of the jeremiad,[7] sorrowfully proclaimed the end of "the faith once delivered to the saints." Somehow, in failing to meet its impossible goals, Puritan salvation had evolved (or, more to the point, bottomed out) into the grumbling stasis of perennial complaint. And, after all, the shibboleth "Things have gone to the dogs," while not a pretty credo, has become a fairly workable ethos.

Even a man whose head reached for higher things had, in his heart, to find the way to function. He, like all of us, looked for the way (in Samuel Beckett's phrase) we "have to go on," for we all have to go on. And at the end of it all, after being the great loser who lost, but being great enough to merit the sop of the ambassadorship, Stevenson must have smiled ruefully, and gone on.

Embodied in a brief moment during the 1956 electoral process is a vignette of oratory which in a succinct way tells much about Stevenson. As unmemorable as this little speech may be for its rhetoric, it is memorable indeed for its consequences. These were events, some years in the future, which were put into movement by the former governor's delivery, at the Democratic National Convention at Chicago, of these words:

> The American people have the solemn obligation to consider with utmost care who will be their President if the elected President is prevented by a Higher Will from serving his full term.
>
> It is a sober reminder that seven out of 34 Presidents have served as the result of such indirect selection. . . . The choice for that office has become almost as important as the choice for the Presidency. . . . I have decided that the selection of the Vice-Presidential nominee should be made through the free processes of this Convention so that the Democratic Party's candidate may join me before the Nation not as one man's selection but as one chosen by our Party as I have been chosen.

In this quiet way—with a theistic reference right in the middle of a political convention—Stevenson invokes the unsettled health of President Eisenhower, and, while he might have been suggesting "Watch Out! Nixon's in the wings!," instead, he let the people decide who would run with him on the ticket. This exemplifies the Stevensonian pull to the larger issues, demonstrating his willingness, in a situation almost defined by self-interest, to embrace those larger issues, and respond in a selfless way. Such a man was Stevenson.

When he lost the convention's close vice-presidential vote (755–589) to Estes Kefauver, John Kennedy made the best of it by giving Stevenson's introduction at the convention—an assignment Stevenson had given JFK after assuming he would be the convention's second-spot choice. Then, after the election, when Stevenson's fate as a two-time loser seemed to convince him to abjure seeking any other elective office, Kennedy considered the turn of fate fortuitous: As a Catholic, as a relative newcomer, he knew that the defeat, had he been a party to it, would have eliminated him forever from a run for the presidency.

So, four years later, though Stevenson again held out hopes of running, the electorate turned without inordinate contortions on its part to Kennedy. The generous and fair-minded gesture of the failed presidential candidate to let the people decide led in time to the inaugural address from the handsome man in the Washington cold; and, merely one thousand days later, it led infelicitously to the streets of Dallas.

That the man around whom developed the 1950s caricature of the intellectual as "egghead" was out in the cold now for good was certainly true, as far as his own ambitions went. From 1960 on, there would be no presidency; there would not even be the desirable offer of the post of secretary of state from the young Bostonian who had first presented him, then bested him. An offer came, to be sure. Kennedy may have had his own ideas for underlings (the recent McCarthy counsel Robert Kennedy; the roué San Francisco newspaperman Salinger; Robert McNamara, with his chilling mien), but he knew the quality of Stevenson, and he knew where he wanted him. The offer went out to Adlai to occupy the U.S. seat at the United Nations. Rebuff generating same, Stevenson demurred at first. But to his credit, he swallowed pride, put his country's best interests before his own, and accepted.[8]

His UN tenure had jagged edges: the beginning of the Southeast Asian mire, the disastrous escapade on Cuba's small Communist isle (which drew Stevenson into lies he didn't know he was making). Then, in 1965, he met an unexpected death on a sidewalk in London. The era of the sparkling-eyed intellectual, with wit and words to match, was now eclipsed; the more mundane style of Lyndon Johnson took full hold. With the era's passing came outrageous war, repetitive assassination, and, ultimately, the lusterless quietude of Republicanism.

So, in their own way, Stevenson's words of "sober reminder" in 1956 became a fulcrum of rhetoric for past and future. Behind them lay the words of others:

Are you now or have you ever been. . . . ?

Now Stevensonian words themselves were forebears, they would be followed by:

Ask not what you can do for your country . . .

and

Ich bin ein Berliner!

and

We seek no wider war. . . .

and

I shall not seek, and I will not accept, your nomination . . .

and

Bring us together . . .

and

I am not a crook.

And, of course,

I shall resign the Presidency at noon tomorrow.

The seeds of rhetoric can sow bittersweet crops.

NOTES

1. The volumes edited by Walter Johnson and others (see Selected Bibliography) represent a lasting contribution to the placement of Stevenson's words in the canon of meaningful public address.

2. Johnson, Walter (Editor). *The Papers of Adlai E. Stevenson.* Volume VII: *Continuing Education and the Unfinished Business of American Society, 1957–1961.* Little, Brown, Boston, 1977.

3. Ibid.

4. Ibid.

5. See Foner, Eric and Garraty, John A. (Editors). *The Reader's Companion to American History.* Houghton Mifflin, New York, 1991.

6. The term *Sophist* (like the term *rhetoric*) has slid from its venerated Greek meaning of a professional teacher who specialized in an area of pedagogic discourse, as ''rhetoric, general culture, politics, or disputation'' (from the *Random House Dictionary of American Usage*). *Sophist*'s more modern connotation is of a canny individual clever in the ingenious presentation of specious argumentation, to legitimize an empty rationale. In the present book, Stevenson is a classical Sophist, McCarthy a modern one.

7. A profound lamentation or complaint (after the prophet Jeremiah, sixth century B.C.).

8. This was, of course, Adlai-come-full-circle: Stevenson had represented his country in San Francisco's 1945 meetings which made actual the concept of the UN.

DWIGHT DAVID EISENHOWER:
LESSONS OF D-DAY,
WARNINGS OF ARMAGEDDON

Supreme Headquarters Allied Expeditionary Force

Soldiers, Sailors and Airmen of the Allied Expeditionary Force!

You are about to embark upon the Great Crusade, toward which we have striven these many months. The eyes of the world are upon you. The hopes and prayers of liberty-loving people everywhere march with you. In company with our brave Allies and brothers-in-arms on other Fronts, you will bring about the destruction of the German war machine, the elimination of Nazi tyranny over the oppressed peoples of Europe, and security for ourselves in a free world.

Your task will not be an easy one. Your enemy is well trained, well equipped and battle-hardened. He will fight savagely.

But this is the year 1944! Much has happened since the Nazi triumphs of 1940–41. The United Nations have inflicted upon the Germans great defeats, in open battle, man-to-man. Our air offensive has seriously reduced their strength in the air and their capacity to wage war on the ground. Our Home Fronts have given us an overwhelming superiority in weapons and munitions of war, and placed at our disposal great reserves of trained fighting men. The tide has turned! The free men of the world are marching together to Victory!

I have full confidence in your courage, devotion to duty and skill in battle. We will accept nothing less than full Victory!

Good Luck! And let us all beseech the blessing of Almighty God upon this great and noble undertaking.

The images are still clear: The ringing words of the supreme Allied commander, piped into the LSTs, resounding in the engine rooms of the destroyers, the cruisers. Baby faces peer up at the loudspeakers mounted on the walls, sailors' eyes wide beneath the starched dimples of their caps' brims.

Dwight David Eisenhower's moments of rhetoric appeared throughout his luminous career; but the ones remembered best—for they were the ones which came from the deepest sources of his feeling—were the one above, "the document which launched the greatest invasion in history,"[1] and the one excerpted below, the statement of consummate rhetoric with which Eisenhower ended his public career in 1961.

In both instances, Ike showed what he did best: to lead, without arrogance or forced suasion, first by exemplary behavior, and then by a refined and modest reportage about the values inherent in such behavior. In the D-Day message, a general's expectations were sobering; the work was cut out for the several hundred thousand troops upon those boats. In the swan song address, a retiring leader essentially wished his people Godspeed—but added that he was holding his breath.

Around that swan song time, in the space of about thirty-six months, the American public received no fewer than three pointed, fearful warnings, by three of its most articulate, accomplished, and highly placed citizens. These warnings, when viewed from the historical standpoint, represent a verbal watershed and a political fulcral point between halves of this century.

Candid warnings about the misuse of the communications media came from Edward R. Murrow, one of its charter practitioners and stellar giants. Some felt that by his pointed remarks at a convention for broadcasters in 1958, Murrow had sacrified himself (in effect, by stating strong beliefs which ran contrary to the grain of the delegates to that meeting). And as it happened, much pain and difficulty would devolve upon Murrow for his outspokenness.

And on May 9, 1961, the president of one of the broadcast networks, CBS's Newton Minow, made his own famous address which, like Murrow's, took American network television to task. Though of far less personal consequence, Minow's stand, and his rhetoric, are remembered today.[2]

The third voice of warning came from the thirty-fourth president of the United States, in one of his last public utterances as chief executive. As a West Pointer, a career military officer, a five-star general, and a supreme commander in the field, he brought much expertise to his views and reviews of the military community and its intentions within the modern sphere of influence. And as the leader of the standard-bearing capitalistic democracy, he was, in a sense, industry incarnate. Ike—who had been indecisive before 1952 whether to run as a Democrat or a Republican—in two terms had become a well-known moderate-conservative politician. And yet it was this individual, at the moment of his departure from public life, who chose to shine light on the military, on industry, and on conservative economics, and take them all to task with his warning.

For these reasons, his "military-industrial complex," or "M-I-C" speech, proves the most meaningful rhetoric of this soft-spoken but remarkable man. And in ways which even he could not foretell, it would represent a harbinger of untold national consternation in the thirty years which followed its televised presentation on January 17, 1961.

Ambrose points out that Eisenhower prided himself on his command of the English language.[3] That pride must perforce have been muted: both during the war, when that province seemed solely occupied by the prime minister, and years later, while campaigning against the higher-profile wordsmith Stevenson. However—and it is noteworthy for the purposes here—Ambrose also reveals that Eisenhower wrote speeches for MacArthur in the 1930s, the very time when Ike was little more than a "batman" for the slightly older but senior West Pointer.

Eisenhower and Mamie had a home in Gettysburg, a fine 300-acre farm where they raised exceptional cattle. The farm was on one edge of the famous battle-

field. Did the former general muse upon the homage his distant Civil War predecessor paid to the Union and Confederate dead? Ambrose thinks this was so;
it would not require the historian's license to imagine the reflections of a general
about the battle enacted so brutally once nearby, nor imagine the admiration of
one president for the words spoken by another.

Ike's character manifested itself early in his first presidential campaign of
1952. He possessed a kind of individualism, muffled or hidden altogether from
public view for so long, which was most in evidence when he was allowed to
do his own thinking.[4] Being motivated by his own ideas was the kind of "true-
character" nature which permitted him, as a relieved "lame duck" president in
1960, to make the M-I-C speech.

Those who had worked with the five-star general during the war knew his
strength of character; but those who only saw him as the more benign side of
a team which comprised the feisty Nixon did not anticipate either the man's
reserves or his expressiveness. One reason for this misapprehension, I believe,
is the horrific espionage case which Eisenhower inherited immediately upon
entering office. For Ike, who took office in late January 1953, this meant that a
clemency appeal for Ethel and Julius Rosenberg awaited him literally upon oath
taking. (Truman had received the clemency appeal on January 10, 1953, and
did not act upon it.) Unfortunately, sometimes the current man in the spotlight
is held responsible for goings-on before his time of responsibility; and Ike,
brand-new on the job, denied the appeal on February 11, 1953.[5] Truman, who
did not care what problems he left for his successor (as Ike, in turn, would not
feel favorably disposed toward the handsome Bostonian who succeeded him),
could easily have handled the case before leaving office. It was a case, like the
committees which were beginning to pick up the pace in their red hunting, that
had been a product of the early years of the Cold War, a product closely as-
sociated with the Truman administration. That he did not finish it brings discredit
to Harry Truman; but in any event it was the former soldier who now bore the
brunt.[6] Perhaps somewhere in this matter Eisenhower took on the reputation for
being a "responsive" rather than an "initiating" president. (The president
"does not initiate leadership," his aide C. D. Jackson confided to his diary in
mid-1953. "But he wants energetic, alert staff to bat things up to him, and when
he approves, he will lead.") As William Ewald puts it, Ike's qualities were
"fealty to principle; aversion to personality; reliance on organization."

When Eisenhower was taking stock before leaving office, these ideals received their toughest test, for eight years of Cold War, McCarthy,[7] and association with Nixon did little to make him feel good about the prospects for his
country. His own principles were intact, certainly; but he had no hope that the
nation would avoid falling for personalities, rather than supporting issues (JFK's
advent certainly suggested to Eisenhower a nation's dangerous veering into cult-
ism); and every conceivable group upon which he had had to depend for two
terms—cabinet, Senate, army, constituency—had become less and less reliable
as he moved through his presidency. Thus, when it came time for his valedictory

of joy, he made it instead a swan song of gloom, predicting that the organizations which had failed the country and failed him now would merge, and form the frightening monolith whose very name was so complex.

Changes in the world, however alarming, might have been expected. Eisenhower had, in fact, done a bit of "world changing" himself. Clearly, the image of Eisenhower as a diffident, "yes-man" kind of politician does not jibe with the facts. And his individual character, depth of thinking, and forcefulness of expression are all qualities which propelled him to take the subject matter and tone of address he assumed before television cameras three days before John F. Kennedy became president of the United States. At the suggestion of Norman Cousins, Eisenhower put together his thoughts for a kind of "farewell address to the country, reviewing your Administration. Telling of your hopes for the future. A great, sweeping document." He delivered the address from the president's office on radio and television the evening of January 17, 1961.

Beginning with homilies about good relations with Congress and his own "half century in service of our country," Ike's speech did not move toward his unsettling thoughts until the section in his draft marked as "III."[8] But then the seriousness of its message revealed the turmoil the old soldier had harbored for an untold time. Those familiar with Washington's Farewell Address will identify a like feeling, even if not a borrowed wording:

> Throughout America's adventure in free government, our basic purposes have been to keep the peace; to foster progress in human achievement, and to enhance liberty, dignity and integrity among people and among nations. To strive for less would be unworthy of a free and religious people. Any failure traceable to arrogance, or our lack of comprehension or readiness to sacrifice would inflict upon us grievous hurt both at home and abroad.
>
> Progress toward these noble goals is persistently threatened by the conflict now engulfing the world. . . .

Though he acknowledged the need for quality-of-life balance from social program spending, the president paid homage to the ethos of vigilance:

> A vital element in keeping the peace is our military establishment. Our arms must be mighty, ready for instant action, so that no potential aggressor may be tempted to risk his own destruction.
>
> Our military organization today bears little relation to that known by any of my predecessors in peacetime, or indeed by the fighting men of World War II or Korea.

The outgoing leader now turned toward his central argument, and evoked swords/plowshares imagery to speak of how the Cold War had changed this either-or scheme. He spoke of the 3.5 million people still engaged in defense work, and noted that U.S. citizens "annually spend on military security more than the net income of all United States corporations."

> This conjunction of an immense military establishment and a large arms industry is new in the American experience. The total influence—economic, political, even spiritual—is felt in every city, every State house, every office of the Federal government. We recognize the imperative need for this development. Yet we must not fail to comprehend its grave implications. . . .Only an alert and knowledgeable citizenry can compel the proper meshing of the huge industrial and military machinery of defense with our peaceful methods and goals, so that security and liberty may prosper together.

And now Eisenhower refined the bipolar concept of his concern:

> [W]e must also be alert to the equal and opposite danger that public policy could itself become the captive of a scientific-technological elite.
>
> It is the task of statesmanship to mold, to balance, and to integrate these and other forces, new and old, within the principles of our democratic system—ever aiming toward the supreme goals of our free society. . . .

Feeling he had given his "word to the wise," Eisenhower left the issue, to let it gel. Now the man who added the words "under God" to the Pledge of Allegiance invited the prayerful thoughts of all those who were seeing and hearing him on one of the last nights of his presidency, those he exorted to be "confident but humble with power," to join his own prayer—an invocation of his secular fears just revealed, placed in the language of the supplicant:

> We pray that peoples of all faiths, all races, all nations, may have their great human needs satisfied; that those now denied opportunity shall come to enjoy it to the full; that all who yearn for freedom may experience its spiritual blessings; that those who have freedom will understand, also, its heavy responsibilities; that all who are insensitive to the needs of others will learn charity; that the scourges of poverty, disease and ignorance will be made to disappear from the earth, and that, in the goodness of time, all peoples will come to live together in a peace guaranteed by the binding force of mutual respect and love.

In a way which only Eisenhower could do, the gauntlet was flung down, and yet all the participants remained smiling. Ike had grave misgivings about Kennedy; indeed, the general took the Democrat's election as a repudiation of his own administration, a statement of public approbation of the charges of the campaign about the Republican administration's lack of sensitivity, its unwise fiscal appropriation philosophy, its "do nothing" leadership. While much of this was sloganeering, and the savvy Ike knew this, still the election victory over his chosen vice president stung the retiring leader.

And yet, during the transition, he became impressed with the young president-elect. Whereas his own taking of the reins from "that man Truman" had proved awkward and tense, with the departing president conducting meetings with his successor in the face of a phalanx of Truman people, Kennedy had come alone to call on Eisenhower during the last days of the outgoing administration's tenure. The grace and respect this alone showed gave Eisenhower a chance to speak both directly and sensitively with the new leader. As a result, the crux of Kennedy's concerns—questions over Southeast Asia, over Cuba, over defense expenditures—were precisely the concerns of the last months of Ike's regime, and the old soldier had the feeling that the advice he was asked to give, on subjects he recognized as important and of administratively overlapping concern, was advice which Kennedy absorbed. The two men may have had vast chasms of differences in many areas of thinking, as well as personal style; but each respected the person and the position of the other.

Eisenhower would later be called to Camp David, when Kennedy misstepped in Cuba and needed his predecessor for a "refresher course."[9] And, less than three years later, in the most unexpected of events, the former president would appear shaken when television newsmen asked his feelings about the Dallas motorcade's disastrous results. The restored five-star general would outlive the dashing new commander in chief by six years.[10]

Ike's personality had a consistent dichotomy: He needed to excel at everything he undertook; and yet, his public and private persona conveyed the modesty which was his character's essence. Whether at war stratagems, cabinet guidance, arbitrating between congressional leaders, or simply golfing or painting, Dwight Eisenhower was not content to do less than his best.

He would have been the first to note that this did not mean "Be competitive!" He did not need to excel *over others;* he merely needed to do *his* best, to meet the mark of his own personal expectations. In this measure, his writing, his rhetoric, met more than his own mark: It left strong marks which continue to work well as standards for anyone else.

NOTES

1. Dust jacket copy from Doubleday's publication of Eisenhower's own version of the war tale, *Crusade in Europe: A Personal Account of World War II.* Doubleday, Garden City, N.Y., 1948.

2. As late as a radio forum in November 1991 memorializing his infamous "television wasteland" address thirty years before, Minow stated that he felt the same problems were still in existence in broadcasting!

3. Ambrose, who helped Eisenhower write his own autobiographical books, devoted a two-volume set to the general in 1984 (see Selected Bibliography).

4. John Gunther tells a wonderful story of a military aide to Ike during the war who

put the initials *A* and *B* next to names of candidates for an important job under the general. "What do 'A' and 'B' stand for?" Ike wanted to know. " 'American' and 'British,' " the aide replied, thinking himself helpful. "Retype the list without the 'A's and 'B's, and then let me have it," Eisenhower said.

5. Eisenhower quickly lost his innocence, however, when clemency appeals reached him. The following paragraph from Ronald Radosh and Joyce Milton's book *The Rosenberg File: A Search for the Truth*, Vintage Books, Random House, New York, 1984 sets the correct—and contemporaneous, that is, McCarthy-related—perspective on the case which Truman's successor inherited, and dispensed with in a summary and passive way:

Eisenhower was not impressed by any of these [clemency] arguments. In a lengthy personal reply to [Columbia professor and old Ike friend Clyde] Miller, the President insisted that the case had already been "reviewed and re-reviewed by every appropriate court in the land" (not quite true since the Supreme Court had dealt with the Rosenberg appeals by declining to review them) and went on to reveal his real reason for deciding against clemency: The executions were necessary to refute "the known convictions of Communist leaders all over the world that free governments . . . are notoriously weak and fearful and that consequently subversive and other kinds of activity can be conducted against them with no real fear of dire punishment. . . ." The full Eisenhower rationale revealed his conviction that the Rosenbergs—"arch criminals," as his term was—were guilty anyway.

6. Anyone who doubts the public's ability to apportion all responsibility for history into the lap of whatever man lands in the job next should remember the Iranian hostage ordeal. With all the months of suffering Jimmy Carter experienced trying to resolve this crisis, his successor had not been in office more than literally five minutes when the "coincidental" freeing of the Americans held captive in Iran took place, and the laurels went to the incumbent-of-minutes, Ronald Reagan.

7. William Ewald was Ike's "advisor" for the autobiography *Mandate for Change*. Whether he was acting as a ghostwriter or merely as an editorial consultant is not clear; but in either capacity, he forced his subject to confront the issues attendant upon the McCarthy questions, regarding both the campaign and the Army-McCarthy hearings. All the president's attempts to remain in the background could not mute the fact that he was not only involved in the issues, he was attempting to manage events as best he could, while still maintaining a posture of aloofness. Ewald's work can be seen in the fundamental section of Book III, Chapter XIII, "Problems of Internal Security." In Ike's own name, the chapter description is telling:

Need for new security regulations and protection of legitimate rights. Investigations by the FBI and Civil Service Commission. Clearance of Dr. J. Robert Oppenheimer denied. Harry Dexter White case. Permanent Investigations Subcommittee; the extremism of Senator McCarthy. 1952 Campaign in Wisconsin. Anti-"Book-burning" speech. Attack on the Army: The Peress case; General Zwicker and Secretary Stevens Accused; investigation of Cohn's actions in behalf of Schine. Censure of McCarthy.

The chapter betrays the wracking concern Eisenhower had with the Wisconsin senator during the period.

8. Roman numerals, present as section dividers in the U.S. Government Printing Office version, are excised in this rendering.

9. Again, photography's "language" works in ways which rhetoric cannot: Paul Vathis' often-seen Pulitzer Prize winning image of the backs of the two presidents walk-

ing along a path at Camp David—the emeritus leader holding his hat, the fresh incumbent slightly stooped in disciple-like respect—reveals Kennedy without hubris, Eisenhower no pasture grazer. The ambience at Camp David (which Ike had renamed after his young grandson) erased any remnants of FDR's image of the retreat, which the wartime president had dubbed "Shangri-la."

10. Ironically, Kennedy's murder took place during the very month when Ike and ghostwriter Ewald's first volume of presidential memoirs, *Mandate for Change: The White House Years, 1953–1956,* was published. Mirroring the passing of the baton of 1961, Eisenhower handed the now-deceased president the literary attention of the nation, for sales of the memoirs fell off in the wake of Dallas.

JOHN FITZGERALD KENNEDY:
"LET THE WORD GO FORTH!"—A PROMISE
PLOWED UNDER

Once during the 1960 campaign against Nixon someone had asked Kennedy
if he was exhausted, and he answered no, he was not, but he felt sorry for
Nixon, he was sure Nixon was tired. "Why?" the friend asked. "Because
I know who I am and I don't have to worry about adapting and changing.
All I have to do at each stop is be myself. But Nixon doesn't know who
he is, and so each time he makes a speech he has to decide which Nixon
he is, and that will be very exhausting."

—David Halberstam,
from *The Best and the Brightest*

I did not realize how bone-tired I really was until I opened my eyes about
noon on Sunday [September 11, 1960, following the first week of the cam-
paign] and found that I could hardly pull myself out of bed to get on with
the mass of preparatory work that had to be done before we started out on
our second week's swing.

—Richard M. Nixon,
from *Six Crises*

One of film's more interesting legacies to the narrative process is the device
known as flash-forward. In contrast to its counterweight, flashback, flash-
forward takes the viewer into the future, for glimpses as swift as one twenty-
fourth of a second. (Sound film flickers by at a normal rate of twenty-four frames
each second.)

With the advent of the flashback, cinema joined forces with Freud: In fleeting
exposures, the retina registered, and sent to the brain, tiny mosaic-pieces of our
past, which the brain could use during its "background" functioning to help
the psyche make sense of ongoing behavior. The little flashbacks now are cliché:
the scene of child abuse, the moment a mother withheld love, the accident which
forever welded fear to the act of travel, the glimpsed lovemaking of parents that
braided pain and passion with the third strand of experience to come.

With the flash-forward, cinema still plays with history; but in reliving all of
a given history—which is what film does by definition—a film has a chance to
toy with causality. This teasing can be humorous—the Monty Python gang
jump-cutting to pantslessness—or it can be searingly grave—a disaster looming
subliminally to tear with harm at a placid psyche.

This last event is a phenomenon which for some has colored in a tragic way
the life of the thirty-fifth president of the United States. When youthful Jack
and pretty Jackie sit side-by-side in 1953 at the wedding feast table, they suddenly appear in the backseat of the 1963 motorcade's presidential car; as the
crisply attractive candidate from Massachusetts raises a pointed finger for a 1960

debating emphasis, an inevitable image seizes our attention as the man in the Lincoln flings his hands to his throat. And as the newly elected president's breath of frost emerges in his brilliant inaugural exhortation, the horrific moment appears in our consciousness of the bloodstained widow standing next to the hulking Texan in the cramped curvature of Air Force One, for an oath taking whose adventitiousness can only be explained by its omniscient but cruel overseer.

It is a melancholy fate for many that any wistful memory of John Fitzgerald Kennedy will be tied to the gut-wrenching events of November 22, 1963. The Bostonian's brief tenure as president (and, of course, its very recency) aids in attaching such quick horror to the facts of the Kennedy administration. Even Lincoln's similar demise does not dominate our thoughts of that martyred president; and indeed, the ratio of positive information to unhappy news with the sixteenth president helps us to focus upon his instrumentality during the 1860s.

The eloquence of Kennedy's inaugural and of several other of his fine oratorical efforts gives them honorable place among achievements of rhetorical greatness.[1] And the serious concerns of the Kennedy administration—the two Cuban crises, disarmament, the Berlin crossroads—all brought "immortal" sayings into the permanent political lexicon. For the purposes of this book, however, a more instructive text for remembering Mr. Kennedy is the first debate against Richard Nixon. On that occasion, polarity was at work, with both participants stressing their differences, despite the then public perception of their similarities. To aid the drawing of distinctions (debates, after all, require contraries), the candidates themselves put forth their personal styles as distractions. And so it appeared inside a television studio when Howard K. Smith stood between the sharp, contrasting tones of the dark-suited senator from Massachusetts, and the gray expressions of uncertainty from the pallid form of the vice president (pallid, that is, in all aspects save that damnably unlucky terrain of his face, with its malevolent blue whiskering).

This "debate"[2] is key because for many individuals, it marked the moment when they decided that Mr. Kennedy's offerings were superior to those of the better-known Nixon. As an act of personal persuasion and effectiveness, no words of Jack Kennedy's ever served him better than those spoken here. They also, of course, in helping bring campaign victory, brought as well his doom.

The event is instructive and signal for even another reason, which also makes it more interesting from the point of view of the effect of rhetoric: A well-known historical corollary of this event is that those members of the debate audience who heard the program on radio, but did not watch it, felt Mr. Nixon had "won" the debate. But those who watched it take place—and thus were exposed to Kennedy's strong eye contact, his slight but confident smile, and who also saw Nixon's unretouched face stifling the pain from a convalescing knee, and saw as well the Californian's shifting eyes,[3]—felt without question that Kennedy not only emerged victorious, but sealed the presidency for himself in this critical one-hour exposure.

In the first televised debate,[4] the candidates elected to have individual opening statements of eight minutes each, and closing statements of three minutes each. Kennedy opened the debate with an historical allusion:

In the election of 1860, Abraham Lincoln said the question was whether this Nation could exist half slave or half free.

In the election of 1960, and with the world around us, the question is whether the world will exist half slave or half free, whether it will move in the direction of freedom, or whether it will move in the direction of slavery.

The "slavery" he meant was not regional, but geopolitically global; for no issue burned as brightly—or was as needed domestically, for presidential candidates—as the perceived threat from the Soviet Union. Kennedy finished his initial statement with another historical allusion, albeit a more recent one:

In 1933 Franklin Roosevelt said in his inaugural that this generation of Americans has a "rendezvous with destiny." I think our generation of Americans has the same "rendezvous." The question now is: Can freedom be maintained under the most severe attack it has ever known? I think it can be, and I think in the final analysis it depends upon what we do here. I think it's time America started moving again.

Positionally, Kennedy drew the "lucky" spots: His beginning and concluding statements "surrounded" the vice president's. This needn't handicap a debater; but on one undeniable score Kennedy got the best of Nixon: The Democrat (and the fact of Republican incumbency) virtually put the vice president on the defensive throughout the debate. The most graphic example of this was that, even excluding the formal greeting of courtesy with which each candidate began his presentation, Nixon used Kennedy's name no fewer than twelve times and referred to Kennedy by pronoun twenty-one times. Kennedy only mentioned Nixon by name twice; never again in the opening statement did he refer to him in any other way. And in the concluding statement, Kennedy only mentions Nixon twice, and only one of those times by name. The implication, and the impact, of this tactic was clear: Already, on their first encounter, Kennedy the challenger had left Nixon behind.

For his final statement, Kennedy concluded this way:

[I]f we meet our responsibilities, I think freedom will conquer. If we fail— if we fail to move ahead, if we fail to develop sufficient military and economic and social strength here in this country, then I think that the tide could begin to run against us, and I don't want historians 10 years from now to say, these were the years when the tide ran out for the United States. I want them to say, these were the years when the tide came in, these were the years when the United States started to move again. That's the question before the American people, and only you can decide what you want, what you want this country to be, what you want to do with the future.

I think we're ready to move. And it is to that great task, if we are successful, that we will address ourselves.

As this crucial confrontation drew to a close, it moved the campaign into a new sphere. There were decided differences noted between the candidates. Kennedy spoke simply. His sentences were short, his ideas clear and flowing. Anyone intellectually curious enough to tune in to the debate was intellectually competent enough to absorb his thinking. Nixon, on the other hand, started with an imposing flow of statistics, and then stopped suddenly, to insult his audience: "Let's put it in terms that all of us can understand."

The vice president's "pitch" was calculated to represent himself as a spokesman for the present administration, and a natural heir to continue in administration—to be the next president. This was the underlying strategy of the Republican campaign in general: Nixon was the man of experience; Kennedy was the "greenhorn." As we know, the people elected to think otherwise. The conditions at issue were the same for both parties: Things were rocky, uncertain, financially unstable, the Republicans said; better stick with the tried commodity. And: Things were rocky, uncertain, financially unstable, the Democrats said; better take a bit of a risk, and try the new face.

The "new face" had much appeal just by itself. And more than the pleasing appearance, it was the *style* of the man beginning to emerge. The last few beats of his concluding statement were vintage Kennedy. Like the vortex of Kennedyana itself (so well described by Garry Wills in his incisive family biography *The Kennedy Imprisonment: A Meditation on Power,* Boston: Little, Brown, 1982), this commanding figure from the special Boston family drew people in, centripetally, by all the means available to him. Come on, he was saying; get on the bandwagon. But in his own lexicon, this invitation soared into a different space, inviting the voter not only "in," but "upward." Noblesse oblige of a unique variety was about to gain the attention of the country.[5] The rich man's rich son (who had never known "what it means to be poor") with his enlightened program of social concerns had convinced the poor that they had the best chance with him. Americans were taking a deeper look at Kennedy now; and it was a riveting look.

To push the point a bit: This televised debate was a moment for Americans which was equivalent to the moment a person looks at another who has been merely a friend, and sees something, a quality, which elevates that person onto an extraordinary plane. That plane might be the plane of romantic attachment, the plane of religious experience, or the plane of "specialness" in deciding between political candidates. When all Nixon's facts and attempted co-opting of incumbency from Eisenhower didn't impress, the people notified the executive branch of its intention to change the executive's party affiliation. America moved onto the plane of John Fitzgerald Kennedy.

Part of the plowed-under promise of John F. Kennedy was the expectation that our lives would flower with riches, as his liberalism, enlightened worldview, confidence, and youthfulness grew alongside us. In the bullet's trajectory an opportunity for insight disappeared for us as well. Now, instead of the vessel of our growth, he was an omen of our circumscribed bounty. The fact of him meant not a history of progress crackling with meaning, as it was with FDR; instead, he was an historical idea almost before the glow of imagination had paled.

That was the essential, physical disruption caused by the Kennedy killing: Time was destroyed. What was first was last and what was last was first, and the middle—JFK's time in office—was a swiftly passing breeze.

With this spare one thousand presidential days to record, history has turned its attention to the shards left after sadness: Was Oswald really a lone and deranged stalker? What bullet went where, into whom? Was this Cuba at work? Russia? The CIA? A New Orleans businessman plotting the world's most despicable act? Here was our rendered emptiness; we tried to fill the void of our love with intrigue. The funniest of us took the rest to task with the sober abruptness of his candor: "Somebody killed our President," Mort Sahl said into the television camera's eye. "Doesn't anybody want to know who it was?"

The flash-forward is complicated now; in fact, it is rendered almost irresolutely complex. The historically narrated image, Kennedy in "real time," flashes forward to the [now historical] assassination scenario and then back to the living president and then ahead to *our* actuality, our deep and long mourning, or rather, forward but still in the historical past, to our present awareness of past events. For now we hear stories of compromise, tales of the human being inside the shining armor: stories of infidelity, and chicanery with criminals; deals, even, shady deals. And then we must have our present mourning: grief, for the loss of the gain made by the loss after the gain. Kennedy has become a metaphor for time; a figure invented by Anthony Burgess, and filmed by Stanley Kubrick.

When a promise is "plowed under," the presumption is that the new crop so fertilized will be of the parent's essence, only stronger. Hope, also, is that the clime will be more hospitable. Thus, when John Kennedy perished during the storms of the 1960s, it was felt that a new Kennedy would emerge from the sifted earth. But Robert was denied a chance to let his Kennedy leaves open fully; and for Ted, last in line, the higher political soil proved unfruitful. The legacy which should have evolved was a legacy, however born, of uplifted hopes, of renewal which could work. No contour plowing, no reconstruction, could survive the inherently bankrupt strictures of war and bullying, secrecy and back-stabbing.

Margaret Mead's measure of time—the length between the boyish grandfather and the grandson as old man (a measure of memory, really)—is apt; but in the case of those grandsons attempting to identify their legacies from the Kennedy idyll, their work is cut out for them. The antecedent's dreams have become cryptic and mouldy shards left for the heirs to come.

Someday, when we hold time in our hands and play with it, perhaps utilizing the brainchild devices of the marriage of video and holography, we may play out this old, old saga, and see where it leads us. Someday, it may show us a pattern in the shards, a set of coordinates which will lead us, pulsing weakly but magnetically, and hence inevitably, back down to the stairway which exits our world of circumstance and pain. Intrigued, then pulled, we may follow, and find more shards, and more coordinates, until we come to the doorway whose invisibility until now was guaranteed by our veil of sadness.

Here, we may scrape at the corroded hinges of our lost childhood suffering. Then there may come a small peephole portal, to which we place a curious eye. And here, behind a vague translucence, we may find a catalogue of treasures to inform and resolve; here are the artifacts of a time our vulnerabilities heretofore have shuddered to let come full-force to our sensibilities. For here are the crystallized indicia of the whole of the Kennedy years, with human failings, quick elation, and then unbridled pain—all molded and shrunk into specimens of historical wonder. Here may lie treasures which we too can have the strength to behold.

NOTES

1. How many of these writings should be ascribed to Theodore M. Sorensen is not precisely known, and is not the focus of this chapter. The present text will ascribe authorship to the political candidate and (later) chief executive from whose mouth, as addresses, these words emerged.

2. Like all modern political "debates," of which this event was indeed the forerunner, there is no actual contesting of issues, or position taking for thrust-counterthrust purposes. Despite each candidate's desire to distinguish himself from the other, the events feature instead mere sequential speech givings, with the follower perhaps taking exception to a point just made by his opponent.

3. Whether the then–vice president was thinking furtive thoughts will never be known; but such an image was unfortunately an often true caricature of Richard M. Nixon.

4. Officially entitled in the Public Papers on the Freedom of Communications the "First Joint Radio-Television Broadcast, Monday, September 26, 1960, Originating CBS, Chicago, Ill., All Networks Carried." Press representatives in attendance were Sander Vanocur, NBC News; Charles Warren, Mutual News; Stuart Novins, CBS News; Bob Fleming, ABC News.

5. Kennedy refused his salary throughout his presidency.

Chapter Eleven

King and Heir

MARTIN LUTHER KING, JR.— "THIS PENDING COSMIC ELEGY": REMEMBERING A CAUSE'S SUPERB WORDSMITH

Martin Luther King's oratory is arguably among the best-known in the world. It ranks, in fact—both in quality and in effectiveness—with the best of the best, with Churchill's. King's speeches have enriched people's lives and motivated their souls and changed their minds or strengthened their convictions. No statement of his necessarily will do all these things; but in an address as he accepted the Nobel Prize for Peace in 1964 he celebrated the motivational power of his words.

Like his fellow martyr of the 1960s, John Kennedy, Martin Luther King has suffered somewhat from the crucible of revisionism. Set aside for some is the resonant King baritone with its motivating messages, and in its place is the more current and newsworthy speculation about the man's private life. This question actually boils down to whether King was a "ladies' man"; while this would not be the most horrific of sins, the charge does tend to turn the idolized one's feet to clay. And, even within the reading of materials contemporaneous with his work, King's political propensities are stressed. So, while both of these traits, in one form or another, were true even of Gandhi, it is the American man of nonviolence who is the object of upstretched arms ready to pull him (or his memory) from its perch of respect.

These factors were not considerations during the heady days of Martin Luther King's nomination, anointing, and acceptance of the Nobel Prize for Peace in

1964. King's widow Coretta has written movingly of the almost rhapsodic quality which circulated about the large party (of thirty travelers) which accompanied the Kings to Oslo, Norway, to honor him with their observance as he received the prize.

Much of the attention directed toward King (and in all probability, the reason he was chosen to receive the prize) resulted specifically from his adaptation of the Gandhian principles of nonviolence in the earlier civil rights struggles. To demonstrate this activity's importance, the Nobel presenter, an official named Dr. Jahn, recited to Norway's reigning monarch and others ceremoniously gathered that "Dr. King has succeeded in keeping his followers to the principle of nonviolence. . . . [W]ithout Dr. King's confirmed effectiveness of this principle, demonstrations and marches could easily have been violent and ended with the spilling of blood." This was not factually accurate, inasmuch as blood, and teeth, and lives *were* shed in the course of King's many efforts to keep a rendezvous with some sort of civil rights legislation. (The new Nobel recipient would point this out in his acceptance speech.)

Erik Erikson,[1] in his discussion of Gandhi's *satyagraha,* or nonviolent warfare, which the Indian pacifist inaugurated in 1919, draws more sharply the distinctions between the spiritual Gandhi and his more practical American disciple, as noted above. Nehru has defined *satyagraha* as meaning, literally, "holding onto truth."[2] Erikson points out that Gandhi's use of a clumsy English rendering of *satyagraha* as "passive resistance" was misleading:

This dilemma [of the confused meanings] has never been resolved: "Truth force" as a term has nowhere come close to having the power of a slogan in the West. "Militant nonviolence" (the term, I think, preferred by Martin Luther King) is at least descriptive of the attitude and the action of the Satyagrahi, but it fails to suggest the spiritual origin of nonviolent courage in Gandhi's "Truth." (*Gandhi's Truth,* "The Past," pp. 198–199.)

Erikson continues to ponder the added confusion of the concept of leverage, as in the "leverage of truth" idea which accompanies the ideas of nonviolence.

Martin Luther King was surprised at his consideration, and ultimate selection, for the Peace Prize, for he felt that his work, as a regionally limited effort, disqualified him for an award provided to honor those whose accomplishments were international in scope. Coretta King, who the year following her husband's murder wrote a personal account of their life together, felt others did not see "the broad implications of [King's] philosophy."[3]

It is possible (and this is hazarded here as hypothesis) that King's humility might have been grounded not in the geographical scope of his peace work, but in the distinction between the Mahatma's maintenance of an aura of ethereality to the practices of *satyagraha,* in comparison with his (King's) more mundane applications. This view preserves the Martin Luther King persona of humility: Bus riders and garbage strikers are earthy; whereas the rendering of salt from an ocean (from blood?) and the spinning of flax as an exercise in philosophy and discipline, as well as being means of obtaining basic commodities, signaled Gandhi's acute sensitivity to symbols. This—his action—was the Indian leader's forte, whereas the American Black man relied more on his *language* for instilling meaning and conveying higher levels of awareness which needed to become part of the process of struggle.

Mrs. King describes her husband's speaking style as that "clear rich voice filling the cathedral" (as happened at St. Paul's in London, on the way to Oslo). "His style of preaching grew out of the tradition of the southern Baptist ministers," she elaborates, "with cadences and timing which he had heard from his father and other ministers as long as he could remember."[4] She takes pains to point out, however, that "what made Martin's sermons memorable was not the oratorical skill with which he was so abundantly blessed, but the message which he brought and which came from his heart, straight to the heart of the listener."[5]

Coretta King uses concepts worthy of King's thinking when she discusses racism. It is "the most vicious and evil sin against humanity anywhere,"[6] she asserts, with its fallacious attachment of superiority to the white race and inferiority to the Black. Much of her writing discusses this central issue, but it appears in a book which remarkably attains an implied goal of her husband's— namely, to face squarely the ugliness of this mammoth problem, but to do so without succumbing to bitterness.

In his acceptance speech at Oslo, Martin Luther King, Jr., addressed both the Nobel official's soft-pedaling of the actual violence engendered, and suffered, by episodes within King's movement, and this overriding garrot of racism. King noted that he accepted the prize at an active time for millions of Americans in fighting racial inequalities. Musing rhetorically that the award was being bestowed not in the wake of triumph over racism but in the very midst of the struggle (no civil rights bill had yet passed in Congress), the civil rights leader concluded that this demonstrated affirmation of the movement's choice of non-violent tactics. Invoking Gandhi's memory, King extolled the profound capacity for change inherent in the energetic application of moral conviction.

Writer Lenwood Davis distills from the award recipient's comments a kind of peroration prayer: " 'Sooner or later all the people of the world will have to live together in peace and thereby transform this pending cosmic elegy into a creative psalm for brotherhood.' " The Davis material then cites King's conclusion: " 'If this is to be achieved, a man must evolve for all human conflict a method which rejects revenge, aggression and retaliation. The foundation of such a method is love' " (*I Have A Dream: The Life and Times of Martin Luther King, Jr.,* n.p., 1969, p. 279).

It is interesting that twice within his short Nobel address, King used the word *audacious,* or *audacity.* This fine old English word means, of course, to be bold, to dare. In the context of a racial group's seeking sanctions for redress, or its attempt to recall humanity's seeming charter of inequity, a cause and its leader crave boldness. And in ways with more report than a thousand blasts of dynamite, each Nobel Peace Prize winner wears a mantle of daring, and fights new battles with a greatly revivified boldness. With the sublime weapon known as laureate status, the philanthropic Swede supplied an armament which, for effectiveness, spectacularly outstrips the fuse and the blasting cap.

STEPS OVER THE BRIDGE BECOME STRIDES INTO STATUTE

The civil rights bill to which King alluded in his acceptance speech marked the first substantial change in the acceptance of racial minorities since Reconstruction. As a piece of legislation, House of Representatives Bill No. 7152 would face every invidious debilitation and sabotage. These included power brokering and an excruciatingly long filibuster. But, as the new president, Lyndon Johnson, said (following the advice of United Nations Ambassador Adlai Stevenson), the new bill should be passed as a memorial to the slain Kennedy, who had worked energetically since June 1963 on this bill's behalf.

What was the new bill? How could it get started? What would be its goals? In their fine new work on the history of American rights, James MacGregor Burns and Stewart Burns state simply the purpose and effect of the 1964 Civil Rights Act.[7] It was, they write, created to implement a national policy prohibiting racial segregation and discrimination. It outlawed discrimination in public accommodation and public schooling, and it also prohibited sex discrimination. It authorized the attorney general of the United States to bring suit against any offenders. In a word, like the voting act which followed it, it enfranchised minorities by providing them the best bully pulpit in the world: the United States judiciary.

Harvard legal scholar Archibald Cox coauthored a book on the constitutional ramifications of civil rights. Cox found, on the question of "sit-in" types of demonstrations, that "[d]isobedience of the commands of local authorities is [not] always morally justified . . . [unless] it may be found to involve the exercise of a constitutional right." He also cautions against the repeated use of disobedient tactics, lest their effect be dulled. However, he notes we "should defend the social and moral right to disobey a law that one sincerely believes will be held unconstitutional, even though he turns out to be wrong. Whatever harm is done to the principle of consent is balanced by the need to conform the law to the demands of conscience."[8]

The bill, H.R. 7152, made its long march, with much debate in the congressional chambers where the bill was entertained. On June 20, 1963, it was introduced, and on July 2, 1964, it was signed into law. The major provisions of the act are the following:

Title I	Voting Rights
Title II	Injunctive Relief against

	Discrimination in Places of Public Accommodation
Title III	Desegregation of Public Facilities
Title IV	Desegregation of Public Education
Title V	Commission on Civil Rights
Title VI	Nondiscrimination in Federally Assisted Programs
Title VII	Equal Employment Opportunity
Title VIII	Registration and Voting Statistics
Title IX	Intervention and Procedure after Remand of Civil Rights Cases
Title X	Establishment of Community Relations Service
Title XI	Miscellaneous (Including Jury Trial Language)

These eleven "titles," or provisions, go through the process of adaptation into workable statutes, which form the basis of the civil and criminal codes. It is this process which takes the basic "ingredients" of the bill, and translates them into specific legal units. Then, it is against these units that alleged offenders can be charged.

These sections are formidable, and delineate the power of law. Each section has a heading, and a few paragraphs of plain-language discussion. Here are some of the headings from Title 18 of the United States Code (Annotated), in which Chapter 13 is dedicated to civil rights (from a variety of pieces of civil rights legislation):

Conspiracy against rights of citizens; Deprivation of rights under color of law; Exclusion of jurors on account of race or color; Discrimination against person wearing uniform of armed forces; Federally protected activities.

Each of these headings has numerous subdivisions, treating the specifics and minutiae of conditions under which violations of civil rights could take place. (The above tenets date from earlier civil rights legislation passed in June 1948.)

These facts might feel tedious to confront; but they have been included here to demonstrate how exacting (if denaturing) the process is of making into law the feelings of the people. The act of Rosa Parks in 1955, when she refused to give up a bus seat, the crossing of the bridge in Selma ten years later, and indignities right up to the mid-1960s consolidation of the people's will into the "landmark legislation" were key elements of a process which is both central and indispensable to the American experience.

WHAT WAS IT THAT WAS OVERCOME?

How do you get a nation to pass a law? How do you get a president to consider a law which he knows will initiate chaos? How do you get a Congress to put forth a law whose backing its members are loath to give until the law's precepts are commonplace, and the precepts cannot become commonplace until they pass the law?

In the mid-1950s, Martin Luther King, Jr., asked himself these questions; and the responses he gave himself he carried to his congregation, and through his words his response was carried to Black people, and through their actions, their response was carried to a nation. And in 1964, there was a law passed in Congress. It was called the Civil Rights Act of 1964.

It had taken two presidents to bring the bill to fruition: one who would be slain, and one whose apex of leadership would revolve around this bill's passage, after which his leadership would fail, and he would shrivel in influence until, forced to relinquish his own expected renomination for office, he failed in health and died two days after the day on which, with better fortune, he would have completed a second term of office.

It is well to recall that the internal motivations which impelled this preacher forward took their cruel toll: For the effort to lead Black people to expressiveness, and to acquaint white people with the need to listen, Martin Luther King, Jr., went to jail, was beaten, was stabbed, was harassed by the director of the Federal Bureau of Investigation, was badgered by the Internal Revenue Service, was made a scapegoat by hostile politicians. And, finally, he was shot through the neck, which shattered his central nervous system. Moments later, he died.

After him, Martin Luther King, Jr., left this law called the Civil Rights Act of 1964, the Nobel medal for his work for peace and humanitarianism, and, most importantly to him, the right for a Black to use a gas station's washroom, or sit at a lunch counter, or walk into a school.

These things are normal things to do, unless you can't do them. And to hundreds of thousands of Americans of African heritage, it was worth the dogs, the water hose assault on the kidneys. And for these hundreds of thousands who had marched with Martin Luther King, Jr., in Selma, in Birmingham, who had boycotted buses and stores, there was born with the Civil Rights Act of 1964 a fervent prayer: that the spirits of countless American citizens of African origin who had died brutal, sickening, and undeserved deaths at the hands of fellow *Homo sapiens* filled with hate, over the centuries since being brought to this country in chains, would somehow hear this cry of anguishingly late, final acquittal from the Congress of the United States; and that their lynchings, their dismemberment, their mutilations and killings would even in this savagery have formed a necessary part of the mosaic of peace and respect which Martin Luther King, Jr., worked to erect. These were the people, the brothers and sisters, the citizens, who would "hold this torch high without faltering because they have weathered the battering storms of persecution and withstood the temptation to retreat to a more quiet and serene life."[9]

To King, it was worth the lesser indignities; and on so many occasions he intoned his expectations that at some future point he would have to pay a greater toll for his act to enlighten, his venture to redeem. This brilliant preacher who grew into a world leader knew that ultimately he would not survive the lethal weapons of his enemies; he also knew he couldn't have survived as long as he did without the recognition of society that it had an obligation. This obligation became formalized, for Martin Luther King's country, in the form of the Civil Rights Act of 1964. It is a stunning legacy. And the simple fact of any white person's watching with unconcern a little Black child leaving a gas station rest room is a fitting epitaph.

On that Washington summer day of July 2, 1964, when President Lyndon Johnson signed the bill into law, a group of people stood around him, watching this ceremony. In Cecil Stoughton's photograph of the scene, fifteen faces can be counted. One is that of Congressman Peter Rodino, after whose intervention one of the title amendments was modified. Another watcher is Congressman John Lindsay of New York City (whose Black population that year totaled 8 percent of its people). Another is Speaker of the House of Representatives John McCormack. Labor's George Meany is present. California Congressman James Roosevelt is another onlooker; he is in one corner of the group, in this room which was central to his father's four terms. The familiar but obscured face of Robert F. Kennedy can be found among the group.

And another person, standing next to Congressman Rodino and directly behind the president, is a man whose look of reflection is eased by a slight but firm expression of smiling. He is in the forefront of these watchers, his gaze looking directly over the president's head and onto the bill itself. His positioning, and his dark suit, add to the great dignity of his witness.

His open face seems to be at peace, as this signing transpires. He is a Black man, and he has walked the longest walk of any in the room to reach this moment.

His name is Martin Luther King, Jr.

NOTES

1. As might be expected, King was a serious student of Eriksonian ideas. His premature death, however, prevented him from exposure to Erikson's work *Gandhi's Truth: On the Origins of Militant Nonviolence*. W. W. Norton, New York, 1969. This title garnered both the Pulitzer Prize and the National Book Award for the year 1970.

2. It is interesting that, while never presuming upon the patriarchal role of Gandhi, Nehru nonetheless often took on the role of interpreter (literally and figuratively) of Hindu philosophical terminology.

3. King, Coretta Scott. *My Life with Martin Luther King, Jr.* Holt, Rinehart and Winston, New York, 1969.

4. Ibid. Note, in the context of Mrs. King's remarks, the discussion in the "Afterthoughts" section of the present text.

5. Ibid.

6. Ibid.

7. The elder member of an able historical writing team, James MacGregor Burns can

trace his authoritative credentials to his firsthand participation in the administrations of Truman and Roosevelt.

8. Cox, of course, "practiced what he preached" in constitutional law by applying that document's principles in his later role as the first Watergate special prosecutor.

9. King, Coretta Scott. *My Life with Martin Luther King, Jr.*

THE REVEREND JESSE JACKSON—
THE PULPIT AND THE PARTY PLATFORM: A
VOICE OF CARING IN THE AGE OF ANECDOTE

He's the only real poet in American politics today.
>   —Richard Nixon of Jesse Jackson

When you listen to Jesse Jackson, . . . you have to hear not only his words, but his music.
>   —Daniel Schorr, National Public Radio,
>   ("Morning Edition," July 16, 1988)

I would rather have Roosevelt in a wheel chair, than Reagan on a horse.
>   —Jesse Jackson at the Democratic
>   National Convention, 1984

Every speaker of moment must be a bit of a soul sayer. He must reveal what is in his own soul, and it must find harmonics with the mettle of the souls who attend him.

The Reverend Jesse M. Jackson's speech at the Democratic National Convention of 1988 is a marvel of oratory. It derived from the themes continually repeated during his year-old candidacy, and thus was refined endlessly on the stump; but this does not detract from the astonishing fact that he delivered it, without notes and without flaw, from the fertile, improvisational fields of his heart, for a solid hour. Its construction, its emotion, its thematic constancy, and its driving thrust make it the paradigmatic statement for the candidate, the leader, the father figure, the giver of inspiration. It conveys, almost without peer, the essential statement of the soul sayer. It fulfills in a first-rate way the demand of the masses: *Lead* us. *Deliver* us from our myopia, our listlessness. In delivering his listeners, Jackson knows better than any other what his listener wants and needs. He understands, in Auden's phrase, the "metaphysics of the crowd."

With the intimacy and presence of television, the camera washed across the faces of the conventioneers as Jackson spoke. It found the feeling, whether the set features of commitment or the overflow of tears from those visibly moved. It lit up the connection between orator and listener. It affirmed the power of the spoken message, the sureness of its reception.

Much of his fine address had the energy and lift of evangelism to it. Jesse was, and is, an advocate—of the people before him, of the nameless ones outside, in society's cold. Little wonder Jackson transforms the speaking ambience with projectile vocalisms. They are memorable, expanding both sound and sensibilities.

Yet, among the more than 3,000 words he spoke, three brief passages were the most revealing of Jesse Jackson's own essence, of the substance of his offering as a candidate, and of the meaning of his life and work from that

moment back to his earliest exposure to Martin Luther King. In these segments
Jackson recounted three incidents to the gathering, almost in passing. They came
quietly, almost plaintively, privately, but they had the weight and impress of
parable. One was a metaphor—the patchwork quilt as a great symbol of the
hybrid strength of peoples linked. One was a vignette of Black American life,
which takes exception to the venerable stereotype of the lazy Black; and one
was the briefest autobiographical sketch, where the elegant speaker in the fine
suit brushes back the granules of soil in his own history, and reveals the roots
of an abject social, cultural, and personal estrangement. It is important to note
that Jackson's thought development, and theatrical effectiveness, can be appreciated fully only by encountering a speech of his in its entirety. But if, as in
this case, abridgment is necessary, the parables form an admirable representative
proxy.

Together, in fact, these three parables form an encyclopedic view of the kind
of problems posed for the nation Jackson wanted to lead. I have framed them
in the parable motif, and named them to match; but I doubt that Jackson sees
them as such. For they, like the yeasty solids of the fermentation starter known
as the "wine mother," bear all the elements of the culture, and so much that is
elemental to that culture are problems. These parables stem from but some of
the problems which emanate directly from the living experience of those who,
like this tall and influential Black man, are on a great migration from a forced
and insidious anomie to a plateau of dignity and recognition.

Here, extracted from Jackson's address, are the three narratives I have chosen
to call parables.

The Parable of the Quilt

When I was a child . . . , and Grandmama could not afford a blanket, she
did not despair, and we did not freeze. Instead, she took pieces of old
cloth, wool, silk, gabardine, coker's sack, only patches. . . . But they didn't
stay that way long. Sturdy hands and a strong cord, she sewed them
together into a quilt, a thing of beauty and power and culture. Now,
Democrats, we must build such a quilt. . . . Alone . . . your patch is not big
enough. . . . But . . . Pull the patches together. . . . When we make a great
quilt of unity and common ground, we will have the power to bring about
health care, and housing, and jobs, and education and hope to our nation.

The Parable of the Lie of the Stereotype

Most poor people are not lazy. . . . They work hard every day. I know. . . .
They catch the early bus. They work every day. They raise other people's
children. They work every day. They clean the streets. They work every
day. They drive dangerous cabs. They work every day. They change the
beds you slept in . . . last night. They work every day. They're *not* lazy!
. . . They work in hospitals. . . . They wipe the bodies of those who are
sick with fever and pain. They empty their bed pans. They clean out their

commodes . . . and yet when they get sick, they cannot lie in the bed they made up every day.

America, that is not right! We are a better nation than that!

The Parable of the Rightness of Low Birth for Future Greatness

You see, I was born of a teenage mother, who was born of a teenage mother. I understand . . . I'm adopted. . . . I understand, when nobody knows your name. I wasn't born in the hospital. Momma didn't have insurance. I was born in the bed . . . in a three-room house. Bathroom in the back yard. Slop jar by the bed. No hot and cold running water.

I understand . . .

The talented popular writer Gay Talese once related to journalist Digby Diehl a wonderful story about his own writing process, which came into place strategically at a certain impasse in finishing his book about the Mafia, *Honor Thy Father.* Unable to "see the forest for the trees" in his writing, Talese went to his basement, and on laundry drying cordage he clothespinned pages of his manuscript. Then, standing as far as he could from the clotheslines, he peered at his typed wordage through binoculars. The result, he claimed, was a new perception, a vantage point of understanding which broke the momentary writing blockage.[1]

The example of this vignette has proven instrumental to me in "seining" Jackson's great "catch" of words. In the midst of a lengthy, emotion-laden address, the "parables" retreat into the supportive structures of verbal color. Yet, I believe they bear great beauty, as well as legends about Jackson's feelings, his people, and their times. One way of appreciating these qualities is, like Talese, to find an isolating stratagem that provides a differing perspective. For the purposes of revealing Jackson's rhetoric, I placed these "parables" within the altered garb of versification. (I have modified the titles I gave the "parables" to make them appropriate to their transformation from parable to verse.)

Here, scanned in a way which courses naturally from the words themselves, are Jackson's parables, seen anew. And here, seen through this special "glass," their excellence glows:

The Quilt

When I was a child,
And Grandmama could not afford a blanket,
She did not despair, and we did not freeze.
Instead, she took pieces of old cloth,
Wool, silk, gabardine, coker's sack, only patches . . .
But they didn't stay that way long.
Sturdy hands and a strong cord, she sewed them together
Into a quilt, a thing of beauty and power and culture.
Now, Democrats, we must build such a quilt. . . .

Alone . . . your patch is not big enough. . . .
But . . . Pull the patches together. . . .
When we make a great quilt of unity and common ground,
We will have the power to bring about health care,
And housing, and jobs, and education
And hope to our nation.

The Stereotype

Most poor people are not lazy. . . .
They work hard every day.
I know. . . .

They catch the early bus.
They work every day.
They raise other people's children.
They work every day.
They clean the streets.
They work every day.
They drive dangerous cabs.
They work every day.
They change the beds you slept in . . . last night.
They work every day.
They're *not* lazy! . . . They work in hospitals. . . .
They wipe the bodies of those
Who are sick with fever and pain.
They empty their bed pans.
They clean out their commodes . . .
And yet when they get sick,
They cannot lie in the bed they made up every day.

America, that is not right!
We are a better nation than that!

The Rightness of Low Birth for Future Greatness

You see,
I was born of a teenage mother,
Who was born of a teenage mother.
I understand . . .
I'm adopted. . . .

I understand, when nobody knows your name.
I wasn't born in the hospital.
Momma didn't have insurance.
I was born in the bed . . . in a three-room house.
Bathroom in the back yard. Slop jar by the bed.
No hot and cold running water.
I understand . . .

The original words which became these parables—these "verses"—are excerpted from the portion of Jackson's speech which used his "mid-range" vocal effort. And yet they have an integral rhythm which is not dependent upon his later higher-energy projection. When Jackson's rhythm "worked," he knew it instinctively; he could feel it bounce back from his audience. It was his impulse to leap into the next gear—a tonal switch, to a higher level of vocal tension. Here, in a stratospheric altitude, the tenor of Jackson's rhetoric resembled a musical harmonic; perhaps a better metaphor would be a rocket ship, freed suddenly of earthly orbit and in sole command of its directional fate. This voice—the "Pentecostal Preacher" quality of it striking—is a plaintive sound and a warble, but it has the overtones of a chain saw. It is Jackson's way of saying, "What I said before is literal, but what I'm saying now is Gospel!" It also implies, especially to white persons: "This is the last stretch, of the final lap. If you have been on board but silent, speak up now! If you have been on the sidelines idly glancing over to see what the noise was, move out of the way." Whatever interpretation is laid upon this locomotive of language and spirit, there is no opportunity to hesitate, to substitute rationality for feeling, or to believe that anything negative can survive the uplifting values being laid out by this preacher.

In this way, Jackson both excelled his mentor King, and appears to remain a step behind him and to one side. King's rising baritone was a clear stream; Jackson's glottal insistence is a foaming water. The bubbles are more dynamic than the stream; but the stream, running clear and running deep, is the most refined distillate of blood.

And yet it must be asserted that, however invidious it may be to compare the great civil rights force of the 1960s with the most promising man among Black leaders in the 1990s, Jesse Jackson is natural heir to America's oratorical Mahatma. Jackson's star has taken longer to ascend than King's;[2] its burn is bright but not yet brilliant; nonetheless, with his comparative youth, and barring a similar fate, he is certain to provide long-lasting guidance to any minority ear listening for the words which assure worth, words which affirm promise, words which incite the release of righteousness from the soul.

Jesse Jackson in that speech has made *himself* the subject of parables, fables in a sense about Black life. And yet, "Black" as those stories are, they also ironically illuminate very "white," even Anglo-Saxon, qualities: rising up from adversity, ingenuity conquering poverty, personal direction replacing an anomic lack of compass. These are immigrant virtues, residues of an Ellis Island ethos more than the tauter, angry energy of the slave past. The hero of these fables is the *Black* man who can make it in the *white* world. More than that, it is *this* Black man who has claim to the "whitest" of the white world: The U.S. presidency. For Jesse Jackson, fables legitimize belongingness; rhetoric induces rights.

Black support turns out for the man because he is an affirmer. His reminders to them are straightforward. In Jackson's speech, there is really no cleverness;

this rhetoric is not self-consciously manipulative. Rather, it moves by the implied chastisement within the stated praise. "You're right"; "I understand"; "Keep hope alive, keep hope alive!"; "Don't submerge your dreams; you must never stop dreaming!" Jesse's affirmations keep the listener in a hammock; never calm or unmoving, and yet no longer vulnerable to falling.

It is simplistic, but true, that Jackson's life can be divided into the years before Dr. King's assassination, and the years which followed that event. Jackson was one of King's "promising young people," and as an aide to the civil rights leader, he still toyed with the symbols of youth and rebellion. (King's last words—spoken to Jackson—were to invite him to dinner that night, and to request, with a smile, that the younger man not wear jeans.) Within two months of the Nobel laureate's murder, Jackson was ordained a minister. Two years later, in 1970, his image was featured on an issue of *Time* magazine.

If persons concerned with Black progress saw Jackson as attempting to replace King as a leader of minorities, they might be forgiven, for in rapid succession, Jackson had involved himself with the 1967 Operation Breadbasket Business Seminar and Exposition; the "Black Christmas" effort of 1967, in which he urged Blacks to buy from other Blacks during the holiday season; the "Black Expo" in 1971, which found a mixed success; and, later in 1971, PUSH (Persons United in Service to Humanity). At this time, Jesse Jackson resigned his membership in the Southern Christian Leadership Conference. In three years, he had moved from a great Black leader's youthful assistant to a responsible initiator of minority political movements, an established preacher, and a man capable of confrontation, deserving of respect, and eminently qualified to enter the rhetorical stream as a major factor.

PUSH, specific issues such as sickle-cell anemia,[3] and travel to South Africa and some Middle Eastern ports characterized the "roving ambassador" period in Jackson's life. By identifying with political prisoners and leaders such as South African Archbishop Desmond Tutu, Jackson was able to "do good works" in keeping with the loose dicta of his minister's creed, and also become better-known. This activity coursed from his "coming of age" period beginning in 1971 until his serious focus upon political opportunities in the United States in the early 1980s. In this new focus, Jackson wanted to see ripen into fruition the growth to personal maturity he felt he had gained since the blood on the balcony in 1968.

Harold Washington's successful effort to unseat Jane Byrne in the mayoralty race in Chicago in 1983 supported Jackson's conviction that Blacks could score significant achievements: (1) A minority candidacy could be advanced in a substantive way; (2) minorities could be motivated to support such a candidacy; and (3) the establishment—in this case, the consummate political machinery of Richard Daley and his successors in Chicago—could be confronted and overcome. Out of these successes, the Rainbow Coalition was born.

The presidential contests of 1984 and 1988 followed, with Jackson being Black gadfly in the first, but candidate of equal stature (with two U.S. senators and one former and one sitting governor) in the second campaign. His personal energy and appeal, his articulate presentation of his issues, and, most important, the critical significance of the Rainbow Coalition's voting bank, made Jackson not only an attractive candidate but a power broker of immense influence.

The swiftly evolving world of the decade beginning in 1990 would challenge even Einstein in its torquing of time. In the fickle world of politics, Jackson is now being considered a creature of the 1980s and hence an archaism in the 1990s, like the Reaganism Jesse posited himself against as foil. And yet, the voluble author of the Rainbow Coalition still earns attention. In the early months of 1992, journalist Marshall Frady carved space out of three issues of the *New Yorker* magazine for an assessment-making profile series.

In this lengthy three-part article, Frady gives us a view of an intensely human individual. Frady's Jackson covets attention, yet seems unwilling or unable to craft the opportunities to make himself known. For example, on the eve of King's assassination, the young man in his entourage tries to wrest a speaking engagement from the civil rights leader, only to be thwarted by King's wariness of the upstart's effort.

Later, from his own labors, Jackson has succeeded in organizing a hostage-release mission to Iraq, which included intimate contact with Aziz, Hussein, and others of the Mideast power clique. Propelling his commanding presence into a persuasive international agency of conviction, Jackson manages to get the president of Iraq to magnify the token release of four ill hostages into three plane-loads of fleeing Americans and other Western nationals. Upon his return, the same press which magnified his "Hymie-Town" remark of 1984 into a campaign-threatening issue all but ignored his herculean accomplishment, and thus encouraged the ongoing questions raised about his "lack of leadership" because he has not been an officeholder.

This purposeful neglect, in his hour of triumph, reduced Jackson to tears. The Black leader is a lachrymose man, given to weeping from compassion. Here, even if seemingly self-serving, he wept justified tears, urged forth in the face of an unsympathetic press. And yet, with high visibility through television, with opportunities ahead (at this writing, the issue of statehood for Washington, D.C., still awaits resolution, along with the choice of its senators), Jackson will keep his own hope alive.

Meanwhile, as uncertain as were these future challenges, some definitive achievements had slipped into history. The first Black man to run a serious, respected, and conceivably successful campaign for the nomination of his party as presidential contender had stepped into the political focal point. His magnificent effort had changed the fortunes of millions. His words, in the longest and most moving address at the 1988 Democratic National Convention, brought to the nation's oldest carnival a rhetorical gift whose inspiration eclipsed all communications from any other candidates, including the words of the nominees from both parties, and the telling vocal inadequacies of the winner.

NOTES

1. Told to the author by Diehl.

2. There is only one mention of Jesse Jackson in Taylor Branch's amazing book *Parting the Waters: America in the King Years 1954–1963,* Simon and Schuster, New York, 1988, and it is made in reference to a "sit-in" action of students at North Carolina A&T led by Jackson, their student body president. In a footnote, Branch states: "Jackson already had attracted notice in the Negro press as a sports star and precocious social leader. He had been elected second vice grand basileus of the national Omego Psy Phi fraternity. In these first political stories, he appeared in a snap-brim hat, telling his followers, 'I'll go to jail and I'll go to the chain gang if necessary.' "

3. This blood disease affects primarily Blacks, and has two phases—a benign "trait" phase and a more virulent and lethal form, the malignant phase, which can develop only if a carrier of the "trait" phase mates with another carrier to produce a child with both traits.

Chapter 12

Afterthoughts on Leadership and Language: How Does History Handle the Rhetorician?

An ironic notion of historical review holds that the "bigger" the concept of an era's history (and the "swifter" the historian's need to move through its mass), the slower was that era's actual evolution. Surely, living through an era's historical evolution—the marginal periods when change becomes palpable—can sometimes feel like eons, the passage of light-years.

It is this way often in the development of governments. In politics, when the rhythm of an era dies, it is not sudden or unexpected. Rather (long after the next epoch is picking up pace), there is a beat, then another beat, then, down the road, another beat, before the old era finally breaks stride, comes slowly to a halt, and then, one long beat later, rolls over and expires. If you are scrutinizing American political life, and for these "beats" you substitute the lengths of presidential terms, then you have gained some chronometric sophistication about the American body politic.

An opposing view—history as cataclysm—takes the same elements to derive a kind of "shock-moment" conclusion. Living as the clock ticks, this theory goes, human beings feel periodic jolts, until time's curve resembles a series of seismic shocks.

This is the way recent history—actuality—feels now. As an example, within a ten-month period a world watched a war in the Persian Gulf, a coup in Soviet Russia, and the collapse of a dozen countries' slavish interstitial bonds with the discredited Communist system (while at home, a law professor publicly questioned the moral fiber of a United States Supreme Court nominee, and in doing so redefined and rejuvenated national gender-discrimination issues).

This ten-month beat seems a record in global cataclysm. Yet, within the short *five* months between April and August 1945,

- The city of Dresden, in Germany, was reduced to ankle-height rubble.
- The leader of the free world died unexpectedly in Washington.
- The creator of world war and instigator of 55 million murders shot himself in a bunker in Berlin.
- A smiling, bespectacled piano player from Missouri announced to the world that his country had just used an atomic bomb in "a harnessing of the basic power of the universe. The force from which the sun draws its power has been loosed against those who brought war to the Far East."
- An island people who had spent thousands of years constructing a code of personal and national dignity, then had become savage enough to kill 2,500 servicemen in two hours of premeditated slaughter, was forced to "think the unthinkable" and capitulate in unprecedented ignominy.

These are periods of a mere handful of calendar pages; and yet these few days have shaken the world.

How do we embrace these cataclysms? How can our psyches absorb these cold, indecorous realities? Human beings, to bring humanness to grasp the indecency of their follies of polity, have but one recourse, one chance at embracing redemption. This redemptive balm can only be found in something alien to most of what happens in politics.

We need to discuss poetry. And in discussing poetry, we need to look again, and a bit closer, at some of the "legends of language" whose words have formed the focus of this book.

A current criticism of the press is that reportage is characterized by exploitation of our leaders' human foibles, and too little column space or television time is devoted to serious explication of policy, or examination of issues. One of this volume's word-warriors has been placed upon the microscope stage, and accorded particular—and particularly harsh—scrutiny. A brief reprise of our attention to Reverend King reflects upon this journalistic vogue, and, more significantly, offers commentary about the effects of time upon the hero's halo.

In the process of securing rights for use of the King Nobel lecture, to my surprise I came upon a burgeoning bureaucracy of institutions, foundations, and agencies. Seeking a source of information more attuned to the spirit of the lecturer himself, I contacted Professor Keith Miller, a teacher of English and writing at Arizona State University. His 1992 book *Voice of Deliverance: The Language of Martin Luther King, Jr. and Its Sources* (New York: The Free Press, 1992) is literate explication, loving homage, and truth-setting research into the borrowings King made from the word-quilt woven by Black preachers throughout the country and throughout the century.

Miller's thesis is that King's greatness came not from his thinking, but from his preaching. The concepts of his sermons and speeches, which were sometimes "lifted" in a wholesale fashion, were simply the material a desperately busy lecturing parson needed to infuse his mission. In the case in point of the Nobel lecture, Miller states that Reverend King simply appropriated for his address the minimally altered entirety of a sermon by one J. Wallace Hamilton, a religious personage from Florida. (In Miller's book, myriad original textual sources and King's well-known derivations are compared, side by side.) The scholar means no disrespect when he demonstrates valid reasons for saying King "mirrors" other preachers, and that King always "fails to acknowledge his source." In a sense, Miller might say that King was goal-, not means-oriented; deliverance of a people was a noble striving which consumed all the time and energy a less driven pastor might more leisurely have employed to flesh out a sermon with more completely original wit and substance.

Moreover, King (in Miller's view) was a paradox, a Black man educated in a white intellectual clime, who quickly realized that the way to achieve renown (in the Adlerian sense of recognition) was to portray neither the "Hallelu-ya!" old-line barnstormer, nor the dusky version of an Eastern intellectual:

> By appropriating the language of well-established white preachers, King created and maintained a self who grappled with urgent public issues and was also a scholar, a philosopher, and a theologian. His magisterial image as a philosopher and his consummate political skill disproved whites' patronizing and stereotypical views of black preachers as uneducated souls ranting in the pulpit to wildly emotional followers. But, while King's philosophical image was a necessary fiction, it was a fiction. Today it is no longer necessary or useful. We should no longer allow this image to conceal his relationship to the folk pulpit, which served as the wellspring of almost all his ideas and values.[1]

Miller concludes that King "triumphed because, by adapting the traditions of the folk pulpit to a massive white audience, he became the greatest folk preacher of all."

Such findings about a man considered a legend of rhetoric strongly suggest the need for revisionist thinking. Reevaluation, however, needs to come not from viewing the worth of the contribution of Martin Luther King, but rather from viewing the role of the rhetorician. Given the wider view of the figures in the present text, the student of language must conclude that, a Churchill notwithstanding, leadership comes less from being able to conceive original ideas than from being able—effectively—to say to an attentive populace: "The time is *now*—so get off your butts!" Rhetorical niceties refine this expressed sentiment; but the essence of the sentiment remains brute suasion. In one important sense, then, leadership is defined by the same terms as rhetoric: moving people to action, by moving their feelings with stirring verbal tools.

Thinking in this vein, I found that my task of acquiring permissions regarding the civil rights leader now bore the impress of a new, reasoned, and insistent conclusion: Inseminated by the word of others, midwifed by the venues of public fora, given birth by this acclaimed preacher, and legitimized by the goals of a receiving public, a King speech by all rights should belong to the *people*.[2] As

Professor Miller showed, the speaker owed much to his preaching forebears; and as King himself would probably have agreed, the *people* were the purpose of the words and the repository of the results. Justifiably, as King took the clay from others, refashioned it, and used it, so now did it appear only right that that which belonged to the people should be returned to the people.

Without wishing to enter into that purgatorial labyrinth called copyright law, I think it is worthwhile to wonder about the nature of contribution and posthumous sharing. This is an issue not of law but of generosity of spirit. What greater implications are there in some of the specific terms of copyright protection—namely, "public domain" and "fair use"? When is one man's utterance his sole province, and what conditions legitimize a legatee's incorporation of those words within his personal lexicon?

Curiously, perhaps an analogy from the world of photography helps illustrate a point about the world of wordsmiths. The late Ansel Adams, arguably the twentieth century's master photographer, took great pains with each print he made from his *oeuvre* of negatives; yet, upon his death, he had arranged for all his negative materials to be housed in an Arizona college, where even the greenest student photographer would be allowed to print from them, in any way such a student desired. More recently, the photographer Brett Weston (a gifted photographer, but by any measure no challenger to Adams' preeminence) faced a similar retirement decision about his own legacy of photographic negatives. Weston's answer was promptly to burn all of his negatives in the fireplace of his home, rather than imagine anyone else "doing them differently" from his own conceptions. What moral emerges from this comparison? One is prompted simply to say: The anxious miser hoards silver, the generous rich man gives away gold.

Martin Luther King's words now generate a similar quandary: Should they be made freely available for a new and eager public, or should they remain under guard and shielded by their guardians against all save the payers of indulgences, and held as sacrosanct among other artifacts in the late preacher's Atlanta reliquary? This, surely, is a saintly dismay.

Canonization carries its own burdens, and the reverent run risks of distraction from the intentions of the one they revere.[3] When the unseemly element of commerce enters into the equation, suspicion can cloud an otherwise admirable purpose. The legacy of Martin Luther King's rhetoric might be managed with a greater grace if that rhetoric were allowed, like that loam of Reverend Hamilton's words, to return and remix, unrestricted, with the slip and glaze of the people's pottery. Making vessels for our ideas, a revered claywork of man, requires continuous kneading of our plastic medium. Reworking vivifies, forces out the trapped air which threatens explosion, and allows our best efforts to accept the crucible of fire, and emerge into permanence. A leader's leavings should not be viewed as a catalogue for brokers, but as the muddy plasma which is powerless to do anything but create new life.

An unsettling dichotomy exists between the lofty and exalted aspirations of politicians, and the (too often) squalid results of their labors. If ever a soaring form of poetry existed, it is in the goals of our leaders. Nowhere are they more succinctly stated than in the Rooseveltian Four Freedoms.[4]

And yet, the comparisons between the stirring promises at the convention podium and the realities of the execution of the office held by at least thirty-six of those forty-two presidents are more than merely unflattering to the office-holders: The comparisons point to an astonishing propensity on the part of the American people to accept the theatergoer's premise of the "willful suspension of disbelief." Were entertainment, or even enlightenment, the only expectations of the people from their leaders, the resultant paucity of anything poetic would not be so alarming. But when feeding hungry people, and eradicating disease, and replacing psychic malaise with nourished mentalities are the goals of the *candidates'* poetry, there remains no acceptable excuse for the fact that the *incumbents'* far from poetic outcomes will neither scan nor embrace a sustainable moral tenor.

Why does a people continue to promote to standing, and then elect into office, ambitious persons 98 percent of whom do not seem to possess morally exacting natures? Moreover, why is it, when every so many decades someone on a higher plane does achieve office, he is followed for several terms by persons who may or may not proclaim lofty intentions, but who haven't a prayer of delivering anything but mediocrity? To name names: Why must the end of Jeffersonianism be characterized by Van Buren, Polk, Pierce, Taylor, Buchanan? Why must Lincoln's genuinely tragic demise mean that Andrew Johnson, and Grant, and Hayes and Harrison and Harding and even Coolidge must of necessity follow? Why is Eisenhower the people's choice merely because Roosevelt is no longer possible? Why is a Nixon empowered, and a Humphrey put to pasture?[5] And why, we ask again, is an Adlai Stevenson thanked and excused, when most can see that his victor, however likable, though he made courageous decisions at the English Channel in 1944, was not in any way a man of noble aspect?

Some psychologists believe that this country punishes itself for its political murders, and expiates guilt over these acts by electing the mediocre and the undeserving. Others, more pragmatic, take a harder political view, deciding that it is easier for the political bosses, or even the people themselves, to be in charge, if the political servants are not too elegant, are not seen as too lofty, too much our "betters." It must be remembered that in a country which rejected elitism and caste, the appearance of aristocrats like FDR and Kennedy—and the unlucky Stevenson—make common people feel ill at ease.[6] With rare exception, the "common man" cannot draw strength from people whom he resents.

Left with poetry as solace, the "aristocrats" named above (or the men like Lincoln who "earned" aristocratic status) can get along fairly well. Stevenson never fell into the kind of depressive morass which appears to have afflicted Mr. Nixon after his narrow loss in 1960, or Mr. Dukakis after he was summarily rejected in 1988. And perhaps Lincoln succeeded because he *was* a poet; he felt on a poetic plane, he suffered from the too acute insights of the poet; he could envision, and express, in poetry.

Moreover, in Stevenson, perhaps as much as in Lincoln, conceits and circumstances of living worthy of poetic consideration abounded. In childhood, an act of play took a neighbor's life. In young adulthood, the ineluctable pull of love drew him to choose a mate with incipient madness. Another mad mind, the one in the diabolical McCarthy, brought Stevenson near the painful flame again. And later, in his last decades, there was the lure of the call, the near taste of the presidential wine, and then the twin defeats.

Many felt—including one who succeeded later in becoming president—that despite his gifts, Adlai Stevenson was somehow almost congenitally aloof from the people. That even with his experience, and his insight, and his feeling—his poetic nature—he was nonetheless isolated from an essential understanding of the passions within the people. It is a charge which must be considered.

There was a kind of fatalism about Stevenson (part of which may have been of some comfort in his losses). It might have explained his relatively easy acceptance of the losses; it might have enabled him to rise with dignity, later on, when given tasks which, however prestigious, had something ignominious about them when offered to this particular person. The poet in him (and a poet is one with a poetic nature, not just one who versifies) made the quick calculations whose usefulness comes with the muse, and arrived at answers, resolutions which lent him balance, acceptance, at-oneness with himself.

This is what happens in a poetic man.

Ten years after first seeking national office, Adlai Stevenson was asked by the editors of *The New Republic* to review a work of Robert Frost, when that illustrious figure had reached his eighty-eighth year. Here is what the statesman said of the poet:

> It is just because there is no naive optimism, and the abyss is recognized for what it is—the possibility of ultimate despair—that Robert Frost's constant extolling of a quiet, unsensational, dogging courage is more than a conventional theme. It is an inspiration and a force.
>
> I, for one, do not believe that these are days of halcyon weather for America or for the world. We need poets who help us to gird ourselves for endurance, and who walk with us on dark roads where the end is not in sight.

For the most part, the political road grew darker after Adlai Stevenson. The end he could not see is an end he could not covet, but did not fear. And that suggests the other aspect of poetry which should be vital to a president, vital to a politician, and was living, and burning brightly, in so many of these warriors whose words have been reflected upon here:

Poetry brings the courage of which Frost wrote and makes it possible for the poet to regenerate fear into something florid with positiveness and potential. And the quintessential poet is he who is humble enough to extract faith from others, all the while exuding unquenchable inner strength.

All the rhetoric in the world is not equal to this purest poetry, this golden language of conviction.

NOTES

1. Miller, Keith. *Voice of Deliverance: The Language of Martin Luther King, Jr., and Its Sources.* The Free Press, New York, 1992.

2. My experience (and that of Professor Miller's) showed clearly that when historians and others desire permission from the several foundations created in King's name, a courteous reception is provided, but such word seekers are expected to pay a sizable fee for the use of these words—a fee which in the King estate's agency's opening discussion is "nonnegotiable." This, despite the undeniable fact that the preacher had borrowed most of these words freely, and dispersed them, under the mantle of his new authorship, to a growing people who (not being otherwise disabused) accepted these words as his own.

3. It has been said of the Jung Institute in California that if the Viennese analyst and renegade Freudian disciple Carl Jung were alive today and attended any of his namesake institute's workshops or lectures, he would be rendered completely confused by what he heard.

4. See the chapter on Roosevelt in Part II of this book.

5. Richard Ketchum reminds us of Woodrow Wilson's view that only once in a generation could the people tolerate a radical change of things; hence, conservatives win three quarters of the time.

6. In FDR's and JFK's cases, this may have been true in concept; but their personal magnetism positively affected all with whom they came into direct contact.

Selected Bibliography

GENERAL REFERENCES

The Scope of History

Alington, C. A. *Europe: A Personal and Political Survey.* Charles Scribner's Sons, New York, 1948.

Baron, Daniel, and Bendiner, Robert. *The Strenuous Decade: A Social and Intellectual Record of the Nineteen-Thirties.* Part of the Documents in American Civilization Series. Anchor Books, Doubleday, Garden City, New York, 1970.

Bullock, Alan (Editor). *The Twentieth Century: A Promethean Age.* Texts by Alan Bullock, W. H. McNeill, Herbert Nicholas, Alistair Hennessy, Hugh Seton-Watson, C. P. Fitzgerald, Elizabeth Monroe, J. D. Fage, John Willett, Anthony Quinton, Stephen Toulmin, John Maddox, Andrew Shonfield, and Reinhard Bendix. McGraw-Hill, New York, 1971.

Commager, Henry Steele (Editor). *Documents of American History* (Fifth Edition). Appleton-Century-Crofts, New York, 1949.

————. *Documents of American History.* Volume II: *Since 1898* (Eighth Edition). Appleton-Century-Crofts, New York, 1968.

Cooke, Alistair. *America Observed: From the 1940s to the 1980s.* Selected and introduced by Ronald A. Wells. Alfred A. Knopf, New York, 1988.

Foner, Eric, and Garraty, John A. (Editors). *The Reader's Companion to American History.* Houghton Mifflin, Boston, 1991.

Gilbert, Martin. *The Second World War: A Complete History.* Henry Holt, New York, 1989.

Grun, Bernard. *The Timetables of History: A Horizontal Linkage of People and Events.* Based upon Werner Stein's *Kulturfahrplan.* A Touchstone Book, Simon and Schuster, New York, 1979.

Howe, Mortimer; Grew, Raymond; Herlihy, David; Rabb, Theodore; and Woloch, Isser.

The Western Experience. With art essays by H. W. Janson. Alfred A. Knopf, New York, 1974.

Luce, Robert B. (Editor). *The Faces of Five Decades: Selections from Fifty Years of "The New Republic."* Simon and Schuster, New York, 1964.

Minow, Newton N.; Martin, John Bartlow; and Mitchell, Lee M. *Presidential Television.* A Twentieth Century Fund Report, Basic Books, New York, 1973.

Morris, Richard B. (Editor). *Encyclopedia of American History.* Harper & Row, New York, 1965.

Neustadt, Richard E. *Presidential Power: The Politics of Leadership.* New American Library, New York and Toronto, 1964.

Smith, Page. *A People's History* (in eight volumes). McGraw-Hill, New York. Volume VI: *The Rise of Industrial America: A People's History of the Post-Reconstruction Era* (1984); Volume VII: *America Enters the World: A People's History of the Progressive Era and World War I* (1985); Volume VIII: *Redeeming the Time: A People's History of the 1920s and the New Deal* (1987).

Van Thal, Herbert (Editor). *The Prime Ministers: From Sir Robert Walpole to Edward Heath.* Stein and Day, New York, 1975.

Voss, Frederick S. *The Smithsonian Treasury: The Presidents.* Smithsonian Institution Press, Washington, D.C., 1991.

White, Theodore H. *In Search of History: A Personal Adventure.* Harper & Row, New York, 1978.

———. *America in Search of Itself: The Making of the President, 1956–1980.* Harper & Row, New York, 1982.

Wilson, Harold. *A Prime Minister on Prime Ministers.* Book Club Associates (by arrangement with Michael Joseph and Weidenfeld & Nicolson), London, 1977.

Rhetoric

Boyle, Kay. *Words That Must Somehow Be Said: Selected Essays of Kay Boyle (1927–1984).* North Point Press, San Francisco, 1985.

Cole, Thomas. *The Origins of Rhetoric in Ancient Greece.* Johns Hopkins University Press, Baltimore and London, 1991.

Corbett, Edward P. J. *The Little Rhetoric & Handbook with Readings.* Scott, Foresman, Glenview, Illinois, 1983.

Jamieson, Kathleen Hall. *Eloquence in an Electronic Age: The Transformation of Political Speechmaking.* Oxford University Press, New York and Oxford, 1988.

Muller, Gilbert H., and Wiener, Harvey S. *The Short Prose Reader* (Sixth Edition). McGraw-Hill, New York, 1991.

Ricoeur, Paul. *The Rule of Metaphor: Multi-Discussional Studies of the Creation of Meaning in Language.* University of Toronto Press, Toronto, 1981.

Rowse, A. L. *The Poet Auden: A Personal Memoir.* Weidenfeld & Nicolson, New York, 1987.

Ryan, Halford Ross. *American Rhetoric from Roosevelt to Reagan: A Collection of Speeches and Critical Essays* (Second Edition), Waveland Press, Prospect Heights, Illinois, 1987.

Shrodes, Caroline; Josephson, Clifford; and Wilson, James R. *Reading for Rhetoric: Applications to Writing.* Macmillan, New York, 1975.

Civil Rights

Abraham, Henry J. *Freedom and the Court: Civil Rights and Liberties in the United States* (Second Edition). Oxford University Press, New York, 1972.

Brigham, John. *Civil Liberties and American Democracy.* CQ Press, Washington, D.C., 1984.

Cox, Archibald; Howe, Mark DeWolfe; and Wiggins, J. R. *Civil Rights, the Constitution, and the Courts.* Harvard University Press, Cambridge, Massachusetts, 1967.

Whalen, Charles and Barbara. *The Longest Debate: A Legislative History of the 1964 Civil Rights Act.* Seven Locks Press/Cabin John, Washington, D.C., 1985.

THEMATIC REFERENCES

Prophets of the New Century

Freud, Sigmund, and Bullitt, William C. *Thomas Woodrow Wilson: A Psychological Study.* Houghton Mifflin, Boston, and Riverside Press, Cambridge, 1967.

Hoffman, Eva. *Lost in Translation: Life in a New Language.* Dutton, New York, 1989.

Mordden, Ethan. *That Jazz! An Idiosyncratic Social History of the American Twenties.* G. P. Putnam's Sons, New York, 1978.

Smith, Gene. *When the Cheering Stopped: The Last Years of Woodrow Wilson.* William Morrow, New York, 1964.

Weintraub, Stanley. *A Stillness Heard round the World.* E. P. Dutton (Truman Talley Books), New York, 1985.

Williams, Wayne C. *William Jennings Bryan: A Study in Political Vindication.* Fleming H. Revell, New York, 1923.

Voices of the Second World War

[Editors of the Columbia Broadcasting System]. *Crisis: A Report from the Columbia Broadcasting System* [on the Czech situation of 1938]. [Published by CBS?], New York, 1938.

Daniel, Jonathan. *The Time between the Wars: Armistice to Pearl Harbor.* Doubleday, Garden City, New York, 1966.

Dollinger, Hans. *The Decline and Fall of Nazi Germany and Imperial Japan: A Pictorial History of the Final Days of World War II.* Bonanza Books, New York, 1965.

Donn, Linda. *Freud and Jung: Years of Friendship, Years of Loss.* Scribners, New York, 1988.

Eisinger, Chester E. (Editor). *The 1940's: Profile of a Nation in Crisis.* Part of the Documents in American Civilization Series. Anchor Books, Doubleday, Garden City, New York, 1969.

Farago, Ladislas (Compiler and Editor). *The Axis Grand Strategy: Blueprints for the Total War.* Farrar & Rinehart, New York, 1942.

Fussell, Paul. *Wartime: Understanding and Behavior in the Second World War.* Oxford University Press, Oxford, 1989.

Hynes, Samuel. *A War Imagined: The First World War and English Culture.* Atheneum, New York, 1991.

Kaltenborn, H. V. *Europe Now: A First-Hand Report.* Didier, New York, 1945.

Maass, Walter B. *Country without a Name: Austria under Nazi Rule 1938–1945.* Frederich Ungar, New York, 1979.

Mosley, Leonard. *On Borrowed Time: How World War II Began.* Random House, New York, 1969.

Mosley, Nicholas. *Rules of the Game—Beyond the Pale: Memoirs of Sir Oswald Mosley and Family.* Dalkey Archive Press, Elmwood Park, Illinois, 1991.

The New Yorker Book of War Pieces. Reynal & Hitchcock, New York, 1947.

Rausch, Basil. *The History of the New Deal 1933–1938.* Creative Age Press, New York, 1944.

Salmaggi, Cesare, and Pallavisini, Alfredo (Compilers). *2194 Days of War: An Illustrated Chronology of the Second World War.* Gallery Books, New York, 1988.

Stone, I. F. *The War Years: 1939–1945.* Little, Brown, New York, 1988.

Strong, Anna Louise. *Spain in Arms 1937.* Henry Holt, New York, 1937.

Weintraub, Stanley. *Long Day's Journey into War: December 7, 1941.* Truman Talley Books, Dutton, New York, 1991.

Postwar Panic

Burns, James MacGregor, and Burns, Stewart. *A People's Charter: The Pursuit of Rights for America.* Alfred A. Knopf, New York, 1991.

Goldman, Eric F. *The Crucial Decade—And After: America, 1945–1960.* Vintage Books, Random House, New York, 1960.

Life magazine, April 23, 1945.

Lilienthal, David E. *This I Do Believe: An American Credo.* Harper & Brothers, New York, 1949.

Navasky, Victor S. *Naming Names.* Viking Press, New York, 1980.

Nizer, Louis. *The Jury Returns.* Doubleday, Garden City, New York, 1966.

Stewart, George R. *The Year of the Oath: The Fight for Academic Freedom at the University of California.* Doubleday, Garden City, New York, 1950.

The Modern Epoch

Broder, David S. *Changing of the Guard: Power and Leadership in America.* Simon and Schuster, New York, 1980.

Grodzins, Morton, and Rabinowitch, Eugene (Editors). *The Atomic Age: Scientists in National and World Affairs—Articles from the Bulletin of the Atomic Scientists 1945–1962.* Basic Books, New York, 1963.

Humphrey, Hubert H. (Editor). *Integration vs. Segregation.* Thomas Y. Crowell, New York, 1964.

Jungk, Robert. *Brighter Than a Thousand Suns: A Personal History of the Atomic Scientists.* Translation by James Cleugh. Harcourt, Brace New York, 1956.

Parmet, Herbert S. *Richard Nixon and His America.* Little, Brown, Boston, 1990.

Schlesinger, Arthur, Jr. *The Imperial Presidency.* Houghton Mifflin, Boston, 1973.

Sulzberger, C. L. *A Long Row of Candles: Memories and Diaries, 1934–1954.* Macmillan, New York, 1969.

———. *Such a Peace: The Roots and Ashes of Yalta.* Continuum, New York, 1982.

United States Code Annotated: Title 18—Crimes and Criminal Procedure Sections 1 to 370. West Publishing, St. Paul, Minnesota, 1969.

Wyman, David S. *The Abandonment of the Jews: America and the Holocaust 1941–1945*. Pantheon Books, New York, 1984.

BIOGRAPHICAL SUBJECT REFERENCES
(IN SEQUENTIAL ORDER)

Jane Addams and Alice Hamilton, M.D.

Abrams, Irwin. *The Nobel Peace Prize and the Laureates: An Illustrated Biographical History, 1901–1987*. G. K. Hall, Boston, 1988. [Jane Addams.]

Blum, John Morton (Editor). *Public Philosopher: Selected Letters of Walter Lippmann*. Ticknor & Fields, New York, 1985. [Alice Hamilton, M.D.]

Davis, Allen F. *American Heroine: The Life and Legend of Jane Addams*. Oxford University Press, New York, 1973.

Grant, Madeleine P. *Alice Hamilton: Pioneer Doctor in Industrial Medicine*. Abelard-Schuman, London and New York, 1967.

Hamilton, Alice, M.D. *Exploring the Dangerous Trades*. Little, Brown, Boston, 1943.

Lovett, Robert Morss. "Jane Addams at Hull House." *The New Republic,* May 14, 1930. In Luce, Robert B. (Editor), *The Faces of Five Decades: Selections from Fifty Years of "The New Republic,"* Simon and Schuster, New York, 1964.

Sicherman, Barbara. *Alice Hamilton: A Life in Letters*. A Commonwealth Fund Book, Harvard University Press, Cambridge, Massachusetts, and London, England, 1984.

Smith, Page. "Jane Addams and Hull House." In Smith, Page, *The Rise of Industrial America: A People's History of the Post-Reconstruction Era* (Volume VI of the eight-volume *A People's History*), pp. 410–421, McGraw-Hill, New York, 1984.

Wasson, Tyler (Editor). *Nobel Prize Winners*. An H. W. Wilson biographical dictionary. H. W. Wilson, New York, 1987. [Jane Addams.]

Wise, Winifred E. *Jane Addams of Hull House*. Harcourt, Brace, New York, 1935.

Clarence Darrow

Darrow, Clarence. *Crime: Its Cause and Treatment*. Reprinted as Publication No. 143: Patterson Smith Reprint Series in Criminology, Law Enforcement and Social Problems. Patterson Smith, Montclair, New Jersey, 1972.

Darrow, Clarence, and Rice, Wallace. *Infidels and Heretics: An Agnostic's Anthology*. Stratford, Boston, 1929.

Tierney, Kevin. *Darrow: A Biography*. Thomas Y. Crowell, New York, 1979.

Wilson, Edmund. *The Twenties*. Edited with an introduction by Leon Edel. Farrar, Straus and Giroux, New York, 1975.

Mohandas K. Gandhi

Andrews, C. F. *Mahatma Gandhi's Ideas*. Includes selections from his writings. Macmillan, New York, 1930.

Brown, Judith M. *Gandhi: Prisoner of Hope.* Yale University Press, New Haven and
    London, 1989.
Collins, Larry, and LaPierre, Dominique. *Freedom at Midnight.* Simon and Schuster,
    New York, 1975.
Erikson, Erik H. *Gandhi's Truth: On the Origins of Militant Nonviolence.* W. W. Norton,
    New York, 1969.
Gandhi, Mohandas K. *Gandhi's Autobiography.* [Edition undetermined; based upon the
    1941 English edition issued by the Navajivan Press.]
Nehru, Jawaharlal. *Nehru on Gandhi.* A selection, arranged in the order of events, from
    the writings and speeches of Jawaharlal Nehru. John Day, New York, 1948.
————. *Gandhi: A Memoir.* Simon and Schuster, New York, 1979.
Sheehan, Vincent. *Lead, Kindly Light* [a remembrance of Mohandas K. Gandhi]. Random
    House, New York, 1949.

Neville Chamberlain (See also Churchill, Winston S.)

Baldwin, Hanson W. *The Crucial Years, 1939–1941: The World at War—From the
    Beginning through Pearl Harbor.* Harper & Row, New York, 1976.
Chamberlain, Neville. *In Search of Peace.* G. P. Putnam's Sons, New York, 1939.
Dilks, David. *Neville Chamberlain.* Volume I: *Pioneering and Reform, 1869–1929.* Cam-
    bridge University Press, Cambridge, 1984.
Fuchser, Larry William. *Neville Chamberlain and Appeasement: A Study in the Politics
    of History.* W. W. Norton, New York, 1982.
MacLeod, Iain. *Neville Chamberlain.* Atheneum, New York, 1962.
Martel, Gordon. *The Origins of the Second World War Reconsidered: The A. J. P. Taylor
    Debate after Twenty-five Years.* Allen & Unwin, Boston, 1986.
Schmidt, Paul (R. H. C. Steed, Editor). *Hitler's Interpreter.* Macmillan, New York, 1951.
    [See also Hitler, Adolf.]
Smith, Gene. *The Dark Summer: An Intimate History of the Events That Led to World
    War II.* Macmillan, New York, 1987.
Taylor, A. J. P. *The Origins of the Second World War.* Hamish Hamilton, London, 1961.
Taylor, Telford. *Munich: The Price of Peace.* Doubleday, New York, 1979.
Watt, Donald Cameron. *How War Came: The Immediate Origins of the Second World
    War, 1938–1939.* Pantheon Books, New York, 1989.

Winston S. Churchill

Churchill, Randolph S. *Winston S. Churchill.* Volume I: *Youth, 1874–1900.* Houghton
    Mifflin, Boston, 1966.
Churchill, Winston S. *The Unrelenting Struggle: War Speeches by Winston S. Churchill.*
    Compiled by Charles Eade. Little, Brown, Boston, 1942.
————. *The End of the Beginning: War Speeches by Winston S. Churchill.* Compiled
    by Charles Eade. Little, Brown, Boston, 1943.
————. *The Second World War.* Volume I: *The Gathering Storm* (1948). Volume II:
    Their Finest Hour (1949). Volume III: *The Grand Alliance* (1949). Volume IV:
    The Hinge of Fate (1950). Volume V: *Closing the Ring* (1951). Volume VI:
    Triumph and Tragedy (1953). Houghton Mifflin, Boston.

————. *A Churchill Reader: The Wit and Wisdom of Sir Winston Churchill, Constructed from His Own Sayings and Writings and Framed with an Introduction by Colin R. Coote.* Houghton Mifflin, Boston, 1954.

Colville, John. *Winston Churchill and His Inner Circle.* Wyndham Books, New York, 1981.

————. *The Fringes of Power: 10 Downing Street Diaries 1939–1955.* W. W. Norton, New York, 1985.

Day, David. *Churchill and Menzies at War: A Controversial Account.* Paragon House, New York, 1988.

Gilbert, Martin. *Winston S. Churchill.* Volume VII: *Road to Victory 1941–1945.* Houghton Mifflin, New York, 1986.

————. *Winston S. Churchill.* Volume VIII: *'Never Despair,' 1945–1965.* Houghton Mifflin, Boston, 1988.

Humes, James C. *Churchill: Speaker of the Century.* Stein & Day, New York, 1980.

Manchester, William. *The Last Lion: Winston Spencer Churchill, 1932–1940.* Little, Brown, Boston, 1988.

Moran, Lord Moran (Charles Wilson). *Churchill: Taken from the Diaries of Lord Moran—The Struggle for Survival, 1940–1965.* Houghton Mifflin, Boston, and Riverside Press, Cambridge, 1966.

Pilpel, Robert H. *Churchill in America, 1935–1961—An Affectionate Portrait.* Harcourt Brace Jovanovich, New York, 1976.

Taylor, A. J. P.; James, Robert Rhodes; Plumb, J. H.; Liddell Hart, Basil; and Storr, Anthony. *Churchill Revised: A Critical Assessment.* Dial Press, New York, 1969.

Adolf Hitler

Berke, Joseph. *The Tyranny of Malice: Exploring the Dark Side of Character and Culture.* Summit Books, Simon and Schuster, New York, 1988.

Borgese, G. A. *Goliath: The March of Fascism.* Viking Press, New York, 1937.

Brill, A. A. (Editor and Translator). *The Basic Writings of Sigmund Freud.* The Modern Library, Random House, New York, 1938.

Dornberg, John. *Munich 1923: The Story of Hitler's First Grab for Power.* Harper & Row, New York, 1982.

Hitler, Adolf. *My Battle (Mein Kampf).* Abridged and translated by E. T. S. Dugdale. Houghton Mifflin, Boston, 1933.

————. *Mein Kampf.* Complete and unabridged and fully annotated. Reynal & Hitchcock, New York, 1939.

Lindbergh, Anne Morrow. *The Wave of the Future: A Confession of Faith.* Quinn & Boden, Rahway, New Jersey, 1940.

Lindbergh, Charles A. *We.* G. P. Putnam's Sons (The Knickerbocker Press), New York and London, 1927.

Ludwig, Arnold M., M.D. *Principles of Clinical Psychiatry* (Second Edition). The Free Press, New York, 1986.

Shirer, William L. *Berlin Diary: The Journal of a Foreign Correspondent 1934–1941.* Alfred A. Knopf, New York, 1942.

————. *20th Century Journey: A Memoir of a Life and the Times—The Start: 1904–1930.* Simon and Schuster, New York, 1976.

————. *20th Century Journey: A Memoir of a Life and the Times—The Nightmare Years: 1930–1940.* Little, Brown, Boston, 1984.

Franklin Delano Roosevelt

Alsop, Joseph. *FDR 1882–1945: A Centenary Remembrance.* Viking Press, New York, 1982.

Asbell, Bernard. *When F.D.R. Died.* Holt, Rinehart and Winston, New York, 1961.

Beschloss, Michael R. *Kennedy and Roosevelt: The Uneasy Alliance.* W. W. Norton, New York, 1980.

Blum, John Morton (Editor). *The Price of Vision: The Diary of Henry A. Wallace 1942–1946.* Houghton Mifflin, Boston, 1973.

Brown, John Mason. *The Worlds of Robert E. Sherwood: Mirror to His Times, 1896–1939.* Harper & Row, New York, 1965.

Burns, James MacGregor. *Roosevelt: The Soldier of Freedom.* Harcourt Brace Jovanovich, New York, 1970.

Ickes, Harold L. *The Secret Diary of Harold L. Ickes—The First Thousand Days 1933–1936.* Simon and Schuster, New York, 1953.

Lash, Joseph P. *Eleanor and Franklin: The Story of Their Relationship, Based on Eleanor Roosevelt's Private Papers.* W. W. Norton, New York, 1971.

————. *Roosevelt and Churchill, 1939–1941: The Partnership That Saved the West.* W. W. Norton, New York, 1976.

McJimsey, George. *Harry Hopkins: Ally of the Poor and Defender of Democracy.* Harvard University Press, Cambridge, Massachusetts, and London, England, 1987.

Perkins, Frances. *The Roosevelt I Knew.* Viking Press, New York, 1946.

Sherwood, Robert E. *Roosevelt and Hopkins: An Intimate History.* Harper & Brothers, New York, 1948.

Joseph R. McCarthy (See also Welch, Joseph N.)

Ewald, William Bragg, Jr. *Who Killed Joe McCarthy?* Simon and Schuster, New York, 1984.

Matusow, Allen J. (Editor). *Joseph R. McCarthy.* From the Great Lives Observed Series. Prentice-Hall, Englewood Cliffs, New Jersey, 1970.

Reeves, Thomas C. *The Life and Times of Joe McCarthy.* Stein & Day, New York, 1982.

Senate Report No. 2508, United States Senate, 83rd Congress, Second Session. *Report on Resolution to Censure: November 8, 1954.* [Select Committee to Study Censure Charges.] United States Government Printing Office, Washington, D.C., 1954.

Wolfe, Alan. *The Seamy Side of Democracy: Repression in America.* David McKay, New York, 1973.

Joseph N. Welch (See also McCarthy, Joseph R.)

Adams, John G. *Without Precedent: The Story of the Death of McCarthyism.* W. W. Norton, New York, 1983.

Fisher, Frederick W., Jr. *Where the Tall Grass Grows.* Unpublished manuscript. Boston, 1966(?).

Thomas, Evan. *The Man to See: Edward Bennett Williams—Ultimate Insider; Legendary Trial Lawyer.* Simon and Schuster, New York, 1991.

Adlai E. Stevenson

Bush, Noel F. *Adlai E. Stevenson of Illinois: A Portrait.* Farrar, Straus & Young, New York, 1952.

Fairlie, Henry. "The Great Hesitator." Review of McKeever, Porter, *Adlai Stevenson: His Life and Legacy,* William Morrow, New York, 1989. *The New Republic,* July 17 and 24, 1989, pp. 25–29.

Johnson, Gerald W. "I'm for Adlai Stevenson." *The New Republic,* July 11, 1960. In Luce, Robert B. (Editor), *The Faces of Five Decades: Selections from Fifty Years of "The New Republic."* Simon and Schuster, New York, 1964.

Johnson, Walter (Editor). *The Papers of Adlai E. Stevenson. Volume VI: Toward a New America, 1955–1957; Volume VII: Continuing Education and the Unfinished Business of American Society, 1957–1961.* Little, Brown, Boston, 1977.

Johnson, Walter; Evans, Carol; and Sears, C. Eric (Editors). *The Papers of Adlai E. Stevenson. Volume IV: "Let's Talk Sense to the American People," 1952–1955.* Little, Brown, 1974.

Martin, John Bartlow. *Adlai Stevenson and the World: The Life of Adlai E. Stevenson.* Doubleday, Garden City, New York, 1977.

McKeever, Porter. *Adlai Stevenson: His Life and Legacy.* William Morrow, New York, 1989.

Steinbeck, John. "The 'Stevenson Spirit.' " *The New Republic,* January 5, 1953. In Luce, Robert B. (Editor), *The Faces of Five Decades: Selections from Fifty Years of "The New Republic,"* Simon and Schuster, New York, 1964.

Stevenson, Adlai E. "Robert Frost at Eighty-Eight." *The New Republic,* April 9, 1962. In Luce, Robert B. (Editor), *The Faces of Five Decades: Selections from Fifty Years of "The New Republic,"* Simon and Schuster, New York, 1964.

Dwight D. Eisenhower

Ambrose, Stephen E. *The Supreme Commander: The War Years of General Dwight D. Eisenhower.* Doubleday, Garden City, New York, 1977.

——. *Eisenhower.* Volume II: *The President.* Simon and Schuster, New York, 1984.

Donovan, Robert J. *Eisenhower: The Inside Story.* Harper & Brothers, New York, 1956.

Eisenhower, Dwight D. *Crusade in Europe: A Personal Account of World War II.* Doubleday, Garden City, New York, 1948.

——. *Mandate for Change: The White House Years 1953–1956.* Doubleday, Garden City, New York, 1963.

——. *Waging Peace: The White House Years 1956–1961.* Doubleday, Garden City, New York, 1965.

Ferrell, Robert H. (Editor). *The Eisenhower Diaries.* W. W. Norton, New York, 1981.

Office of the Federal Register. *Public Papers of the Presidents of the United States: Dwight D. Eisenhower, 1960–61, Containing the Public Messages, Speeches, and*

Statements of the President, January 1, 1960 to January 20, 1961. National Ar-
    chives and Records Service, General Services Administration. United States Gov-
    ernment Printing Office, Washington, D.C., 1961.
Radosh, Ronald, and Milton, Joyce. *The Rosenberg File: A Search for the Truth.* Vintage
    Books, Random House, New York, 1984.

John Fitzgerald Kennedy

Ambrose, Stephen E. *Nixon: The Education of a Politician 1913–1962.* Simon and Schus-
    ter. New York, 1987.
Collier, Peter, and Horowitz, David. *The Kennedys: An American Drama.* Summit Books,
    New York, 1984.
Halberstam, David. *The Best and the Brightest.* Random House, New York, 1972.
Nixon, Richard M. *Six Crises.* Doubleday, Garden City, New York, 1962.
Paper, Lewis J. *The Promise and the Performance: The Leadership of John F. Kennedy.*
    Crown Publishers, New York, 1975.
Schlesinger, Arthur M., Jr. *Kennedy or Nixon: Does It Make Any Difference?* Macmillan,
    New York, 1960.
Wicker, Tom. *One of Us: Richard Nixon and the American Dream.* Random House, New
    York, 1991.
Wills, Garry. *Nixon Agonistes: The Crisis of the Self-made Man.* Houghton Mifflin,
    Boston, 1970.
———. *The Kennedy Imprisonment: A Meditation on Power.* Little, Brown, Boston,
    1982.

Martin Luther King, Jr.

Abrams, Irwin. *The Nobel Peace Prize and the Laureates: An Illustrated Biographical
    History, 1901–1987.* G. K. Hall, Boston, 1988.
Branch, Taylor. *Parting the Waters: America in the King Years 1954–1963.* Simon and
    Schuster, New York, 1988. (See also Jackson, Jesse.)
Davis, Lenwood G. *I Have a Dream: The Life and Times of Martin Luther King, Jr.*
    [Publisher unknown], 1969.
King, Coretta Scott. *My Life with Martin Luther King, Jr.* Holt, Rinehart and Winston,
    New York, 1969.
Lewis, David L. *King: A Critical Biography.* Praeger Publishers, New York, 1970. (See
    also Jackson, Jesse.)
Wasson, Tyler (Editor). *Nobel Prize Winners.* An H. W. Wilson biographical dictionary.
    H. W. Wilson, New York, 1987.

Jesse M. Jackson

Branch, Taylor. *Parting the Waters: America in the King Years 1954–1963.* Simon and
    Schuster, New York, 1988. (See also King, Martin Luther, Jr.)
Colton, Elizabeth O. *The Jackson Phenomenon: The Man, the Power, the Message.*
    Doubleday, New York, 1989.
Frady, Marshall. "Outsider: A Profile of Jesse Jackson." Part I: "The Gift" (February

3, 1992); Part II: "History Is upon Us" (February 10, 1992); Part III: "Without Portfolio" (February 17, 1992). *The New Yorker.*

Lewis, David L. *King: A Critical Biography.* Praeger Publishers, New York, 1970. (See also King, Martin Luther, Jr.)

McKissack, Patricia C. *Jesse Jackson: A Biography.* Scholastic, New York, 1989.

Otfinoski, Steven. *Jesse Jackson: A Voice for Change.* From the Great Lives in 20th Century Politics and Government Series. Fawcette Columbine, New York, 1989.

Index

Addams, Jane. *See also* Hamilton, Alice
as political activist: focus upon wom-
ens' rights and peace, 13–15; as
founder of American Civil Liberties
Union (ACLU), 15; at Progressive
Party Convention of 1912 (seconds
T. Roosevelt nomination), 15
work with Hamilton, Alice: character
as "match" for Hamilton, 14; professional and personal association,
9–20 *passim*
as pioneer in social welfare—credentials and distinctions: Chicago charities at beginning of life work, 9;
discovery of Toynbee Hall, London,
12; evolving character as seen by
Davis, A.F., 13–14; first interest in
social welfare, 10; Hull House, 9–20
passim
place in American social history: compared with Gandhi, 25; of equal importance to Hamilton, Alice, xxiii
n.2; as pioneering role model, 13; as
winner of Nobel Prize, 15
ahimsa (noninjury to animal life), 21, 25.
See also King, Martin Luther, Jr.
Amery, Leo (M.P.) quoting Cromwell,
xvii

anemia, sickle-cell, 166, 168 n.3
Army-McCarthy Hearings. *See* McCarthy,
Joseph R.; Welch, Joseph N.
Atlantic Charter: outcome of Churchill-
FDR meeting, 72; proclamation,
Churchill's hopes from meeting, 88;
text of, 90–91. *See also* Churchill,
Winston S.; Newfoundland; Roose-
velt, Franklin Delano

Banting, Frederick (discoverer of insulin),
18, 20 n.9
Black Christmas (1967). *See* Jackson,
Jesse
the Blitz, xvii
Bourke-White, Margaret, 22
brahmacharya (sexual abstinence), 22
Branch, Taylor, 168 n.2
Bryan, William Jennings: as adversary of
Clarence Darrow, 6; as Biblical
expert, 6; as early 20th-century relig-
ious figure, 4; at Scopes Trial, 6, 7

Chamberlain, Neville, xvii, xix; brings
Churchill back into government, 74;
eulogized by Churchill, 78–81; leadership compared with Churchill, 76;
and Munich crisis, 51–54; sacrifice

About the Author

KEITH SPENCER FELTON's published works include a prize-winning play and internationally syndicated articles for the *Los Angeles Times Book Review*. A past recipient of the Phelan Award in Literature for a novel, Felton holds degrees in writing from Grinnell College and the University of California at Los Angeles. Presently he is working on a book about English diarists and European languages.